THE NIMBLE READER

Literary Theory and Children's Literature

THE NIMBLE READER

Literary Theory and Children's Literature

Roderick McGillis

TWAYNE PUBLISHERS
An Imprint of Simon & Schuster Macmillan
New York

PRENTICE HALL INTERNATIONAL
London   Mexico City   New Delhi   Singapore   Sydney   Toronto

Twayne Publishers
An Imprint of Simon & Schuster Macmillan
866 Third Avenue
New York, New York 10022

Library of Congress Cataloging-in-Publication Data

McGillis, Roderick
    The nimble reader : literary theory and children's literature / Roderick McGillis.
      p. cm.
    Includes bibliographical references (p.) and index.
    ISBN 0-8057-9033-0
    1. Children's literature—History and criticism. 2. Criticism. I. Title.
PN1009.A1M234   1996
809'.89282—dc20   95-36099
                                                     CIP

10 9 8 7 6 5 4 3 2 1

Printed in the United States of America

Contents

Preface

One's "definite position" is one's weakness, the source of one's lia-
bility to error and prejudice, and to gain adherents to a definite position is only to multiply one's weakness like an infection.
                                                    —Northrop Frye

At the outset, I planned to write a handbook to literary theory, one of
those books that describes through analysis of major voices the various
current literary theories and then shows how they perform in practical
criticism. As I proceeded with the writing, I became aware that things
were not unfolding as I had imagined they would. For one thing, in
this book you will find no extended discussions of any one critic and
even the absence of some whom you might consider essential reading
today. At first I was uneasy about the shape the book was taking, but I
quickly realized that I could not write the book I had set out to write.
The reasons for this are clear: I do not know enough about all the
influential critical writers working since mid-century, or even working
today; and anyway, the book is not long enough for me to write
detailed descriptions of so many theorists. Also, despite being deeply
committed to a social vision that seems tailor-made for recent trends in
literary discussion, I am fundamentally a formalist. Consequently, you
will find much practical criticism in this book. My interests as the focus
changes from chapter to chapter remain strongly bound to the texts I
write about. I like the challenge to creative play that each text offers
the reader.

dd

Having said this, I do not want to leave you with the impression that this is a work of practical criticism disguising itself in a wrapper labeled "literary theory." You will find theoretical discussions in the pages that follow, and you will find too (at least implicitly) a theory. My discussions are not exhaustive by any means. I take up the following: Formalism and the New Criticism, archetypal criticism, psychoanalytical criticism, political criticism, structuralist criticism, poststructuralist criticism (feminism and deconstruction), and reader response criticism. I have had no room to take up such subjects as stylistics, speech-act theory, the new historicism, postcolonial theory, or even textual studies. I have, however, tried to make it apparent that every approach to a literary text must navigate the seas and large inland lakes of what have been termed "extrinsic" and "intrinsic" reading. And I have tried also to indicate that all reading demands a theoretical position on the part of the reader. My hope is that my choice of primary texts, my manner of discussing the various topics, and the structure of this book itself will communicate my own position. And I further hope that readers without extensive theoretical backgrounds will find something here to rouse them into critical activity. I have learned from all the critics whose work I refer to here, and although I do not go out of my way to avoid contention, I take literary study to be a constructive, creative activity, rather than a debate. Critical activity should bring us together, even when it investigates our differences.

My choice of texts, then, is important. You will find many children's books mentioned in the following pages. I have tried, however, to concentrate on books for children between the ages of, say, four and fourteen. In other words, I have tried to avoid the issue of what exactly constitutes a children's book. Knowing, however, that some readers will want to know what I mean by "children's literature" and by "children," I offer the following definitions. For purposes of this book, "children" includes any and all persons who fall between the ages from birth to eighteen, when in most areas of North American society the person becomes an adult (i.e., of voting age). My inclusion of infants, children, adolescents, and teenagers necessitates an inclusory definition of "children's literature." "Children's literature," again for purposes of this book, includes all books published and marketed for people falling between the ages I set out above. In other words, I share Perry Nodelman's belief that "the pleasures of children's litera-ture are essentially the pleasures of all literature" (*The Pleasures of Children's Literature*, 11).

As Sharon Shaloo points out in a recent issue of *The Lion and the Unicorn*, children's books take many forms: "traditional hardcov-er, paperback, board book, toddler-pocket board book, bath book, singing book, coloring book, and, only very recently, interactive disk" (1). I have not used all of these formats, although I have tried to focus on both "classic" children's books and popular ones. Three books appear in most of the chapters: E. B. White's *Charlotte's Web*, Maurice Sendak's *Where the Wild Things Are*, and Chris Van Allsburg's *The Mysteries of Harris Burdick*. The first two are by now classics of chil-dren's literature, and the third, a more recent book, might well become a classic. These, and the other books I discuss, serve as exam-ples; the idea is that the various approaches I bring to each of these books might be used to aid readers in understanding and engaging with any book for young readers. Although my subject is not illustra-tion, you will be aware that the critical methods I discuss and put to work are relevant to pictures as well as to print.

Anyone who writes about children's literature must be acutely aware of the subject's unique demands and its distinctive position within our culture. Whether children read books or not seems less the question than the larger question concerning the world in which chil-dren grow up. This world happens to contain books, books that attempt to capture children's interests, to draw them in. Indeed, every-thing in a culture attempts to draw its people in, to make complicity seem natural; we are all in it together. This "it" we all inhabit is a world of terrorism, child abuse, fright, warfare, poverty and staggering wealth, starvation and unforgivable waste, and division at every turn. In this context, writing about ways of reading books for children might appear hopelessly impractical. I continue, however, to think this enter-prise is intensely practical; I continue to believe that active, engaged, even complicit reading can remind us that the only real power to change the world exists within our own imaginations. Peter Hunt's call for a "childist" criticism, that is, a criticism that approaches texts from a child's point of view in the way that a feminist criticism approaches texts from a female's point of view, is quite simply a criticism dedicated to opening doors of perception.

I have presented some of the material in this book to audiences of various sorts, and I have benefited from these occasions. Parts of the first chapter I read at the Upper Plains Conference on Children's and Adolescent Literature at Northern State University in Aberdeen, South Dakota, in July 1992 and at the University of Winnipeg in 1994. I have Wally Hastings to thank for the invitation to South Dakota. Parts of chapters 1 and 5 I presented at the University of Puerto Rico in the spring of 1993, and I have Michael Sharp and Maria Rodriguez to thank for this opportunity to share ideas with colleagues in the tropics. Again, some of chapter 5 I presented at the Children's Literature Association Conference in Fredericton, New Brunswick, in 1993. A portion of chapter 4 I read at the Ninth International Research Society for Children's Literature Congress held in Salamanca, Spain, in 1989. And, of course, I have my students at the University of Calgary to thank for listening tolerantly to many of the ideas in this book, and for taking me to task on several issues. In chapter 8 you will meet Bev McKay, Nita Ross, and the student I refer to as Helen; they are only three of many students who have a genuine desire to explore and share ideas and who have taught me more than I can acknowledge fully.

Some paragraphs in chapter 8, on reader response criticism, have appeared in the pages of the *Children's Literature Association Quarterly*: "Reader Response: Literature and Subjectivity" (volume 6, 1981, pp. 31–34) and "When Intention Meets Response: Affective and Objective Reading" (volume 17, 1992, pp. 43–45).

A good part of the research for this book I carried out while on an Annual Fellowship in the Calgary Institute for the Humanities, 1990–91. I am especially indebted to the Institute for office space, companionship, and encouragement. Both Gerry Dyer and Cindy Atkinson deserve special accolades for their kindness in facilitating my work at the Institute. And as the work progressed, I incurred other debts. My thanks to Sylvia K. Miller and the people at Twayne for their patience and trust. Without Ruth MacDonald, I would never have begun this project. Many colleagues and friends have supported me in one way or another: Michael Steig, Perry Nodelman, Jean Perrot, Jill May, Jon Stott, Anita Moss, Saad El-Gabalawy, Keath Fraser, Ashraf Rushdy, Adrienne Kertzer, Mavis Reimer, Lois Kuznets, Allan Reid, John Stephens, and Abe Friesen. My friend Victor Ramraj read portions of the manuscript and kept me from several serious blunders. This does not mean, however, that I have escaped all blunders; those that remain are entirely my own.

My greatest debt is, of course, to my family, who understand how a project such as this preoccupies the mind even while the body swims, hikes, or tosses a Frisbee. Thanks to Kate and Kyla; thanks to Donna. The three of you chart my course.

1

Beginnings

Jack be nimble,
Jack be quick,
Jack jump over
The candle stick.

Here is a simple, well-known nursery rhyme. I offer it as an example of writing we think of as children's literature, an example of literature for the very young child. But how do we know this is literature for the very young child? Our calling it a "nursery rhyme" indicates that we think it is suitable for children, and indeed this rhyme appears in countless collections of such rhymes lavishly illustrated and marketed for a child audience. Its brevity, its bounce, and its bumptious fun mark it suitable for children. Nothing complicated lurks between the lines; nothing polysemous calls out to us from the nine different words. No author's name comes tagged to this rhyme, and consequently we need not worry ourselves about unconscious expressions of an author's anxieties or wishes. Further, we do not have a date of composition, something that is usually available when a work of literature comes to us from a named author. The rhyme appears to exist in a timeless zone; it actualizes a freedom that confirms our hope that once upon a time purity and innocence were ours. We want our children's literature—we want our children—to signify the truth of an absolute beginning when nothing needed to be explained, analyzed, scrutinized, or interpreted. We accept this truth to be self-evident: to dissect is to murder. And that, dear reader, is that.

But of course that, dear reader, is not that. We all know that rhymes, for children or for adults, are not found beneath trees; nor do they emerge fully formed, pristine and transparent, from mysterious vaults presided over by powerful publishers. We know that someone someplace and at some time made up this rhyme, just as we know Lewis Carroll made up *Alice's Adventures in Wonderland* while living in Oxford in the 1860s or William Wordsworth made up *The Prelude* in stages between 1798 and 1805 and then tinkered with it until he died forty-five years later, and knowing this prompts us to speculate on or investigate the rhyme's origins.

Now, I confess to meeting readers each year in my university classes who are content to say this rhyme jauntily, without manifesting a desire to know where it came from or what it is about. The best of such readers do genuinely appreciate the experience of reading; they read for innocent pleasure. Others, however, are more canny; they sense that this apparently innocent rhyme might have once had a design upon its readers. The most cynical of such readers wish to recast many of the well-known nursery rhymes to bring them up to date, to smooth away rough edges, to remove all vestiges of violence, sexuality, and disorder that might lurk between the lines. The best of such readers, however, wish to re-create the experience of the rhyme, not to destroy it, and such re-creation may take the form of critical commentary, commentary based on knowledge of literature, its forms and conventions. These canny readers wish to become competent, that is, informed, readers.

The canny reader wants to know something about this apparent piece of trivia not only because anything perpetuated in and by our culture tweaks our curiosity, but more importantly because our children are implicated in this rhyme. We offer it to them as something valuable when they are very young, and we rightly ask ourselves, why do we do this? What does this rhyme have to offer children? What effect will it have on them? What meanings does it hold? What meanings will be apparent to children? What meanings will be accessible, even unconsciously, to them? Such questions beg others: What is the meaning of meaning? Is meaning important at all, and if so, then how do we arrive at the meaning of this or any text? What do we want children to get from this rhyme and why?

In short, anyone who offers this rhyme or any other work of literature to a child must do so for a reason, and that reason must have some connection to a sense of what the rhyme or work of literature is and does. For example, a mother or father might offer "Jack be nimble" to a child in order to initiate a period of quietude in the home, and in so doing she or he tacitly accepts a critical sense that the words of this rhyme work in opposition to their obvious meaning. Whereas the words describe a rambunctious activity—leaping over a presumably lighted candlestick—their effect on the child will be to calm the rambunctious spirit. These words work to internalize gusto, and in internalizing gusto they might happily lead to nap time. On another occasion the father or mother might wish to promote verbal exercise by encouraging the child to play with language by learning to say the rhyme. Something about the rhyme and its rhythm makes it fun to repeat. To make this judgment, the father or mother implicitly accepts the form of the rhyme as valuable. On yet another occasion a parent might repeat the rhyme simply to elicit laughter from a child. Laughter is life affirming, and to speak the rhyme in this context is to sense something life affirming either in the very fact of the rhyme or in its meaning, its theme. Whatever the occasion for the repetition of this or any other rhyme, implicit or explicit reasons must accompany the decision to repeat it, and these decisions have something to do with the literary merit or coherence of the rhyme. In other words, we all bring some literary analysis, however incipient, to our experience of what we read, even if what we read is nothing more intricate than "Jack be nimble."

Partly because I hope that mothers and fathers, as well as professional academics and researchers, want to know more about the rhymes and other literature children receive either directly or through the mediation of adult readers, I embark on this examination of the ways we have of reading. My intent, however, is not to provide information regarding specific works of literature nor to offer authoritative interpretations of specific works. Instead, I hope to describe the possibilities for each reader finding out about works of literature herself, in a manner most suited to the individual reader. My assumption is that no one interpretation of a work of the imagination is perfect, and that interpretations are the work of individual readers at particular times and in particular places. What any reader in his or her particular time and place needs to know in order to experience a work of literature as fully as he or she might varies. Take the two-year-old child who listens to "Jack be nimble," for example. What she needs to know will have more to do with the occasion in which the rhyme comes to life and with the voice that brings it to life than with the rhyme's internal consistencies of diction and rhythm. She quickly learns that the tone of voice and the accompanying bounce on the seat of her diapers that form her experience of this rhyme are its meaning. What this two-year-old needs to know has more to do with what Wellek and Warren, in *Theory of Literature* (1942), call the "extrinsic" approach to literature. The adult who reads or recites the rhyme to the child will need to know different things: the rhythmic pattern of the rhyme, its theme or themes, its type. These are matters Wellek and Warren term "intrinsic" to literature, and they are necessary to the adult for two reasons: so that he or she can read the rhyme aloud effectively, and so that he or she can decide whether the rhyme is suitable to read to a particular child. Now we might add to this brief summary of readers the adult reader who is either a professional researcher or someone who is simply curious about our culture and its creative products. This reader might wish to know where the rhyme comes from or what it tells us about the person or people who invented it. This reader might want to know something about the symbolic import of the rhyme's image: the candlestick. To satisfy such curiosity, this reader will employ methods of inquiry that might be "extrinsic" or "intrinsic." It is these methods, either "extrinsic" or "intrinsic," which are my subject.

Extrinsic approaches might take us in four directions. We might study the historical circumstances of the origin of the rhyme as the Opies have done in *The Oxford Dictionary of Nursery Rhymes*, and consider the centuries-old custom of candle leaping "both as a sport and as a form of fortune-telling" (Opie, 227). Such an approach might shift into a consideration of various appearances of this rhyme in collections over a period of years, and we might wish to note how, if at all, the audience for the rhyme changes both in its profile and in its reception of the rhyme. For example, an obvious change in the audience is the narrowing down to children what was at one time a community experience. Another possibility, since we are speaking of audience, is to examine individual responses to the rhyme, raw data, as it were. One child might express joy at the image of a young person leaping over a candlestick, accomplishing successfully a feat that in most houses would probably be frowned on. I know that my own response involves the appreciation of subversive or transgressive activity in this rhyme. This shift to personal response might move again toward the psychological impact or implication of a rhyme such as "Jack be nimble." Does my interest in the rhyme actually have to do with a castration anxiety? Or is it more positively a phallic joy, the release of libidinal energies in a suitably subliminal way?

These four ways of reading the rhyme take us away from the rhyme itself as we try to place it in a historical, emotional, or psychological perspective. The four approaches might look something like this: History–Reception–Response–Psychology. The movement is from context to audience to intertext (I mean here by "intertext" the connection between the text in words, the rhyme, and the text in motion, the mind). Each of these—context, audience, intertext—has balancing subjects in an intrinsic approach to the text. (See Figure 1.)

Whereas an extrinsic approach to literature looks to historical circumstances related to the origin and reception of the works of literature or to their psychological implications for a specific reader or for the general reader, an intrinsic approach looks at literary history, conventionally thought of as the study of genres or literary types, or at the influences on, or the form and message in, specific works. In short, the intrinsic approach is what we think of as "close reading" and *explication du texte*. In the case of "Jack be nimble," we might concern ourselves with the type of literature called "nursery rhyme," and trace its development from early collections of rhymes in the eighteenth century or from appearances of the rhymes in Renaissance works to argue for the radical nature of this type of poetry, its connections to a countertradition to court poetry or later to what came to be known as high art. The rhyme joins a tradition of accentual poetry in English that for centuries finds itself associated with folk art, primitive art, nonsense, nonserious verse. It is, from an ideological perspective, an expression of antibourgeois feeling.

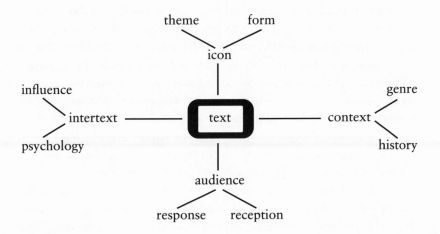

Figure 1.

If we concentrate on the form of the rhyme, we might conclude that the form *is* the content or the theme and that this content is self-referential; that is, the rhyme draws our attention to its language because this—the musical sound of the rhyme—is the meaning. Like music and dance, rhyme celebrates life. In fact, the words communicate this celebratory sense: to jump or cross over an object is to exhibit speed, agility, and energy. "Nimble" means "take quickly," "agile," "quick." But "quick," as well as meaning "fast," also means "alive." The potential pleonasm—nimble, quick—accentuates Jack's lively behavior, his seizing the day. Whatever that candlestick signifies, Jack's agility in jumping it testifies to his engagement in life. Having said this, however, we still have not explained the rhyme. Who is Jack, and why does he jump the candlestick? What does it mean that he jumps a candlestick and not some other object? For answers to these questions, we will have to set the rhyme in another context.

The context for the rhyme is forever renewed each time someone reads it. Although we might think that the act of jumping over a candlestick, just like the act of reading the four-line rhyme itself, has a beginning and an ending, we are mistaken. Jack is, like the figures on Keats's Grecian urn, suspended forever above the candlestick. Or perhaps the image of the repeated jump cut in film serves us better here; Jack forever jumps that stick, and he does so precisely because we have no original context for his action. Readers will provide the context they think most appropriate for an understanding of the rhyme. And the context they provide will depend upon their experience of the rhyme. Do they *see* the text, that is, read it silently? Do they *hear* it, that is, hear themselves or another person read it aloud? Do they read it for themselves or for others such as their children; do they read it as part of a community of readers, as part of a class assignment, for example? Do they read it because they want to or because they have to? Do they read to confirm their sense of things, to lose themselves, to have experiences only available in language, to learn something?

What I want to indicate is that an understanding of something as simple as "Jack be nimble" may take us in several directions. No single meaning, beyond the obvious meaning (what E. D. Hirsch in *Validity in Interpretation* terms intentional meaning) that someone observes a fellow named Jack jump over a candlestick, is available ready-made to the reader of this rhyme. Even my assumption of an "obvious meaning" is rather a presumption since it does not take into account that this might be an exhortation and not simply a description, and that Jack is a person and not an animal. The punctuation would suggest description ("Jack be nimble" rather than "Jack, be nimble"), but the syntax and grammar suggest exhortation ("Jack jump over" rather than "Jack jumps over"). Despite the possibility of general agreement to my assertions, the possibility remains for another reading. And another.

But this talk of multiple readings, familiar enough to readers of literary criticism and theory, presumes we know *what* we are reading. In this case, what we are reading is a rhyme conventionally placed in that body of work we in literary studies call children's literature. If I practiced a different discipline, anthropology say, then I might well consider this rhyme as part of a different body of material called folklore. My purpose here is not to debate the naming of academic territory, but rather to point out that what I call children's literature is itself problematic. What is children's literature? The easy answer is that it is literature written for or by children. The difficulty here is that in many cases we must accept what publishers publish in their children's lists as "children's literature," thereby accepting as fact that specific authors wrote with children in mind. But we know that the authors of some books (e.g., *A Sound of Chariots* by Mollie Hunter, *Red Shift* by Alan Garner, and *The Tin-Pot Foreign General and the Old Iron Woman* by Raymond Briggs, to name only three) did not write with children specifically in mind and were surprised when their books ended up in the children's lists. And publishers have recently complicated matters by publishing fiction for adolescent readers under the tag YA (Young Adult) Fiction. The best of this fiction—by such authors as Robert Cormier, Virginia Hamilton, Alice Childress, Margaret Mahy, William Mayne, and Kevin Major—may be read with pleasure and thoughtfulness by adults as well as by young adults.

As for literature written by children, this is almost never considered by professional literary critics or theorists, presumably because they either do not have access to a body of this work or because they do not consider it worthy of the nomenclature "literature" (my guess is the latter). Whatever definition we subscribe to, we tacitly indicate that we know what "literature" is when we offer our definition of "children's literature." I suspect, however, that Northrop Frye was right when he noted that we "have no real standards to distinguish a verbal structure that is literary from one that is not" (*Anatomy of Criticism*, 13), and Terry Eagleton, more recently, voices a similar truism: "There is no 'essence' of literature whatsoever" (9). Clearly, we all behave as if we do know what literature is because we all have a sense of what we perceive as literature. The attempt of the Children's Literature Association to create a canon of children's literature in the 1980s indicates what we should have known all along: canons of literature for adult and child readers have existed for centuries because people who think about these things and who are in positions of influence and power have ideas

canon

about what literature is and does. Whatever it is and can do, we can say several things about it without defining it in any more rigorous way than I have done in the preface to this volume.

Literature, according to Wellek and Warren, must include "oral literature" (10), and this is worth stressing when we consider the use of oral forms with young children. It might not be too much to say that all children's literature is the ghost of an oral form. The visual, in the sense of graphic art—book illustration—is also an important aspect in children's literature. Wellek and Warren further argue that literature distinguishes itself through a particular use of language; "it stresses the awareness of the sign itself" (12). This seems adequately appropriate to children's literature, especially to literature for the very young that stresses sound above sense. The very young child needs to like language before he or she needs to understand it. Yet from the eighteenth century to the present, those who assume responsibility for children have also stressed the sense that literature should contain. "Good" literature is good for children. The nineteenth century was rich in platitudes on the importance of reading literature, platitudes that we still echo: reading literature strengthens the imagination, toughens the moral fiber, sharpens our sense of beauty consequently improving our sense of taste, and deepens our spiritual awareness. In short, the reading of literature is a civilizing activity; it makes us better human beings. It makes us more discriminating than we are if we do not read. Knowing good from bad in literature helps us know good from bad in life. And make no mistake, we can know good from bad; we can find truth in literature and in life. This line of thought would see a rhyme such as "Jack be nimble" as preparatory; it is a piece of ephemera, useful, if at all, only as material to help children begin to read and become comfortable with the language of poetry.

The nineteenth century generally accepted Matthew Arnold's championing of poetry; to read poetry was to receive fine impressions as well as cogent criticisms of life. Fine impressions, although they seem as important to many now as they did a hundred years ago, began to lose their luster as investigations into the psychology of reading indicated that readers need not respond to a poem or a novel in similar ways. Impressions also proved inadequate to account for the complexities of form and language we could perceive in the literary text. Comparing a poem to music or to the true voice of feeling, even describing a novel as a comic epic in prose, proved inadequate to account for the vagaries of form in fiction or the nuances of ambiguity in poetry. The early decades of the twentieth century saw forms of close critical reading become popular—either the practical criticism of I. A. Richards, the morally rigorous reading of F. R. Leavis and the *Scrutiny* group, or the writers influenced by the Formalist trends in Russia. In the United States, as Gerald Graff points out, "much of the program of the latter-day New Criticism had already been formulated by the mid-nineties" (*Professing Literature*, 123). By mid-century the work of literature came to be revered as an icon; this was especially true of poetry. What we still refer to as the New Criticism—a form of careful close reading practiced by American and British critics in the 1930s, 1940s, and 1950s—articulated a new vocabulary for literary discussion: ambiguity, irony, paradox, coherence. For the New Critics, the study of literature as a coherent discipline was, in itself, valuable: "our starting point must be the development of literature as literature" (Wellek and Warren, 255).

The New Critics saw no use for psychology as a method for literary study: "In the sense of a conscious and systematic theory of the mind and its workings, psychology is unnecessary to art and not in itself of artistic value" (Wellek and Warren, 81). The study of psychology had, however, affected some readers' interpretations of literature for years; Freud himself had written about literature and drawn many of his ideas from it, ideas that go beyond the famous Oedipal complex into areas such as the family romance, narcissistic neuroses, the uncanny, and the creative process. Freudian concepts proved useful to many practicing critics during the years of New Criticism's ascendancy; for example, see the work of Lionel Trilling. Somewhat more recently, we can find in Norman Holland's Freudian analysis of literary response, *The Dynamics of Literary Response* (1975 edition), the following: "In this day and age, few of us have not heard of phallic and feminine symbols—they have even penetrated the nursery rhymes:

> Jack be quick, Jack be nimble,
> Jack jump over the phallic symbol." (56)

The impact of psychology, though, did not derive from Freud alone. Jung, Rank, and others began to influence not only the interpretation of literature, but also the way we think about the totality of literature. New Criticism accepted the work of literature as discrete, but Jungian oriented critics, as well as anthropologists such as Jesse Weston and James Frazer, who furthered the investigations of such nineteenth-century scholars as Andrew Lang and Max Müller, drew attention to recurring symbols, motifs, and characters within literature. The connection with myth also became clearly apparent and available to critical thinking. The result was myth criticism, or the study of archetypes and archetypal patterns in literary works, often associated with the influential studies of Northrop Frye.

Whereas the New Critics viewed literature as a number of discrete texts that formed a canon of great works, Frye was willing to include any and all works of the imagination in the literary universe. New Criticism is unlikely to take serious scrutiny of something as apparently frivolous as "Jack be nimble," but Frye would include it in the structure of words that forms the literary universe. As the fragment of a myth, "Jack be nimble" tells the story of someone named Jack—a name with connections to folk traditions of the peasantry (Fr. *jacque*, ME *jacke*) with its various associations: jack-of-all-trades, jack-in-the-box, jack-in-the-pulpit, jackanapes, jack-o'-lantern, and of course, the coarser connotations concerning toilets and phalluses. The jack-o'-lantern shows a connection between Jack and light also apparent in the jacklight, a light used for hunting or fishing at night. The connection here between Jack, light, and fishing might lead the mythically inclined reader to think of biblical types, and the name "Jack" has connections both to James and John. Jack is, we might remember from our reading of traditional fairy tales, a giant killer and a rescuer. His jumping the candle testifies to his luck, and perhaps to his heroic association with the light of the world. To jump the candle successfully is to preserve life. This connection between Jack and the life force might remind us that Jack is that most paradoxical of creatures: the trickster.

Frye, however, had another end in view than the study of mythic patterns in literature; he was deeply committed to the view that literature presented the reader with a total world, one that stands over against our world with its own conventions and its own structures. Unlike the New Critics, Frye wanted to see how individual works cohere in a body of work, the totality of what the human imagination has created. How does a particular story relate to the traditions of story? His aim was to articulate the conventions and structures of literature so that the readers, any readers, could better grasp the imaginative possibilities in whatever work of literature they read. The study of literature, then, was based on a growing body of knowledge, the knowledge of how literature works. What the student of literature studied was criticism and critical thinking, rather than literature per se. Knowledge of literature is dependent upon knowledge of "the criticism of literature," which is "all that can be directly taught" (*Anatomy of Criticism*, 11). And this knowledge has a liberating power; the critic becomes a Blakean creator "able to construct and dwell in a conceptual universe of his own" (12). Frye implicitly attacked the canon-making activity of New Criticism; his was a democratizing activity. Despite his fierce championing of the work of art's independence from ideology, he argued that we must consider "the participation of the work of art in the vision of the goal of social effort, the idea of complete and classless civilization" (348).

Frye's "liberal humanism" came under attack from both the right and the left, from conservative critics such as E. D. Hirsch who maintain the authority of the author's intention, and from those who viewed literature from a political and sociological perspective. Hirsch's criticism, perhaps more implicit than explicit, lies in his attempt to reinstate the author as final arbiter of meaning. Finally, however, both Hirsch and Frye share an Arnoldian faith in the power of literature to civilize and humanize. A more radical attack on Frye comes from Marxist and feminist critics who argue that literature is not above ideology, that it does not liberate us from social codes but rather enforces those codes. Literature has a powerful and direct effect on the reader; it has a socializing power because readers assume a one-to-one relationship with the characters and actions depicted in a work of literature. To put it plainly, if a sympathetic character in a novel accepts as a good the authority of state, church, gender, or institution, then the reader is apt to accept these as a good in life. The best that can be said for the New Critics and Frye as exemplars of liberal humanism is that they are "impotent" to alter social reality (Eagleton, 199). The liberal humanist cannot make the social implications of a rhyme such as "Jack be nimble" apparent. The Marxist critic, however, will point to the connection between candle jumping and the working class. Historically, the practice of jumping over a lighted candle is associated with guilds such as the lace makers of Wendover, Buckinghamshire, who did their jumping on November 25, Saint Catherine's Day. The rhyme, then, becomes an expression of working class solidarity, and perhaps a reminder of the working man's jump into the light of a new day, as much as an expression of superstition. Might we even go so far as to say that this rhyme contains a call to action?

If it does, then the call to action is oblique. And I daresay Frye's liberal humanism divorced from action ought not to be glibly dismissed. Clearly, Frye has a social vision, a radical one. But what he also generated within literary studies was an interest in the structure of a literary work. Frye's interest is in the structures or building blocks of literature, whether these be traditional symbols, recurring character types, or shapes of plot. According to John Carlos Rowe, Frye's *Anatomy of Criticism* "may be the only 'native' version of structuralism that we have had" (34). This interest in structures Frye holds in common with critics whose work derives from structuralism, a term deriving from both linguistics and anthropology and dating from the early years of this century and the work of Ferdinand de Saussure (1857–1913) and, later, Claude Lévi-Strauss (b. 1908).

Structuralists from linguistics, anthropology, and psychology had for some time previous to the work of Frye investigated humanity's instinct for creating structures. Unlike Frye, who focuses his attention on literature, structuralists turn their attention to all aspects of the human sciences. They study anything seriously, from the color of traffic lights to wrestling matches. In literature, they will take any work seriously, not worrying over its "greatness"; for the structuralist there is no great tradition. Each object of study is a structure of images, effects, characters, actions, whatever, that reflects on itself in a series of binary opposites. By organizing the binary oppositions of a work, we can come to understand the significance of that work, the tensions that hold it together, and the gaps that might weaken it. For example, a structuralist might draw our attention to the opposition between animate and inanimate objects in "Jack be nimble": Jack and the candlestick. This drawing into tension of a moving and an immobile object is accentuated in the rhyme "quick" and "candlestick." Examination of the two objects might bring us to an awareness that life and death are not as opposed as we might at first assume; Jack may leap, but the candle also burns. Both objects function through energy. Nothing is static. The candlestick, too, is quick. But whereas structuralism tends to privilege one aspect of the binary opposite—life as opposed to death, Jack as opposed to the candle—and to see the poem or whatever it looks at as a closed system, the so-called poststructuralists focus on the energy that refuses to allow Jack to land or to envisage the candle as burning out.

Poststructuralism finds fragments everywhere. Nothing is neatly packaged except nothing. In literary criticism, deconstruction is the most pertinent form of poststructuralism. To deconstruct a work of literature is to show how it does not cohere. As Alvin Kernan puts it: "The razor-close readings of deconstruction always eventuate in discovering that all texts, because of the indeterminate nature of language, contradict themselves in ways that cancel out even the possibility of any meaning, however ironic or ambiguous, and this is about as far away as it is possible to get from the position of the new criticism that works of literature are sacred texts so intensely meaningful that any paraphrase is heresy" (*The Death of Literature*, 81). The deconstructive critical activity gives free play to the interpreting mind and focuses on the point in the text in which gaps appear, gaps that indicate language's tendency to contradict itself. The written work leaves traces of different meanings, and it is these traces that prevent interpretation from ever closing a text. Unlike the New Critics, who ground interpretation in a belief in the unified work of art, the deconstructionist ungrounds interpretation. The power of the text to create meaning weakens, and deconstruction, in Jonathan Culler's words, "puts in question the claim that anything in particular is definitively in the text" (*On Deconstruction: Theory and Criticism after Structuralism*, 83).

The reason for this refusal to delimit meaning lies in an attitude to language. In traditional formulations, language is, in effect, imitative. That is, human beings choose a word (sign) to signify some object or concept that exists in the phenomenal world. For example, "dog" signifies a creature all of us blessed with the power of sight can perceive with our eyes; it has four legs and a tail that wags when it is happy or content, and it appears to enjoy fetching. In a similar fashion, "blue" signifies that an object has a certain color. Users of the language take it for granted that such words put us in touch with reality, the world as it really is. For purposes of literary criticism, this means that readers can assume that a text has definite meaning that derives from the transparency of its language. The linguist Ferdinand de Saussure, however, unsettled this commonsense view of language when he pointed out that words such as "dog" and "blue" are arbitrary. Clearly, for a French-speaking person the three letters "d-o-g" do not signify a four-legged animal who enjoys fetching. In English, the word "dog" is a purely conventional sign; it only means what we allow it to mean. It means something different from "dig" or "dot" or "dip," and so on, because we agree that it does. But "dog" has other meanings: a lazy fellow, an andiron, affected stylishness (to put on the dog), an inferior thing, and so on. Then we have many expressions that use the word "dog": hot dog, dogtrot, dog days, dog-ear, and so on. Any and all of these variant meanings and implications are potentially effective when we hear the word "dog" in a context, and it is not completely possible for a speaker (and even less so for a writer) to control what sense(s) of the word are active in a listener. Language is, as Belsey notes, "in an important sense arbitrary" (41). For purposes of literary criticism, the arbitrary aspect of language means that texts do not have absolute meaning. Instead, they mean whatever a community of readers agrees that they mean.

Since the rhyme before us uses the word "candle stick" and not "candle," we might ask whether Jack jumps over something that contains a candle, or whether the candlestick is empty. Or we could approach the candlestick from another perspective: is it silver or brass, shining or dull? Is the absence of such details accidental or intentional? The fact that we cannot know the answer to these questions, or the many others we might ask, leaves the implications of the rhyme forever open to the free play of the reader. Deconstruction is interested in that free play, but we might note again the authority that has passed from text to interpreter or to the interpretive community.

The interest in the interpreter is, of course, an interest in the reader. How does the reader receive a work of literature? Does the text create its reader or does the reader create the text? Such questions lead to what we know as reception theory and reader response theory. Reception involves, among other things, the implied reader of a text or the kind of person a text supplies as its ideal recipient (Iser, 27–38), or what Chatman refers to as "the audience presupposed by the narrative itself" (150). Response, on the other hand, involves what happens in the mind when we read a text. The response critic is interested in the web of connections the reader inevitably makes to his or her literary or extraliterary experiences. Our response, the feelings and thoughts we have when we read, directs our interpretation and our evaluation of texts. To a large extent, we read the book we wish to read; we make the text as we read it. All reading occurs within a context, perhaps most often the context of a community: a classroom, or a book discussion group, or a community of fans (fandom). The result is that readers, in Stanley Fish's nifty expression, "mispreread" texts (311); that is, they inevitably shape the words they read to fit prior assumptions about both the world and the literature they are reading. Our interpretation, then, may have little or nothing to do with what the author intended when he or she wrote the book. In the most extreme reader response criticism, exemplified by the work of David Bleich and Michael Steig for example, interpretation recedes in importance. What really matters is both our awareness of ourselves as we read and the understanding of our own psychic lives that reading can help us attain. Books that attract us do so because they speak to something deep within our psychological makeup. To talk about these books is to open a path into our emotional lives. The term "bibliotherapy" is appropriate here.

All these theoretical approaches may be, and have been, used by critics of children's literature. Recent criticism has forthrightly applied the work of structuralists, deconstruction, feminism, Marxism, Freud,

Jung, and so on to children's books. Unease, however, accompanies such treatment of children's books simply because books for the young are hardly thought of as "difficult," and even if they are, young readers are unlikely to turn to critical readings of *Charlotte's Web* to understand the myth of eternal return and the nature of the hero, or to learn of their own psychological dependence on the mother and of their emergence from that dependence. The audience for critical readings of and approaches to children's books is, generally, other critical readers: in other words, professional "book people." The hope is, I guess, that sophisticated readings of children's books will affect how and what children read by reaching those (teachers, librarians, parents) who influence children's reading habits. Does this, in fact, actually happen? Or does the hermeneutic activity in this instance produce a particularly vicious circle? Critics speak to critics and not to the people directly involved with children's books: teachers, librarians, parents, and most important, children themselves. But because the texts upon which critics of children's literature write are for children, and because the audience for these texts is relatively unlettered, children's literature critics find themselves looked upon with some suspicion by academic critics who work on mainstream literature. From the other end, the teachers, librarians, parents, and children who read children's literature look with some suspicion on those who spend their lives intellectualizing these ostensibly simple books. This double estranging of the children's literature critic puts him or her in an awkward position: wanting to speak to those both within and without the academy and finding, if not hostility, then at least disrespect from both groups. In the middle, the children's literature critics speak among themselves, more often than not forgetting the children who are the impetus for the enterprise in the first place.

In part, this is the burden of Jacqueline Rose's *The Case of Peter Pan, or the Impossibility of Children's Fiction* (1984). Rose argues that adults write children's fiction and evaluate it, and in doing this they take into account not children, but their conception of what children ought to be and ought to learn. Children themselves are powerless to create their own literature or to control what they receive. They do not, generally, have the economic power to purchase books for themselves; they do not control what books their school or local library places on its shelves. Some adult authority figure mediates most, if not all, of a child's reading, and that mediation is not disinterested. Adults want children to read certain books for social reasons. Consequently, children's books and the criticism of children's books are a form of social power.

Many commentators on children's books readily accept this function of literature to form its readers; for example, Fred Inglis in *The Promise of Happiness* (1981) sets out to show that the "best prose is itself evidence of human goodness and a way of learning how to be virtuous." "Only a monster," he writes, would not want to give a child books "which will teach her to be good." Literature helps the reader to "live well" (4). Speaking specifically about fairy tales and from quite a different ideological position from Inglis, Jack Zipes insistently points out that fairy tales inscribe cultural values in order to perpetuate the power of the male bourgeoisie in this our capitalist system (see such works as *Breaking the Magic Spell, Fairy Tales and the Art of Subversion*, and *Don't Bet on the Prince*). Zohar Shavit, in *Poetics of Children's Literature* (1986), explains the formative aspect of children's literature as a feature of its connection to "the educational apparatus." In Shavit's view of the "literary polysystem" (33), children's literature is "a vehicle for education, a major means of teaching and indoctrinating" (35). A similar view is implicit in E. D. Hirsch's *A First Dictionary of Cultural Literacy* (1989), which sets out to provide the "specific knowledge that is the true foundation of our children's academic skills" (xii). And for a writer such as Robert Leeson (*Reading and Righting*, 1985), both the child and the oral tradition are pure sources of communal value that we have left behind and are in danger of losing (13 and passim).

By setting up the child as a "pure point of origin in relation to language, sexuality and the state" (Rose, 8), children's fiction and the criticism of children's fiction cover the traces of their own weakness. For these writers and critics, the child serves as the touchstone for all that is instinctively and purely human; the child is truly father of the man. Yet Wordsworth's famous words hold an ambiguity: the child might teach us what we are, inscribe us, author us, serve as the authoritative version of what we should be, but at the same time the child is that from which we come and from which we tear ourselves away. In other words, the child and the father represent an impossibility: that which we have been, that which we continuously seek, and that which we can never find. Both child and father are unknowable in any absolute sense. What we know is what we create, and we create both fathers and children through language: we create an identity in language. As Rose argues, creating an identity in language is not the same as reflecting an identity. Language does not simply state truths; it creates them. We forget this when we blithely assume that we know what is best for our children, that we know what literature they should and should not read. Yet much criticism of children's books insists on an evaluative stance: "The shocking ugliness and cruelty of image and action in the latest horror comics and movies can only be horrible and harmful, and any sane teacher will want to keep his children out of such harm's way" (Inglis, 6).

This assertion by Inglis is an extreme example of evaluative criticism. Evaluation implies moral worth, and just as children's books themselves have traditionally had a strong didactic element, so has the criticism of children's books. Good books make us better people than we would have been had we not read these good books. Even the formulaic approach to literature traditionally used in the schools rests on the notion that the competent reader is a humane reader. Evaluation suggests a standard of value that transcends historical fashion. It rests on the belief in the "concrete universal," which the "objective critic" can explain to the uninitiated reader:

> The function of the objective critic is by approximate descriptions of poems, or multiple restatements of their meaning, to aid other readers to come to an intuitive and full realization of poems themselves and hence to know good poems and distinguish them from bad ones. (Wimsatt, 83)

This passage, a fundamental statement of New Criticism's credo, assumes objectivity is unproblematic; it implies in its use of the singular "meaning" that a work of literature has a unified and single meaning; and it is confident that standards of value, which all readers can and should accept, exist. Yet contradiction lurks in these lines. If meaning is single, then why do we need "multiple restatements" of this meaning? Would not one statement suffice for all readers? Further, what does Wimsatt imply by the words "approximate descriptions"? The answer to this question is available in the title of another New Critical essay, Brooks's "The Heresy of Paraphrase" (*The Well Wrought Urn*, 192–214). Language can never reproduce a work of literature without simply repeating the words of that work of literature. And even then, as Borges's "Pierre Menard, Author of the 'Quixote'" shows, a literal transcription of *Don Quixote* in the 1990s must render the meaning and significance of the work different from its meaning and significance in the seventeenth century. Questions as to why someone would transcribe it arise, as do questions of historicity. For Wimsatt and the New Critics, this irreducibility and unrepeatability of the work of literature argues the sanctity of the verbal icon, the power of logos to invest a work of literature with inviolable power.

Recent literary and cultural theory, however, takes up Saussure's argument in *Course in General Linguistics* (1916) that language is a system of signs which is purely conventional. The relationship between words (signifiers) and the objects to which they refer (signifieds) is arbitrary and unstable. The meaning of words is something that social groups agree on, and this agreement is an important aspect of social coherence. Clearly the best interests of a social group are in maintaining existing connections between signifieds and signifiers. Whatever disrupts or extends such connections must present a threat to social cohesion. This is one explanation for the powerful conservative force of most canonical children's literature, and for the attempt over the years to denigrate what Shavit refers to as noncanonical works (comic books, pulp or chapbook material, the fairy tale in the late eighteenth and early nineteenth centuries). Inevitably, however, the meaning and significance of words, and by extension works of literature, change as accommodation and adaptation and downright subversive tendencies affect what authors write. A critical activity that concentrates on the polysemous nature of language has the potential to liberate readers from reified codes of meaning.

If interpretation of literary works is ongoing, without closure as they say, then how are we to understand what we read? And how are we to teach children to become competent—even insightful—readers? As practicing critics, we answer these questions through example; our interpretations of literary works implicitly or explicitly imply a theoretical position, and because of the nature of language as a social institution, our theoretical position must reflect an ideology. Most intrinsic approaches to works of literature accept the notion that language expresses reality; the text expresses a vision of social reality, a vision of the way things really are, or it articulates coherently and fully an author's intention. Most extrinsic approaches accept the idea that texts participate in the nonliterary as well as the literary world; the text expresses cultural beliefs and emotional content beyond the control of the author. Of course, some intrinsic approaches exhibit a belief in language's inherent instability, and some extrinsic approaches exhibit a belief in its stability. The important thing is that we, as practicing critics and teachers, raise to consciousness our own presuppositions when we interpret literature. What is our theoretical position? Why do we read texts the way we do? At the very least, we should be aware of the possibilities for reading texts and of the implications of choosing a particular methodology.

The possibilities for reading texts form the substance of this book. But before I can begin to examine specific methods of reading and interpreting, I must acknowledge some of the difficulties that have silently moved through this first chapter. I have spoken of "works of literature," "children's literature," "children's books," "oral literature," and "texts." These are not simple formulations, nor are they synonymous. "Works of literature" refers to printed books of an imaginative nature (although this definition in itself is problematic), whereas "oral literature" is oxymoronic in that oral forms of discourse are not written and therefore are preliterate. Should we include oral forms such as story and rhyme in a discussion of literature? Are "children's books" the same as "children's literature"? Not necessarily. And what is children's literature? This question returns us to the beginning of this chapter. Children's literature, like all literature, lives two lives: an institutional one and a wandering one. More and more, as Alvin Kernan has argued in *The Death of Literature*, literature survives not by wandering but by its tenuous existence within an institution. But what we need to point out here is that whatever children's literature is, it is not only lettered. In other words, children's literature includes words accompanied by pictures as well as words spoken without the aid of a printed book. In fact, children's literature includes pictures without words. And when words and pictures occur together, their relationship varies as Perry Nodelman has brilliantly shown in *Words About Pictures* (1989).

The most accurate word to use when speaking of stories and poems for children, as it is the most accurate word to use for any narrative or other form of poetic discourse, is "text." "Text" is not only fashionable, it is also precise. It signifies a change in attitude to the "work" of literature. Whereas "work" suits the New Critical notion of the literary object—closed and coherent—"text," coming as it does from the Latin *textus* (that which is woven), suggests the bringing together of disparate things in an inchoate process that is literature, whether for children or adults. As Barbara Johnson says: "'Work' and 'text' are thus not two different kinds of object but two different ways of viewing the written word" (40). My own position has always moved in the direction of what Georges Bataille terms the heterological theory of knowledge; that is, a theory of knowledge that respects scientific rigor and also opposes "any homogeneous representation of the world" (Bataille, 97). Heterology does not reject closed systems; rather, it delights in that which closed systems leave behind. The notion of "text" suits such a theory of knowledge. The text can never be closed, for to close it is to shelve it, fit it into a neat and repeatable system. To accept heterogeneity is to subvert our desire for certainty, for the comforting swaddle of single meaning.

Children, like adults, exhibit both conservative and subversive tendencies. Whatever meaning we may ascribe to "Jack be nimble," children are quick to offer another, as naughty versions indicate. Mary and Herbert Knapp cite this version:

> Jack be nimble, Jack be quick,
> Jack jump over the candlestick.
> But Jack wasn't nimble, Jack wasn't quick,
> Now Jack's in the hospital with a French-fried dick.
>
> (180)

The creator of this version is not as literal-minded as we might first suspect. No, the allusion to French fries turns Jack into something akin to Mr. Potato. From my own childhood, I recall: "Jack be nimble, Jack be quick/Jack jumped over the candlestick/Great balls of fire!" The intertextual allusion here takes us, I have no doubt, to a famous song by Jerry Lee Lewis. The Knapps suggest that rhymes such as these are means by which sixth-grade boys "get used to their own sexuality" (180), and, who knows, this may be the case. What interests me, however, is the impetus to keep the rhyme going, to let its meaning escape reification, especially when reification means, in Bataille's terms, "the establishment of the homogeneity of the world" (96). How exciting for me, then, to discover just this last March (1993) on a visit to a local elementary school, a collection of poems by the students themselves. The third poem in the collection is:

> Cat be nimble
> Cat be quick
> Cat see doggie
> Cat give kick
> Cat show quickness
> Cat show skill
> Cat find dog paw
> Quicker still

Here the transgressive and libidinous energy of the school-yard versions finds expression in understated but very present violence. The rhyme shows considerable sophistication in its linguistic transgressions too.

My concern as a practicing critic of literature is, then, to stain the pellucid consciousness of my reader clear again, and I can accomplish this only by the force of my readings. In other words, theory and practice must connect. To read with understanding we must have some means of entering the system of discourse that we confront, and to read with some chance of situating ourselves outside dominant beliefs we must have several means (strategies of reading) at our disposal. We must, as Eagleton has argued, be pluralists: "Any method or theory which will contribute to the strategic goal of human emancipation" will do (211). The reader who knows the passage from Eagleton's *Literary Theory: An Introduction* that I cite here will note that I do not include the rest of his sentence, which speaks of method and theory contributing to "the production of 'better people' through the socialist transformation of society." "Human emancipation," it seems to me, does not necessarily produce "better people," if "better" means morally superior to others. What Eagleton must refer to is people better than those who subscribe to a capitalist system. I have no design to offer a series of methodologies that we can use to "better" our child readers in this way. It seems to me naive to assume that either literature or theory can make people "better," either morally or politically. The position that it can and does is one that links, surely, the radical theorist Eagleton with the conservative program of someone like F. R. Leavis.

Literary theory is for the adult reader a means of self-consciousness. Why do we read what we read? Why do we interpret one way and not another? What do we wish to do when we read and interpret? Without some answers to questions like these, we remain innocent readers, happy in our ignorance that we are imposed upon by what we read, that we are powerless to escape the enforced quiescence reading can put upon us. But if we read with the confidence of knowing why we read and how we interpret, then we have some chance of passing on such knowledge to our children, thereby encouraging them to become active readers too. Making children active, self-aware readers like the ones who originated the subversive rhymes quoted above offers them the opportunity of understanding the codes and conventions they meet with at every turn in their daily lives from their television viewing to their experience of urban sprawl. In this sense, then, they have the opportunity of standing aside from the whirligig of the market system to understand how it impinges upon them.

The difficulty arises when we ask how we might teach critical theory to children. How do we bring an end to their innocence? This is a pedagogic question, and questions of pedagogy are often divorced from questions of critical practice. Such a divorce is fatal to the study of children's literature, and I will take note of this issue late in the book when I speak of reader response criticism.

Beginnings

In the chapters that follow, I will outline the most significant changes in literary criticism from the time of the Formalists and later the Anglo-American New Critics to the more recent strategies provided by feminist, deconstructionist, reader response, and other theories. More significantly, I will attempt to show how these critical practices can affect readings of children's books. My examples will be many, but I concentrate on three books: *Where the Wild Things Are* by Maurice Sendak, *The Mysteries of Harris Burdick* by Chris Van Allsburg, and *Charlotte's Web* by E. B. White. My examples cover the range from the picture book to books for young adults, and they include contemporary as well as "classic" children's books. At times I will discuss unfamiliar works—for example, Harriet Childe-Pemberton's "All My Doing; or Red Riding Over Again" (1882)—and works that children no longer read. I trust that my procedure here requires no explanation, that the message of my choices is implicit.

This last point regarding older and more recent books for the young raises an issue dealt with in Peter Hunt's *Criticism, Theory, and Children's Literature* (1991). Hunt argues that the study of children's literature must take into account what children actually read. No canon exists in children's literature; rather, what we have are canons. The only literature that we can truly call "children's literature" is that which is "alive" (Hunt, 14). What literature remains alive, of course, depends on what literature we as a social and educational group keep alive. Recently, at a conference on children's literature, I heard one educationalist remark that in the inner city schools of New York children did not, in fact, read anything; rather, they received their stories and narratives from television and other visual media. Be this as it may, my passionate belief is that the competent and informed reading of literature prepares us to understand and stand apart from the narratives we receive in whatever form. Further, because narrative feeds on narrative, because all forms of imaginative thinking partake of previous constructions of the human imagination, knowledge of the past and its cultural products is formative. To deprive children access to—indeed, to fail to encourage knowledge of—the so-called classics of children's literature is to deprive them access to their history as well as to ours. Purely practical concerns keep us from knowing everything, but tolerance and perpetuation of texts from past and present are surely as important in children's literature as they are in adult literature. Consequently, in the following chapters I will supplement my references to the three books mentioned above with reference to a broad selection of books for the young. My readings are illustrative, not prescriptive or exclusive. My intention is to rouse the reader's faculties to act; my hope is that we all rouse our children's capacities to act. Reading is, after all, an activity. And to act is to affirm life. Jack acts when he jumps the candlestick.

2

The Science of Literature: Formalism and the New Criticism

I propose to treat of Poetry in itself and of its various kinds, noting the essential quality of each.

—Aristotle

The so-called "formal method" grew out of a struggle for a science of literature that would be both independent and factual.

—Boris Eichenbaum

The Poet writes under one restriction only, namely, that of the necessity of giving immediate pleasure to a human Being possessed of that information which may be expected from him, not as a lawyer, a physician, a mariner, an astronomer or a natural philosopher, but as a Man.

—William Wordsworth

The New Criticism proved to be dangerously narrowing.

—Geoffrey Hartman

Both the Russian Formalism of the 1920s and the New Criticism of the 1930s and after share a desire to bring the rigor of scientific thought to the study of literature. This desire, as my first epigraph to this chapter indicates, is not new. Essentially, writers of the Formalist and New Critical schools treat literature as a pure discipline: "literary scholarship has its own valid methods which are not always those of the natural sciences but are nevertheless intellectual methods" (Wellek and Warren, 5). The work of literature is an organic object existing for our scrutiny, and we should scrutinize it objectively and rationally to find out how its parts cohere into a unified whole. What is valuable in a work of literature is the experience of the harmonious work in itself; the reader, after long and deep thought, perceives the quiddity of the object. As Brooks and Warren say in their hugely influential book *Understanding Poetry* (first published in 1938):

> We speak of an enlarged capacity for the experience of poetry as an end to be gained. But some people assume that no preparation, no effort, no study, no thought, is necessary for that experience, and that if a poem seems to make such demands it is so much the less poetry. This assumption is sadly erroneous, but the error represents the distortion of a fundamental truth. When we do truly make contact with a poem, when we are deeply affected by it, the experience *seems* to come with total immediacy, with total naturalness, without effort. It comes with the ease of a revelation. (15)

Both the Formalist's emphasis on poetic language and the New Critic's insistence on the universal nature of the poetic experience continue to have an influence on the way we read, especially in such areas as structuralist poetics and semiotics, about which I will speak in a later chapter. As Cleanth Brooks argues in *The Well Wrought Urn*, poetry is "distinct from other kinds of discourse which employ words" (216), and the basis of the Russian Formalist approach to literature is, as Bakhtin and Medvedev point out, the "juxtaposition of two language systems—poetic and practical (communicative) language" (86).

For both the Formalist and the New Critic, the work of literature is "a closed-off unity, each element of which receives its meaning, not in interaction with something outside the work (nature, reality, idea), but only within the structure of the whole, which has meaning in itself" (Bakhtin and Medvedev, 45). In such an objective and absolutist approach to the text, a negligence to history is apparent. So, too, is discussion of the author, whose intention, the critic argues, is not only unavailable, but also irrelevant to an objective evaluation of the verbal icon. Wimsatt and Beardsley have referred, in a well-known turn of phrase, to the "intentional fallacy." Bakhtin and Medvedev speak of the Russian Formalist's treatment of intention:

> Artistic intention itself, being artistic, is from the very beginning given in technical terms, so to speak. And the object of this intention, its content, is not thought of outside the system of the means of its representation. (47)

In this chapter, I will concentrate on Anglo-American New Criticism because its critical practice dominated our schools for the better part of the mid-century. In fact, a 1989–90 survey of English departments in American universities shows that this theoretical approach remains the second most popular in the classroom ("MLA Survey," 14).

The New Critic seeks to experience the ontology of the poem. "A poem should not mean but be," Archibald MacLeish's famous dictum, appears approvingly in many New Critical works. As Wimsatt's use of the word "icon," and Brooks and Warren's use of the word "revelation" in the passage quoted above indicate, the poem is a sacred object. In this, the New Critics are the heirs of Coleridge and Romantic aesthetics generally. The reader comes to the work of literature, most often a poem in the New Critical view of things, to experience truth and beauty, what Wimsatt calls the "concrete universal" (69–83).

Both the Russian Formalists and the New Critics develop the Romantic notion of literature's power to provide the reader with what

Coleridge, in *Biographia Literaria*, calls "that freshness of sensation" (49). This idea turns up in Formalist thought in Victor Shklovsky's suggestion that what differentiates literature from other uses of language is its power of "defamilarization": "The purpose of art is to impart the sensation of things as they are perceived and not as they are known" (Lemon and Reis, 18 and 12). Using an equally Romantic formulation, Brooks and Warren speak of the poem "awakening" the reader "to the significance of our own experience and of the world" (11). One way the poem does this is to use what Brooks, in *The Well Wrought Urn*, calls the "language of paradox" (3–21), a deliberately difficult language that dispenses with the fiction of transparency. Shklovsky refers to poetry as "*attenuated, tortuous* speech" (23; Shklovsky's italics).

Both Formalism and the New Criticism focus resolutely on the work of literature, believing that its estranged and estranging language calls for dispassionate and dedicated reading. Every student of the mid-century learned to think of the literary work as autonomous and to read this autonomous work closely (see Culler, *The Pursuit of Signs*, 3). And every student of the mid-century learned from Wimsatt and Beardsley to avoid two "fallacies": the intentional and the affective. In other words, information of a biographical or historical nature is unnecessary for an understanding of a literary text; so too are the reader's personal responses. The critical reader is, in the words of Wimsatt and Beardsley, "a teacher or explicator of meanings" (34). What such ideas imply is the belief that literature, and more importantly language, is meaningful. The literary work can inform us, in truth, about reality; it is "a simulacrum of reality" (Brooks, *The Well Wrought Urn*, 213).

Certainly, all serious readers of literature must acknowledge a debt to the work of the New Critics and the Formalists. As my epigraph from Wordsworth suggests, the turn to the text, accompanied by a rejection of literary gossip and historical chat, called to all readers. Everyone has the ability to read and comprehend a work of literature; one does not require special knowledge provided by extraliterary disciplines such as psychology, sociology, philosophy, or whatever. And the rejection of both the hunt for an author's intention and the indi-

vidual reader's emotional response served the valuable purpose of freeing literary judgment from moral questions. As Wimsatt candidly put
it: "I seek a formulation which will enable us to say frankly that a
poem is a great poem, yet immoral" (96).

New Criticism is Formalistic in its championing of disinterested
analysis of literary works; but whereas the Formalists eschewed interpretation (saw no reason for the reader to look for meaning in a literary work), the New Critics' tendency was to articulate a poem's
unified statement: "To analyse a poem was to show how all its parts
contributed to a complex statement about human problems" (Culler,
The Pursuit of Signs, 5). A poem may not mean but instead simply be,
and yet the New Critic took pains to show how this "being" works
both formally and thematically. Wimsatt puts the familiar maxim this
way: "A poem can *be* only through its *meaning*—since its medium is
words—yet it *is*, simply *is*, in the sense that we have no excuse for
inquiring what part is intended or meant" (4). Everything, or nearly
everything, in a great work is functional: "Poetry succeeds because all
or most of what is said or implied is relevant" (4). Put another way,
the New Critic shows how form and content reflect each other in a
unified work of literature. And to do so is to participate in a fully
human and humane act. The successful critical activity stands in opposition to the scientific positivism that is our legacy from the
Enlightenment (see Graff, *Literature Against Itself*, 133). Like their
Romantic forebears, the New Critics conceive of poetry as the image
of life expressed in its eternal truth.

These are high words, and critical activity took its place squarely
at the center of liberal education during the mid-century, when such
words were most strongly accepted by academic critics and teachers of
literature. As early as 1947, Cleanth Brooks clearly perceived of the
New Critical enterprise as essential to the survival of the humanities:
"The issue is nothing less than the defense of the Humanities in the
hard days that lie ahead" (*The Well Wrought Urn*, 235). In these days,
which see liberal humanism under the gun, Brooks's words carry a
prophetic ring. Now critical voices speak of the "insidious legacy of the
New Criticism" (Culler, *The Pursuit of Signs,* 5), and catching up to
those students who have spoken for years about the English teacher's

eager murdering to dissect (pulling a poem apart), we have critics who speak of the New Criticism as a reflection of "the modern technological way of thinking and the will-to-power that lies at its root." The dispassionate critical analysis of a literary work is really "a forcible seizure, a 'rape' of the text" (Richard Palmer, quoted in *Literature Against Itself*, 131). The teacher or explicator assumes authority over both the text and the reader; in a classroom, this means that the students/readers accept the explications of the teacher/critic. And of course the isolationism of this activity—the argument that both literature itself and the study of literature are disciplines unto themselves—gradually resulted, in the words of Catherine Belsey, "in an increasingly over-ingenious and sterile quest for complexities and ambiguities" (18).

In the schools, a simplified version of the New Criticism (perhaps crossed with the neo-Aristotelian "species" criticism of the Chicago school) pretty much held sway for the better part of this century. It is as if Aristotle had written curriculum guides. Students were to learn about the kinds of literature (the various genres), the parts of literary works, and what distinguishes the work of literature from other kinds of writing (the word "discourse" had yet to make its way into the common lexicon). As I remember English classes from my days as a high school student and later a high school teacher, I recall the usual breakdown of a fictional work into the following categories: plot, conflict, character, setting (time, place, circumstances), and theme. Poetry was similarly separated into component parts: metrics, similes and metaphors, and sound patterns such as alliteration and onomatopoeia. We learned not how to "read" poems; we learned how to recognize certain formal features. As Belsey notes in her remarks on New Criticism, the New Critics paid little or no attention to the possibilities that follow from an awareness that language is slippery and fundamentally nonrepresentational, and we in the schools followed suit. A metaphor was simply a comparison without the use of either "like" or "as." In the words of Robert Probst, such words as metaphor and symbol "too often become technicalities for students to trip over, rather than statements about how the poem works" (92).

Does the New Critical practice have anything to offer the study of children's books? As I have indicated, close reading based on both genre classification and identification of the parts of a literary work is familiar to readers of children's books. For the student reader, comfort resides in an approach to a text that offers clear guidelines on how to break down the text for discussion and that offers a clear belief in the communicability of fundamental truths. In other words, the New Criticism in some form or other is eminently teachable to students of any age, and it has the added virtue of being welcomed by older students because it now stands as a beacon in the dark seas of late twentieth-century relativism.

I am not sure how successful Rebecca Lukens's *A Critical Handbook of Children's Literature* (1976) has been, but the book is as clear an example of what the New Criticism produced in children's literary commentary as we could wish for. Lukens tells her reader in a preface that her book discusses "the elements common to all imaginative literature—character, plot, setting, point of view, style, tone, and theme" (n.p.). In this, Lukens's book offers the reader what many fat handbooks and guides to children's literature offer: definitions and classifications that allow the inexperienced (I am tempted to say "incompetent") reader to feel that he or she has mastered a literary text. Books of this kind are many: e.g., Constantine Georgiou's *Children and Their Literature*, Charlotte Huck's *Children's Literature in the Elementary School*, Bernice Cullinen's *Literature and the Child*, and John Warren Stewig's *Children and Literature*. It might be useful to examine Lukens's procedure, and then repeat the question regarding the usefulness of the New Critical approach.

Chapter 4 of *A Critical Handbook of Children's Literature* offers a discussion of "Setting." Lukens proceeds carefully, first defining setting as the time and place of a novel's action, and assuring her reader that setting influences plot and character just as these two influence each other and the setting. While dissecting the various aspects of a fiction, the critic must assure the reader that such dissection does not, in fact, destroy the unity of the text. Although Lukens does not employ the metaphor, New Critics such as Brooks speak of the work of literature, in true Romantic fashion, as an "organism" (*The Well Wrought Urn*, 218).

Having defined setting in a general sense, Lukens goes on to isolate two types of setting: "the **backdrop** or relatively unimportant setting and . . . the **integral** or essential setting" (62). I suppose these two types of setting are self-explanatory, the one nonfunctional in a thematic sense and the other functional. One of Lukens's examples of a book with a "backdrop" setting is Milne's *Winnie-the-Pooh*. Christopher Robin, she writes, "might live anywhere at all—from England's Land's End to Lancashire, or from America's Bangor to Sacramento" (63). She writes more, but this is sufficient to illustrate a problem with this approach. From a purely formal perspective, nothing is irrelevant in a unified work of art, and in *Winnie-the-Pooh*, the Hundred Acre Wood not only could not be anywhere at all, it is also deeply important to the other "elements" of literature Lukens isolates. First, where is the Hundred Acre Wood? In the book it remains in a sort of magical retreat from what Kenneth Grahame, in *The Wind in the Willows*, calls the Wide World. It is a retreat: safe, picturesque, cozy, and familiar. Nothing in this place threatens humanity; gorse bushes do not hurt, forests are not dark and forbidding, and rivers do not rage. In this felicitous space, tigers play with kangaroos and rabbits and donkeys talk with owls. Real animals mix with stuffed animals. This space is, of course, a fantasy space; it has to do with desire, the desire to maintain contact with the other as if it were the self. In a sense, the setting in *Winnie-the-Pooh* is Christopher Robin, just as all the denizens of the Hundred Acre Wood are him, too. The father who tells the stories to Christopher Robin creates the Hundred Acre Wood and the characters that inhabit it, keeping a sensitive ear and eye turned to the child's world. His purpose is to comfort and reassure the child, not to unsettle him.

When description of setting occurs in *Winnie-the-Pooh*, it reflects the characters; in a sense, as I indicated, it *is* the characters. Take, for example, the following passage:

> It was a fine spring morning in the forest as [Pooh] started out. Little soft clouds played happily in a blue sky, skipping from time to time in front of the sun as if they had come to put it out, and then sliding away suddenly so that the next might have his turn. Through them and between them the sun shone bravely; and a

copse which had worn its firs all the year round seemed old and dowdy now beside the new green lace which the beeches had put on so prettily. (47–48)

The animism evident here is familiar in works for children, but the personification plays an even more pointed role. The clouds playing happily echo Pooh, Piglet, and the others who also play happily in this little world. Taking turns is, of course, something children learn to do at an early age. Dressing up also appears here, but with the turn of a pun and the hint of time that ages all things. My point, however, is simply that the setting directly reflects the world and its inhabitants in this book. An even clearer passage than the one I have quoted is available in the first paragraph of the book's final chapter. Here, little pools lie dreaming of the life they have seen and the big things they have done, the cuckoo tests his voice, and the wood-pigeons complain about something unimportant. These are the children, and evident in all this is Milne's (or the adult narrator's) amused and superior voice. The Hundred Acre Wood is a place of hectic daily activity, none of it particularly important in the adult scheme of things.

We might still ask, however, where the Hundred Acre Wood is. If we go a little further beyond the book itself—as Lukens does in her references to Land's End, Sacramento, and so on—we should be clear that the setting in *Winnie-the-Pooh* could not be anywhere. The south and central regions of England are precisely appropriate because of their domestic and pastoral qualities. Sussex, Berkshire, Shropshire, and Somerset, for example, with their rolling downs and peaceful woodlands, perfectly complement the Hundred Acre Wood's unthreatening landscape. The grandeur, the sublimity, of the English Lake District or of Maine or northern California is far away from the spirit of the Hundred Acre Wood. And yes, as Lukens says, the Forest, "with a capital *F*," "is the proper place for Pooh and Piglet to track the fearful Woozle/Wizzle." She goes on to note the "minimal description of the beech tree beyond its being in the middle of the Forest" (63). Description of the beech is unnecessary beyond its very existence in the Forest because the beech, in its mythological associations, is a holy tree, feminine and protecting. It perfectly suits this pastoral world that appears made for human activity and not against it.

Lukens's "touchstone" book, *Charlotte's Web* (65), provides her longest example of how setting may be integral to a work of fiction, and White's fantasy is indeed a useful work to examine from a New Critical perspective. Most of the critical work devoted to this novel takes an intrinsic stance (I think of Landes, Nodelman, Alberghene, and Kinghorn). The close reading of the genuine New Critic, however, will go beyond Lukens's description of the importance of setting to the book's themes and conflicts. Rather than isolating aspects of the book such as setting, conflict, character, plot, and so on, such a reading will articulate the unity of the book by focusing on interconnectedness. It will also show a sensitivity to irony and ambiguity, to what Brooks calls the language of paradox. Look, for example, at the description of the barn from the beginning of chapter 3:

> The barn was very large. It was very old. It smelled of hay and it smelled of manure. It smelled of the perspiration of tired horses and the wonderful sweet breath of patient cows. It often had a sort of peaceful smell—as though nothing bad could happen ever again in the world. It smelled of grain and of harness dressing and of axle grease and of rubber boots and of new rope. And whenever the cat was given a fish-head to eat, the barn would smell of fish. But mostly it smelled of hay, for there was always hay being pitched down to the cows and the horses and the sheep. (13)

Lukens quotes this passage and rightly comments that "because [the barn's] description is so vivid, we are alerted to its importance in the total story" (65). She does not, however, explain what that importance is. Instead, she goes on to speak of the importance of the Fair Grounds to Wilbur's character and the conflict he faces. But if the passage in which White describes the barn is integral to the book, then it must also somehow relate to all elements of the novel. It must reveal something about the plot, and it must communicate some aspect of the book's overall thematic meaning. I think that it does these things, subtly and surely, and while in the process of revealing and communicating plot and theme it serves as an excellent guide to young readers on how to read fiction.

Perry Nodelman has pointed out that the story begins again in chapter 3, and this set piece on the barn might well indicate this second beginning (see "Text as Teacher"). It also contains virtually the entire novel in miniature, at least from the perspective of plot and theme. First we might note the style: simple declarative sentences for the most part. These sentences grow as the paragraph moves on, and then they become compound, and finally inverted complex. The simplicity is suitable for a children's novel; it is also nicely modulated to introduce young readers to the possibilities of both the rhetorical force of repetition (virtually anaphoric in its effect) and sentence variation. As the sentences grow, they are the same and yet not the same, perhaps echoing the process of growth in children. Things change, yet change is not necessarily discontinuity. Far from it. The paragraph rounds back to its beginning in its ending, returning to the hay, the horses, and the cows. And yet, it does not quite end where it began, with the size and age of the barn. A lesson is here. The lesson is that things, of course, do change.

We can look back to the paragraph to find other indications of change and what it implies: death. The first smells mentioned are those of hay and manure, that which goes in one end and that which comes out the other. Growth and decay, life and death are what the reader encounters here. Later in the paragraph, we read of a fish-head eaten by a cat, and the same quiet reminder of death, predator and prey perhaps, sounds. But near the middle of the paragraph we read about a "peaceful smell—as though nothing bad could happen ever again in the world." The "as though" gives the lie to certainty; something bad will happen again in the world, although right now in this barn peace reigns. The barn, like this paragraph and like this book as a whole, is a favored place, a "felicitous space," as Gaston Bachelard would have it. The barn, like the garden in Burnett's *The Secret Garden*, is an enclosed space that contains images of both life and death, growth and decay, organic things and inorganic objects. The barn is a small world complete with its unseen deity who pitches hay from above. The patient cows and the horses simply wait, like the lilies, and good things come their way. Comfort is here for the reader, too; this book, like nearly all children's books, contains comfort for the reader. Even in the presence of change and death, comfort is possible. This is one of the lessons of the book.

Charlotte's Web, then, is an excellent book for young readers because it introduces them in a careful way to the interdependence of style and theme. The prose acts as a teaching device. Nodelman's point about this text as a teacher is a fine one, and staunchly New Critical in its thrust. The reader requires little or no special knowledge to understand the meaning of the book; Kinghorn would have it that the reader requires only some experience relevant to the book she reads (9). We might look again at the paragraph on the barn and note its circular structure. This is the structure of the entire novel, beginning as it does with birth (Wilbur's) and the reminder of death (Wilbur's before Fern steps in to save him), and ending with birth (of Charlotte's children) and the reminder of death (the remembrance of Charlotte's). Life moves in cycles, like the seasons, and the book makes this clear in its evocation of the seasonal round. But that fishhead in the description of the barn should remind us of something else: premature death. Not all things in nature live their appointed time. Chance has dictated that this fish meet its end through human intervention; presumably someone has caught the fish, eaten it, and now given the remains to the cat. Chance and human intervention in the natural round constantly interrupt the evocation of pastoral bliss in *Charlotte's Web*.

Take, for example, another passage that Lukens quotes. This is a description of the Fair Grounds:

> After the heat of the day, the evening came as a welcome relief to all. The Ferris wheel was lighted now. It went round and round in the sky and seemed twice as high as by day. There were lights on the midway, and you could hear the crackle of the gambling machines and the music of the merry-go-round and the voice of the man in the beano booth calling numbers. (138)

Lukens states that this description is an "essential part of the story" (66), and she is right. Everything in *Charlotte's Web* is an essential part of the story. But this description is important more for its power to evoke the entire complex of meaning in the book, than because at the Fair Wilbur's character matures. Wilbur matures, but to do so is to grow and to grow is to participate in the diurnal round, here represented not only by the turning Ferris wheel and merry-go-round, but also—and perhaps more significantly—by the gambling machines and beano booth. Life is a bit of a gamble, as the image of the tiny spiders drifting on the breeze under their balloons at the end of the novel might indicate.

As others—Roger Sale, for example—have pointed out, *Charlotte's Web* is about "the glory of everything" (183): the sights, smells, sounds, tastes, and feel of nature in all its facets. Yet this glory is tinged with sadness, the sadness of inevitable good-byes, inevitable change. "Glory" is a strikingly apt word for White to use because it nicely captures the religiosity of this secular scripture. For White, in *Charlotte's Web* in any case, this very world, this world of all of us, is the place where, in the end, we find our happiness, or not at all. The halo of light reminds us not only of holiness, but also of sacrifice and death.

This reading of *Charlotte's Web* is, in Wellek and Warren's terms, intrinsic. It proceeds through an examination of aspects of the literary text, what Lukens calls "elements," and attempts to show the tight unity between form and content. New Criticism is always happiest when working with poetry, and this reading of *Charlotte's Web* treats the novel poetically by discussing aspects of setting as if they were poetic images, and by showing a sensitivity to the prose rhythms, their anaphoric effect. We can simplify a discussion by relying on definition of the parts (Lukens's "elements") of a narrative: plot, character, setting, theme, point of view, and tone. Or we can bring all these together through focusing on a single aspect such as setting. And obviously, we could do a more thorough reading of the novel than I have attempted here. What I want to indicate is simply how an intrinsic reading might proceed.

Charlotte's Web is an effective choice for such a demonstration because the book is tightly constructed; form and content fit snugly together. The book is, in Barthes's terms, "readerly," that is, a book that offers little in the way of an impediment to the reader. The reader may remain passive, in the clutches of a strong story told in a linear fashion. What matters is the reader's enchantment with the story. The reader enters the world of the book in the way Fern and Avery Arable enter the Fair in *Charlotte's Web*:

> The children grabbed each other by the hand and danced off in the direction of the merry-go-round, toward the wonderful music and the wonderful adventure and the wonderful excitement, into the wonderful midway where there would be no parents to guard them and guide them, and where they could be happy and free and do as they pleased. (131)

Pleasure derives from exploration, from a giving of oneself to the experience. The book, like the Fair, is an enchanted space to which we as readers submit, and we take anything from the book only by playing its games, not by bringing our own sensibilities to it. It is in this respect that the New Criticism fails young readers; it tells them the rules of reading exist prior to them and they must learn and accept these rules. This translates in my experience into a familiar question from students when they begin to work on essays in literature: "what does the prof. want?" Rather than rely on their own instincts, knowledge, and imaginative powers, students look to an instructor to unlock for them the mysteries of the sacred object, in this case either a novel, a poem, a story, or a drama.

Most children's books welcome an intrinsic reading for fairly obvious reasons. We continue to consider children incapable of difficult linguistic and literary types. Children's books exhibit a strong tendency toward the traditional, avoiding the "writerly" conventions (or anticonventions) of postmodernism. This is, however, only a tendency. A New Critical history of children's books might well point out that the earliest books for children, or at least those published in the mid-

and late eighteenth century, often consisted of loosely plotted, even discontinuous, narratives. I think of Sarah Fielding's *The Governess* (1749), Mary Wollstonecraft's *Original Stories from Real Life* (1788), Catherine Sinclair's *Holiday House* (1839), and somewhat later, Frances Browne's *Granny's Wonderful Chair* (1856). These books have remained, until recently, mostly unread and undiscussed by critics; one reason is their resistance to New Critical methods of literary criticism. Another work that exhibits apparent disunity in its structure and plot is Kenneth Grahame's *The Wind in the Willows* (1908), yet this book has received considerable attention. The reasons for this must surely take us outside an intrinsic approach to literature; the author of *The Wind in the Willows* is a male who shows restless, indeed radical, desires, yet he controls these desires and conforms to a traditionally class-structured society. Indeed, at the center of the book is a divinity who sanctions an antirational acceptance of passivity. On the other hand, *The Wind in the Willows* is receptive to New Critical reading because of its unifying (or at least apparently unifying) central images—river, road, woods, homes—and its unifying theme—divine discontent and longing.

One might argue that the New Critical approach is only useful for an examination of traditional literary forms. What, for instance, might a New Critical approach do with a picture book, a form that combines words and pictures? For decades critics who studied William Blake's work avoided discussion of what has come to be called Blake's "composite art" (Hagstrum, vii); only in the wake of the New Criticism has the connection between Blake's two artistic methods been explored. The study of the children's picture book, still itself in its infancy, can usefully turn to the intrinsic close reading of New Criticism.

This is clear in Sonia Landes's work on Maurice Sendak's *Where the Wild Things Are* (1963). True to New Criticism's desire for unity and neatness, Landes argues that a "good story is a tight story. It begins with a complication and derives its resolution from it. Start and finish pictures are the visual expression of this closure" ("Picture Books as Literature," 53). She is sensitive to the rhythms of Sendak's prose. Speaking of the first sentence of *Wild Things*, Landes notes that

41

Sendak has "caught the alliteration and the caesura that characterize Beowulf or Gawain and other heroes going off to do battle" (54). Her focus, like Lukens's, is rigorously intrinsic, and she reads Sendak's pictures much the way she reads his prose:

> *Wild Things* is the most spectacular example of a book that uses size and shape of illustrations to tell the story. Watch the first six illustrations explode from the confined world of Max's make-believe to the full world of his imagination. No borders, no limitations, and, within the pictures, the cross-hatching of reality has disappeared and all the straight lines have been transformed into nature's curves. (53)

In fact, "the cross-hatching of reality" has disappeared, but not for long. Once Max arrives in the land of the Wild Things, the cross-hatching reappears, now displaced from that which contains the characters to the characters themselves. Whereas in the first five pictures the cross-hatching appears most noticeably on the walls, floor, and ceiling of Max's room, the pictures in the land of the Wild Things show this working of the pen on the bodies of the Wild Things themselves. We cannot simply equate cross-hatching with reality and watercolor with imagination. Sendak's method seems to remind us that even the creatures of Max's fantasy have some basis in reality. As Landes herself notes, for Sendak fantasy is rooted "ten feet deep in reality" (54).

Where the Wild Things Are is receptive to New Critical close reading because it is, as Landes again points out, a tightly constructed story. Perhaps even more relevant is its language of paradox, evident in those cross-hatched bodies of the Wild Things. The ambiguity rests in the question, What is the difference between dream and reality? In this book wish fulfillment is a fact in both realms. We might notice the full moon in the final picture and compare it with the first appearance of the moon in the book. Here we have the new moon with the old moon in her arms, an ill omen. What, we might ask, does this omen portend? Certainly, the trip Max takes, unlike the one taken by Sir

The Science of Literature

Patrick Spens in the medieval ballad that recounts his story, does not prove tragic. Nor is it as harrowing as the one taken by Coleridge's famous mariner. It is, however, closer to the latter than to the former journey, and Max returns to his room, as the mariner returned to his community, with a sense of the unity of things, even dream and reality.

Unity is the operative word for the New Critical approach, but what would the new critic do with a patently disunified text? Faced with a fragmented, postmodern text such as Chris Van Allsburg's *The Mysteries of Harris Burdick* (1984), should this method of reading prove less useful? This book looks like a typical children's picture book; it is published and marketed as a typical children's picture book. It is, however, anything but typical. The book begins with an introduction in which Van Allsburg attributes the drawings in the book we are about to enter ("read" seems too lame a word here) to a mysterious man named Harris Burdick. Van Allsburg first saw Burdick's drawings at the house of Peter Wenders (to whom the book is dedicated). Wenders, now retired from a children's publishing house, recalls his meeting Burdick once thirty years ago when Burdick entered his office carrying one drawing each from fourteen stories he claimed to have written. Wenders liked the pictures and asked to see the stories, but Burdick never returned. All that remains of Burdick's visit are fourteen drawings, each with a title and caption. Van Allsburg offers these drawings with their titles and captions in the hope that children will be inspired to complete the stories so mysteriously and tantalizingly begun by Harris Burdick.

What can unify a book so evidently lacking unity? Each drawing is discrete, one illustration of a lost story. Of course, we could turn the tables on the book and say that what unifies the book is its very disunity; in disunity the book stretches for the unity of the imagination, that unity in multeity so beloved of the Romantic poets. Similitude in dissimilitude is the watchword here. Although each drawing has a subject markedly different from that in the other drawings, the artist's style remains the same. The images are carefully—even meticulously—drawn and shaded with pencil to give the effect of a super-, or rather magic, realism. The focus is soft to create an atmosphere of unreality, of dream. And yet, like dream images, the images in these drawings are closely realized, even to the point of capturing styles, fashions, and shapes of thirty years ago, when the drawings were supposed to have been done (i.e., in the early 1950s). Clearly, this book draws the reader in, and in doing so it asks for an intrinsic approach to reading, intrinsic to the extent that the reader need not reflect on such issues as the author's intention, the psychological implications of the text, or the ideological position of the author or publisher vis-à-vis the reader (and vice versa).

For practical purposes, the intrinsic approach I am examining in this chapter encourages the teacher to get on with active things. *Charlotte's Web* invites activity; Sonia Landes reports that one fourth-grade class tried making the culinary masterpiece that is Wilbur's slops ("Caught in the Web," 275). The book also offers material for activities in both language and science. *The Mysteries of Harris Burdick* asks to be used as a lesson plan for elementary school; it fits neatly into the scheme outlined by John Willinsky in *The New Literacy: Redefining Reading and Writing in the Schools* (1990). Willinsky argues that "the principle thing about reading is that you are to read for yourself, for the sense which books can make of, or add to, your own experience and understanding, which you then have a responsibility to share with others" (85). Readers of *Harris Burdick* receive an invitation to become, not critics, but authors, and the connection between reading and writing is explicit.

I should point out that until very recently few children's books were taken seriously by literary critics. When criticism began to consider children's books in a coherent way—perhaps only fifteen to twenty years ago—nearly all the literature for children until the mid-nineteenth century remained lost to serious aesthetic and critical study. The works that did receive critical treatment did so in predictable New Critical ways. Most important here is the New Critical absolutism in critical judgments (something the New Critics share with an evaluative critic such as F. R. Leavis). Evaluation is important to the New Critic. Brooks worries that "once we are committed to critical relativism, there can be no stopping short of a complete relativism in which critical judgements will disappear altogether" (*The Well Wrought Urn*, 234).

One consequence of the New Critical approach is the creation of a hierarchy of good works: in short, a canon. The criticism of children's literature shares in this desire to promote "good works." The most striking illustration of this desire in action was the formation of a "Canon Committee" in the Children's Literature Association some sixteen years ago. The result of this committee's labor was, first, a pamphlet, *Touchstones: A List of Distinguished Children's Books* (1985), and second, a three-volume collection of essays on the books considered touchstones by the Children's Literature Association (*Touchstones: Reflections on the Best in Children's Literature*, edited by Perry Nodelman, 1985–1989). And yes, volume 1 contains an essay on *Charlotte's Web*: "E. B. White's *Charlotte's Web*: Caught in the Web," by Sonia Landes. This essay is a splendid example of New Criticism at work; Landes examines the conjunction of meaning and form. Terry Eagleton has suggested that American New Criticism imbued the literary work "with an absolute mystical authority which brooked no rational argument." New Criticism for him "was at root a full-blooded irrationalism" (49). When Landes writes that *Charlotte's Web* is about "the triumph of staying death, of love and friendship winning out at least this time against the apparently natural and rational order of things" (274), she appears to confirm Eagleton's description.

Writing in 1957, Northrop Frye summed up the situation with regard to the study of literature this way: "What critics now have is a mystery-religion without a gospel, and they are initiates who can communicate, or quarrel, only with one another" (*Anatomy of Criticism*, 14). Thirty-eight years have not altered this situation markedly. The irony in the New Critical method and its enterprise is that what purported to open literary studies to all readers in fact closed literary study to all but novitiates. When Geoffrey Hartman writes that "the New Criticism proved to be dangerously narrowing" (*Beyond Formalism*, xii), he is thinking about New Criticism's tendency to form a canon, "a new and exclusive line of modern classics." Hartman continues:

> An emphasis on words is discriminatory as well as discriminating unless it guides us to larger structures of the imagination: to forms like drama and epic, but also to what Northrop Frye calls "arche-

types" and Levi-Strauss "mythemes." Since these structures are
present in popular as well as learned poetry, no special acculturation or very refined training is required to observe them. (xii)

Indeed, the democratizing of literary-critical activity remains one
of the main contributions of Northrop Frye's theory of literary criticism, and I will turn to this in the next chapter.

But let me return now to my question: what does New Criticism
have to offer the study of children's books? First, it is eminently teachable. Even quite young children can learn to understand and appreciate literary figures and the language of paradox. Poetry for the very
young depends on this. Take for example, "Bleezer's Ice Cream," a
poem by Jack Prelutsky. The greater part of this poem consists of a list
of ice cream flavors sold at Bleezer's Ice Cream Store, flavors such as
"COCOA MOCHA MACARONI/TAPIOCA SMOKED BALONEY/CHECKERBERRY
CHEDDAR CHEW/CHICKEN CHERRY HONEYDEW" (*The New Kid on the
Block*, 48). Of course the effect here is largely the absurd juxtaposition
of familiar foodstuffs with ice cream, but something of the actual
absurdity of regular ice cream boards with their hundred and fifty or
however many flavors surely comes through. But more to the point is
the incantatory effect of this lengthy list of alliterative frozen lumps of
liquid and solid foodstuff. Another example from the same book is the
eponymously titled "The New Kid on the Block," which turns on the
paradoxical, or at least unexpected, use of the pronoun "she." Once
the reader comes upon this pronoun at the end of the poem, everything that came before takes on an ironic meaning.

The New Critical method of reading is teachable to young children precisely because it does not demand a great deal of extraliterary knowledge. And it is useful because it lays emphasis on language
and its nuances. To know something of the power of language, its
potential for rhythm, and its range of uses in various figures is to
begin to take authority over our main communicative faculty: our
ability to use language, either to speak it or to write it. To be able to
read closely is to be a competent reader. This skill of reading closely
transfers to nonliterary language, where irony, ambiguity, figures of

speech, and rhetorical patterns also appear. More than simply learning to read recipes and tax forms is necessary in a world where the hectoring marketplace uses all the rhetorical powers it can to affect the minds of consumers. We must learn more than to consume language; we must learn to use it.

So New Criticism does have a use. The downside is that the New Criticism does not emphasize the interrelatedness of one book to another, one poem to another, one play to another. Catherine Belsey puts it this way:

> It [the New Criticism] ignores the intertextual elements of intelligibility, the recognition of similarities and differences between a text and all the other texts we have read, a growing "knowledge" that enables us to identify *a* story as *this* story, and indeed to know it to be a story at all, or which makes it possible to understand one poem as a lyric, another as an epic, with all the expectations and assumptions that that understanding entails. (21)

New Criticism, Belsey also notes, "remained fundamentally non-theoretical and non-explanatory" (20). It does not address questions of what constitutes meaning or whether meaning is important or what language is or how a literary language really differs from ordinary language or how we situate an author in relation to the text or how we situate a text in history or how we construct the relations between text and reader or the many other questions that post–New Criticism criticism asks and attempts to answer.

In short, the New Critical method is without a system. It cannot provide a coherent syllabus for young readers, other than the one provided by the many and myriad anthologies of literature for first-year college courses. These anthologies invariably provide the young reader with a list of canonical works placed in generic and/or thematic categories. Children's literature is not without similar anthologies. For the academic, we have Griffith and Frey's *Classics of Children's Literature* (second edition, 1987), the Opies' several collections, including *The Classic Fairy Tales* (1974) and *The Oxford Book of*

Children's Verse (1973), or Judith Saltman's comprehensive *Riverside Anthology of Children's Literature* (sixth edition, 1988). For the child herself or himself we have such canon-making enterprises as Clifton Fadiman's two-volume *The World Treasury of Children's Literature* (1984). I could list far more titles in both categories, but my point is that the critical method I have been discussing results in a scattershot approach to literature. The young reader can find no sense of order to the literary discourse, and order is precisely what Northrop Frye hoped to bring to the study of literature. One result of his work is an anthology of a different type, Stott and Moss's *The Family of Stories* (1985). This work attempts to present the order inherent in literary symbolism and structure, and it is to this approach that we will turn in the next chapter.

3

The Totality of Literature: Myth and Archetype

While myth criticism endorses the autonomy of literature and its study, it does not consign the critic to the vacuum-sealed container of his own brain. Instead it links him to other disciplines, notably anthropology and psychology, and so broadens his approach to reality and the modes of experiencing it. In this it aspires to reverse the practical achievement of the New Criticism which was largely to cut off the critic from direct, explicit access to the resources of science, sociology, and philosophy.

—John B. Vickery

The reason for studying mythology is that mythology as a whole provides a kind of diagram or blueprint of what literature as a whole is all about, an imaginative survey of the human situation from the beginning to the end, from the height to the depth, of what is imaginatively conceivable.

—Northrop Frye

Criticism has to be based in literature itself. A conceptual framework within which study may be systematic and developmental needs to come from organizing principles actually present in literary works.
—Glenna Davis Sloan

A public that tries to do without criticism, and asserts that it knows what it wants or likes, brutalizes the arts and loses its cultural memory.
—Northrop Frye

My epigraphs do not, perhaps, point out clearly enough the division between a "myth critic," such as John Vickery, and Northrop Frye, who agrees with the Formalists and New Critics to the extent that they ground their critical principles in literature itself rather than in some extraliterary discipline such as anthropology or psychology or whatever. For Frye, "myth" means something slightly different from what it means for someone like Vickery. Indeed, as Vickery himself points out, myth criticism "has more than its share of antagonistic sub-groups, internecine rivalries, and just plain mavericks" (*Myth and Literature*, ix). In Vickery's terms, myth provides source material for much literature, and he is interested, as in his essay "Myth and Ritual in the Shorter Fiction of D. H. Lawrence" (*Myth and Literature*, 299–313), in describing the mythic analogues to characters and their "physical background." But for Frye, all of literature, the structure of words stretching back from our own time to the Greeks and Romans and beyond, forms the literary universe. All of literature takes its shape from the myths with which the ancient poets animated all sensible objects, and these myths, in displaced form, structure all the literature we experience. The connection to metaphor should be apparent from the last sentence; for Frye, "myth is inseparable from . . . metaphor" (*Myth and Metaphor*, 7). The important point for Frye is to maintain the autonomy of these mythic, and hence metaphoric, structures. Consequently, although Frye knows and admires the work of Jung, Frazer, Eliade, Neumann, Campbell, and others, his aim is not to incorporate other disciplines—anthropology or psychology—into the study of literature. Rather he admires a book such as Jung's *Psychology and Alchemy* precisely because it presents "a grammar of literary symbolism which for all serious students of literature is as important as it is endlessly fascinating" (*Northrop Frye on Culture and Literature*, 129).

This chapter will take us from Frye's totalizing vision of literary activity to the psychological aspect most closely linked to Frye's system, the idea of Identity, what in Jung is the end result of the individuation process and what Frye perceives as the vision of all literature: the "story of the loss and regaining of identity" (*Educated Imagination*, 21). Both Frye's comprehensive schematics of literature's structure of words and Jung's expansive description of the archetypes of the collective unconscious present us with a grammar of the imagination, its symbols, forms, and structures. The difference is that Frye's poetics inform us about the nature of literature, whereas Jung's analytical psychology seeks to provide the reader with a means to a healthy psychic life. A Jungian reading of literature presupposes a psychological significance to images and characters; Frye, ultimately, argues that the totality of literature expresses a social significance. Both accept the literary text as a form of and a manifestation of desire: for Jung it is a desire for psychic wholeness; for Frye it is a desire for a better world, for a "complete and classless civilization" (*Anatomy of Criticism*, 348).

Frye's theory of literature rests on his idea of myth. Myths, he says, "represent the structural principles of literature" (*Stubborn Structure*, 102). And somewhat akin to Joseph Campbell, Frye posits a seminal myth: the story told most encyclopedically in the Bible of creation and its paradisal beginning, the Fall, the displacement and wandering of man and woman, and the final return to a renewed and re-created paradise. All narratives present some aspect of this grand myth of human history. Narratives that deal with either the first or last paradises are pastorals and romances; those that focus on the Fall are tragedies; those that deal with the time of alienation and wandering are works of satire and irony; and those that deal with a fall from social cohesion and a restoration of community are comedies. Frye equates these four modes with the four seasons: spring (comedy), summer (romance), autumn (tragedy), winter (irony and satire) (see *Anatomy of Criticism*, 163–239). He suggests, as Glenna Sloan points out in *The Child as Critic*, an explication of Frye for classroom teachers, that these four *mythoi* (Frye's term for generic narratives) occur in historical sequence.

For reasons that are fairly obvious, children's literature does not fall neatly into Frye's historical conception. For one thing, as nearly all the handbooks and histories of children's literature state, literature for children as we know it—a distinct body of works written and published for the edification and enjoyment of children—only came into being in an organized way in the eighteenth century. Whereas Frye suggests that the period from the early eighteenth century to the present saw the dominance of low mimetic (comedy) and then irony and satire, children's literature moves from realistic forms of low mimetic in the eighteenth century (for example, Sarah Fielding's *The Governess* [1749], a work often attributed to Oliver Goldsmith, *The History of Little Goody Two-Shoes* [1765], Thomas Day's *Sandford and Merton* [1783–1789], and Mary Wollstonecraft's *Original Stories from Real Life* [1788]) to the Victorian era's interest in romance. The twentieth century has seen a proliferation of fantasy works for the young, and more recently the conventions of realism are evident in the works published as YA (young adult) novels. Whatever label we use to categorize books for the young—historical novels, fantasy, realistic fiction, animal story, domestic drama, and so on—I think it is useful to point out that most children's books take up the first two of these narrative patterns: romance and comedy.

Of the two, romance is undoubtedly the dominant influence in children's books. Romance is appropriate for children not only because its plots turn on adventures that tend to end happily, thus reassuring the reader that the world is, ultimately, human in shape and meaning, but also because in romance the structural patterns of myth are less displaced than in other forms of literary expression. Most books for children are romances with the sexual aspects displaced into respectable relationships between the hero and authority figures such as parents, wizards, wise old men, white rabbits, or kindly fairies. Frye outlines the stages of the romance plot: the birth of the hero, the youth of the hero, the quest of the hero to rescue someone or to restore order (*agon*, or conflict), the crucial struggle with extreme villainy (*pathos*, or death struggle), and the "exaltation of the hero" (*anagnorisis*, or discovery) (*Anatomy of Criticism*, 187). In children's literature this pattern is perhaps clearest in works of fantasy such as Tolkien's *The Hobbit* (1937), where the first chapter presents, as Randal Helms has shown, a rather witty (and Freudian) version of the hero's birth. There follows the quest to regain the ancestral home for the dwarves, the crucial struggle against the villainy of Smaug, and the revelation of the hero's true worth.

The quest plot, as Moss and Stott (*The Family of Stories*) and others have noted, is either linear or circular. The linear journey takes the hero away from home, through a series of conflicts, to a final resting place that proves to be a truer home than the one left behind at the beginning. Bunyan's *The Pilgrim's Progress* (1678) is as clear an example of such a quest as we could ask for. More recent examples for young readers include Jean Craighead George's *Julie of the Wolves* (1972) and Fiona French's *City of Gold* (1974). George's book offers an ironic version of the linear journey in that the book's hero, Julie/Miyax, discovers that she cannot go home again; instead, she must face the future with the knowledge that all she has held dear is past, the hour of the Eskimo and the wolf is over. *City of Gold*, on the other hand, is a picture book for younger children, and consequently it is closer to the type of linear journey found in Bunyan; here, the hero, after a long and arduous journey, reaches the City of Gold, the golden city of the title.

The circular journey is, perhaps, the more familiar in books for children. The subtitle of *The Hobbit* is "There and Back Again," and this well articulates the pattern of the circular journey. Many of the most famous characters in children's literature take circular journeys: Alice, Jim Hawkins, Peter Rabbit, Hansel and Grethel, Toad and his friends, Wanda Gág's very old man, the children in the Narnia series, and so on. This journey may also be implicit. For example, although near the beginning of *The Secret Garden* (1911) Mary Lennox travels from India to Yorkshire and remains there for the duration of the book, her more important journey takes place in her emotional and psychological life. From the beginning, we know that Mary desires to make a garden. She pretends to grow flowers in the garden of her Indian home, and later at the English clergyman's house she tries vain-

ly to make a garden with heaps of earth. Clearly, Mary desires a world
that is beautiful and bountiful; she instinctively knows a better world
than the one she has inhabited can and does exist if only she can fashion it. Consequently, when Mary finds the abandoned garden at
Misselthwaite Manor, she sets about re-creating it. Her act of renovation is as much internal as it is external, and as the garden grows and
blooms, so too does Mary. Mary ends where she began: in a garden.
But of course the renewed garden differs from the original one, just as
the garden of Revelation differs from the one at the beginning of
Genesis. This is always the case with the circular journeys of romance.
Stories end where they began, but on a higher level of being. The pattern is also familiar from much Romantic poetry, as M. H. Abrams has
shown in *Natural Supernaturalism*.

The title of Abrams's book derives from Carlyle's *Sartor Resartus*
(1839), and it refers to the sense of the numinous implicit in the phenomenal world, but it also nicely indicates the movement in circular
journey stories from a world of apparent hopelessness, of nature as a
one-dimensional object, to a world of glory where nature is symbolic
of a greater world immanent within it. *Charlotte's Web* conforms to
this pattern of romance. It chronicles the loss of the familiar world,
symbolized by the loss of parents and the threat of winter and death.
The hero's removal from his parents is tantamount to a loss of identity
or the loss of the hero's sense both of his own individuality and of his
relationship with his community, his sense of security and authority.
The hero, Wilbur, is a pig of surprising distinction, whose birth, like
that of most archetypal heroes, is obscure. At the beginning of the
story, this young innocent must be rescued from slaughter; then he
must suffer exile and descend into loneliness and fear; he later receives
divine assistance from a matronly spider; with her help, his true stature
as "some pig" is revealed; in an act both self-sacrificing and daring, he
rescues several hundred endangered and as yet unborn spiders; and
finally he succeeds in bringing order to his barnyard community. In
short, Wilbur creates a home in what was once a place of exile.

The child who follows Wilbur's struggle follows an imaginative
re-creation of the quest to create a home in this world, with its attendant themes of life and death. What E. B. White does is to conjoin the

myth of the descent of a divine figure who defeats death with the myth of the earth mother who signifies that death is an integral part of the natural cycle. These two myths we may relate to the two versions of the creation myth that Frye examines in *The Great Code*. The one is linear and masculine in that it posits creation as the product of a sky father (in the case of *Charlotte's Web*, we have a sky mother) and takes no account of sexuality; the other is circular and feminine in that it posits creation as a birth from an earth mother and hence takes account of sexuality (106–7). It is the tension between these two myths that gives the book its complexity. The spider Charlotte is both a magical creature who literally hovers above Wilbur and his world bringing him a life without (apparently) death, and a creature who is part of nature and its diurnal round. At the center of this book is the paradox of life-within-death and death-within-life; at the center of this book is the miracle of writing, the written words "Some Pig" on Charlotte's web. After a fashion, Charlotte gives Wilbur life by inscribing him on her web; or we might say she speaks him into life. The web itself, like the words woven into it, signifies both death and life, connectedness and separation. It is both miraculous and natural; it is, as Dr. Dorian intimates, an example of natural supernaturalism. It is, in short, itself a myth, and as such it structures the way people think. After seeing the words "Some Pig" in the web, the Zuckerman's hired hand, Lurvy, says, "I've always noticed that pig. He's quite a pig. . . . He's as smooth as they come. He's some pig" (82). By the time of the fall Fair and the pig judging, the power of the web to structure not only the way people think, but also their very vocabulary, is clear. As Wilbur is brought to the front of the judge's booth, the loudspeaker booms out praise for the special pig using all the words that have previously appeared in the web: "some pig . . . truly terrific . . . general radiance . . . this humble pig" (158).

The web in *Charlotte's Web* is mythic in its power to structure belief; it creates a story that asserts Wilbur is some pig, a pig out of the ordinary, a pig worthy of grand treatment instead of a premature death so that he can grace someone's dinner table. The web implicitly speaks of Wilbur as *cochon* rather than *jambon*, and its speech governs the way people think; it creates reality (see Rushdy). The desire to believe what the words in the web say, rather than to ask how they got there in the first place, reflects society's desire to focus on words of power, that is, words that convey "primarily the sense of forces and energies rather than analogues of physical bodies" (*The Great Code*, 17). Wilbur becomes something more than a prizewinning pig: "this pig was completely out of the ordinary" (157). The web itself recedes before the influence of its story. In other words, the web as myth is what Frye speaks of as a "myth of concern" (*The Critical Path*, 36–37), that is, a story that holds a community together.

Interestingly, the power of White's book shows itself in the many pigs that have turned up in children's literature since 1954. Even a cursory list would contain *Roland the Minstrel Pig* (William Steig), Hen Wen from Lloyd Alexander's Prydain series, *The Peppermint Pig* (Nina Bawden), *Pig* (Alan Gibbons), *The Sheep-Pig* (Dick King-Smith), all the pigs who populate Arnold Lobel's *The Book of Pigericks*, and even Paul Zindel's *The Pigman*. Wilbur, himself, culminates a long line of pigs from the three little ones, to the one with the ring in its nose in Edward Lear's "The Owl and the Pussycat," to Beatrix Potter's Pigling Bland, to A. A. Milne's Piglet, to Walter R. Brooks's Freddy, to Porky Pig. We could say that an invisible web connects these apparently disparate pigs, and it would be possible to write a poetics of the pig in children's literature.

As for the web itself, its mythic connections are many: Ariadne, Arachnea, the Fates, Penelope, Philomela, and so on. The child who knows such myths or who has experienced folktales such as "Sleeping Beauty," "The Lazy Spinner," "The Three Spinners," or the picture book by Elinor Lander Horwitz, *When the Sky Is Like Lace* (illus. Barbara Cooney, 1975), or Charles Keeping's illustrated version of Tennyson's *The Lady of Shalott* has grounding in the webs and patterns of romance. The web signals an enchanted time and place; as long as it holds, enchantment continues. The triumph of the web is the triumph of guile, cunning, creativity, and wisdom—the triumph of a female force as opposed to the force of masculinity, aggressive force. Mary Daly reminds us of the transcending power of spinning and its connection to female energy (*Gyn/Ecology*, 385–422).

The Totality of Literature

When I speak of the webs of romance, I acknowledge not only familiar patterns of plot, but also recurring images. Frye nicely categorizes literary imagery as either apocalyptic or demonic, and although his explanation of these categories has developed in a complex manner over the years, we can simplify this through the following table:

	APOCALYPTIC IMAGERY	DEMONIC IMAGERY
Divine	God, gods, Heaven	Satan, fates, Hell
Paradisal	Garden of Eden, water of life	wasteland, sea of death
Human	marriage, community	isolation, desiring self
Animal	sheep, lamb	dragon, wolf
Vegetable	garden or park	desert, moor, forest
Mineral	city, temple, home	ruins, tower, furnace, cave
Magic object	branch, ring, sword, cup	wand, ball, amulet, chain
Elemental	spring and summer	fall and winter

Figure 2.

The list, of course, is far from complete, but it does give the idea of a recurring pattern of images. Such a pattern is propaedeutic to an understanding of how the images work in literature, and we can take *Charlotte's Web* as an example. The plot takes us through the cycle of one year, from spring as a time of birth and hope, to summer's content and richness of experience, to the bittersweet experience of both triumph and death in the fall, to winter's period of latency, to spring again with its upspringing of joy. From the perspective of the table of imagery and its relation to plot, we can see that *Charlotte's Web* is about the emergence into life, followed by inevitable descent into the knowledge of good and evil, and the final reemergence or rise into renewed life. In other words, Wilbur grows from his initial innocent delight in life with Fern to an awareness of life's dangers and its loneliness, only to discover a hope of companionship and community. This discovery leads Wilbur to take on a position of authority and responsibility, and to accept life's fullness—the glory of life and death. In its own way, *Charlotte's Web* offers a version of the Romantic myth of a utopian place here on earth, "the place where, in the end,/We find our happiness, or not at all" (Wordsworth, *The Prelude*, 11:143–44).

The narrative of Wilbur's successful struggle to overcome death has, like all narratives, both temporal and spatial dimensions. As we have seen, the temporal dimension is connected to the cycle of seasons. The cycle of day and night also functions to reveal a character's move from a state of innocence to one of experience. The day of Wilbur's most intense feelings of loneliness ends when "darkness settled over everything" (31), and the morning brings him a true friend. Wilbur, like every hero, must suffer through the dark night of the soul. He does so in a barnyard turned dreary from rain and unfriendliness. Wilbur's space is a wasteland as long as he has no companion. In other words, time and space both reflect mood, or more accurately, they reflect the state in which the character finds himself or herself. Myth criticism invariably sees landscape or setting as mythical in resonance. Indeed, the world's great myths begin with the creation of land. Land and human psyche are intimately connected. For example, the barnyard as wasteland expresses the ancient myth of the fisher king in which the land reflects the age and incapacity of the elderly king. The land awaits renewal, just as the king awaits his death. Death and renewal go together. The king dies only to be replaced by a younger king whose coming transforms the land. In *Charlotte's Web* this myth is attenuated, but evident nonetheless. For Wilbur the friendless, rain-soaked barnyard is a wasteland, and he feels despair. In the morning, however, he finds a friend and sunshine. The wasteland transforms into a land of plenty.

This mythic connection between land and psyche is even more clearly evident in a work such as *The Secret Garden*, which also follows the seasonal cycle. When Mary is most depressed, most crimped like an old woman, she finds herself in wintertime on a dreary moor she thinks resembles a sea. The sea is a familiar image of arrested growth, an infertile and alien place. By the time spring rolls around, the moor has become a place of beauty. Its beauty, we learn, has always existed, but Mary's melancholy outlook on things had prevented her from seeing it.

The images in *Charlotte's Web* are also unflinchingly archetypal. I have already spoken of the web and its associations here with connectedness. Connectedness is typical of pastorals, and *Charlotte's Web* is a pastoral romance. The barn and its yard have their sheep and lambs, their geese and goslings, horses and cows. Their smells are rich and satisfying. This may not be a garden or a park, but it is equally as sustaining as these. The barnyard has its community of animals who get along. Food comes without work for Wilbur. He feels at home here. And just as the original edenic place had its snake, so the barnyard has its rat. Templeton reminds us, both in his name and in his actions, of the completeness of this holy place. Without Templeton, White's barnyard would be too good to believe. Whereas *The Secret Garden* moves in the direction of a truly utopian space, *Charlotte's Web* insists on the glory of this world complete with its rats.

If there is a counterworld to the barnyard in the book, it is the Fair Grounds. With its Ferris wheel, gambling machines, and beano games, the Fair Grounds reminds us of chance, contingency, and death. Here Fern enters the world of sexual politics. Here contest, whether it be horse racing, bump-'em-cars, the wheel of fortune, or a pig judging contest, is the order of the day. Here money is strongly in evidence. Here food is synonymous with gluttony. And here Charlotte dies. Her death coincides with the removal of the midway, and left in its place is a wasteland, an infield "littered with bottles and trash" (171). Whereas the barnyard is the place of community, predictability, and permanence, the Fair Grounds is the place of self-gratification, unpredictability, and impermanence. The Fair Grounds offer seductive pleasure that is as ephemeral as a ride on the merry-go-round. The farm offers the quieter pleasures of family, relationship, and love.

Romance, then, provides a form of wish fulfillment. From the point of view of romance, the world is a glorious place, and this explains why so much commentary on romance focuses on its power to console and to strengthen the reader spiritually, to provide what Tolkien refers to as Escape, Recovery, and Consolation (*Tree and*

Leaf). Romance, myth, fantasy—these words go together in many discussions of children's literature. In his article, "Fantasy in a Mythless Age," John S. Morris says myth contains supernatural and extraordinary actions and events. At one time it was richly meaningful. Primitive people believed in their myths; myths organized their world. They had the authority of belief. In time myths coalesced; they stuck together with other myths to form a system of belief upon which an organization of authority could be based. This is how myths cease to be myths in their original instinctive, unconscious form. Myths, which arise out of the human desire for security, comfort, and knowledge of beginnings and endings, are still with us, as *Charlotte's Web* should indicate. We cannot escape myths. But some myths are sillier than others. The social mythology of advertising, education, the news media, and the home encourage us with news that life is a mutual affair in which Fred and the boys get together every weekend to watch sports and drink some beer. An education in the real thing—not the hectoring voices of the marketplace, but the conventions of literary expression—will expose the speciousness of such impositions. The magic objects of television advertising—cans of pop, squeezable toilet paper, musical chocolate-covered peanuts, soap that makes us sing, packaged foods, and so on and on—exist within a decadent version of myth. Here the objects are offered for their own sake (the idea is that the viewer buys something), whereas the objects in literary myths free us to see that they have no reality beyond our imaginations. The rotten egg and the egg sac protected by Wilbur in *Charlotte's Web* are genuine magic objects; the one saves Charlotte's life, and the other ensures that Charlotte's children will survive and be there to help Wilbur remember his friend.

So far I have concentrated on romance because this is, arguably, the most important type of story for children. The other three types, however, are also relevant to any study of children's books. Romance turns into tragedy when the death of a hero occurs, as in Katherine Paterson's *Bridge to Terabithia* (1977) or, for younger children, Raymond Briggs's *The Snowman* (1978) and John Burningham's *Grandpa* (1984). Something between a tragic bittersweetness and the more darkly mysterious notion of irony touches books such as Robert

McCloskey's *Time of Wonder* (1957) and Milne's *The House at Pooh Corner* (1928). Turning romance on its head are satire and irony. Perhaps the most famous satire for children is Carroll's *Alice's Adventures in Wonderland*, but the more recent work of Raymond Briggs offers as spectacular examples of satiric works published (ostensibly at least) for children as we could ask for: *Fungus the Bogeyman* (1977), *Gentleman Jim* (1980), *The Tin-Pot Foreign General and the Old Iron Woman* (1984), for example. The world as darkened by ironic forces beyond human control appears in a book I mentioned above, *Julie of the Wolves*. An even more resolutely ironic writer is Robert Cormier, whose *I Am the Cheese* (1977) depicts an ironic quest in a world where the forces of oppression and doublethink are dominant. Mind control, thought control, and physical control are the realities of Adam Farmer's life. Even a picture book for young children may take the form of an ironic quest: see, for example, Dr. Seuss's *The Lorax* (1971) with the Once-ler's quest for money. This brings us back to happier stories: comedies. In comedy, family or social disruption is followed by family or social harmony, as in Beverly Cleary's Ramona books or many of William Steig's books (e.g., *The Amazing Bone* (1976), *Sylvester and the Magic Pebble* (1969), and *Caleb and Kate* (1977).

The four types of story together form what Alvin and Hope Lee call the circle of stories (see their two-volume anthology, *Circle of Stories*, 1972). Romance, tragedy, satire and irony, and comedy form a circle in which all that can happen to human beings is set out. As Frye says in his introduction to the Lee's *Circle of Stories*, the totality of literature (comprising these four types of stories) reveals to us "what we already know, but we can never know that we know it" unless the poets inform us (x). The echo in Frye's words is from the poet Shelley, who tells us that the poetic faculty allows us to "imagine that which we know" (69). We know what literature has to tell us because mythic knowledge is part of our heritage. Frye does not accede to Jung's notion of the collective unconscious; rather, he suggests that literature organizes life in such a way as to make that which we know in a ragged disorganized way clear. Literature can, so to speak, stain the waters clear. We return again to the substructure of myth that holds all types of stories together.

Morris's definition of myth takes us back to primitive peoples who, so we are told, lived in unconscious participation with their environment. They did not divide the world into subject and object: "Human life was not individual, separated, and remote; men and women were not isolated fragmented dots in a world of isolated fragmented things, but were united with the cosmic power" (Morris, 79). Now this is not only a simplistic view of primitive people, but it is also a shaky beginning for an interpretation of fantasy. Fantasy, as Morris defines it, is the modern response to a mythless world; it attempts to do for us what myth did for primitive people. This assumes there is a different motivating force behind the writing of fantasy than behind other literature, that fantasy intentionally tries to re-create primitive responses, responses that, *in rerum natura, cannot consciously* be re-created.

Fantasy, like all literature, expresses an imaginative vision of human potential. In it we read about ourselves, or as Tolkien puts it, we read about "man in the Perilous realm" (*Tree and Leaf*, 16; see also Ann Swinfen, 1–11). If we react to fantasy in the way primitive people supposedly reacted to myth (or more precisely, lived in their mythic world), then we remain in a preliterate state vulnerable to the fears and anxieties of our deepest fantasies, vulnerable to the impressions we receive. This seems the ultimate end of Morris's program for fantasy. He informs us that fantasy "is not just story, it is enchantment" (83), a word he picks up from Tolkien. This word "enchantment," like another favorite word of critics of children's literature, "magic," alludes to the power the narrative has over its reader. But we know magic can be black or white, enchantment sinister or benign. In any case, the suggestion directs us toward sacred rather than secular scripture. Why fantasy should place the reader under "the domination of an extrinsic power" (83) any more than, say, *Great Expectations* (1861) or *The Great Gilly Hopkins* (1978) remains unclear. Both Dickens's world and Paterson's are self-contained, and certainly they are mythic in the sense that both authors employ the structures of myth and folklore. Morris's argument tends toward a conception of fantasy closer to theology than to literature. Fantasy suggests, he says, "that we are able to live fully only when we accept a basic sense of dependence upon an order beyond ourselves" (85). Thus fantasy encourages us to believe in an absolute value above life rather than to understand our imaginations. Fantasy testifies to something greater than this world rather than presenting a metaphor for the possibilities in this world. The difference lies in seeing fantasy as a re-creation of primitive experience or as a renewed expression of literary conventions. Acceptance of the theory expressed by Morris does not take us beyond the point of intuition, acceptance or rejection on the basis of our likes and dislikes, or our openness to enchantment. Acceptance of fantasy as a renewal of literary conventions leads to an imaginative grasp of the literary universe; it leads to consciousness.

We can see that Morris's description of fantasy leaves us in innocence vis-à-vis the texts themselves. This is because it tries to tell us what fantasy is and how it affects us, rather than describing its structures. This will always be the result of working at one remove from actual texts. An a priori assumption brought to bear on fantasy will only lead us away from literature. Morris's approach is, ultimately, extrinsic. Until we confront the texts, we can generate no useful or accurate generalizations.

Fantasy, which I take to be an extreme form of romance (see McGillis, "Novelty and Romancement: Fantasy in Children's Literature"; and Bloom, *Agon*, 200–223), abounds in children's books. Sendak's *Where the Wild Things Are* is probably the best-known picture book outside the nursery. The hero, young Max, is a rambunctious lad, his aggression manifesting itself in his wolf suit and his behavior. He hammers nails into the wall; he molests the dog with a fork; he draws grotesque figures on the wall. He also threatens to eat his mother, revealing his desire for power rather than relationship. In short, Max is a boy full of vinegar; his wolfish nature is taking over. He is the type of boy sure to turn into someone like Avery Arable in *Charlotte's Web*, with his toy gun and knife, and his instinct for violence.

From a mythic perspective, however, Max might be the young hero revealing his special powers. Heroes often show a penchant for aggressive deeds in childhood. For example, Hercules while still in his cradle strangled two serpents, or David while still a boy slew the giant Goliath. Max's aggressive behavior serves as a foreshadowing of his ability to dominate the Wild Things. Sendak's story, however, is more complex than this simple snippet from the cycle of ancient hero tales might suggest. Max's wolf suit alerts us to the sinister dark side of his character, his shadow self, which desires to dominate and control others. He is, perhaps, akin to Odysseus, a hero who must learn to curb his rashness, and who needs the influence of a benign feminine presence in his life.

Max's mother functions as something of a superego. She disapproves of his mischief, calls him a wild thing, and sends him to bed without his supper. The bedroom, as usual, is a child's microcosm. In a sour mood, Max watches his room uncivilize itself. He perceives what he wants to perceive, and what he perceives is not a home. Max finds himself in a night world of exotic splendor, under the influence of the moon, a feminine principle often associated with the huntress. As Max's night world expands into his fantasy world—what comes to my mind is the entrance into color as Dorothy in the film version of *The Wizard of Oz* enters her fantasy world—the book's pictures grow until they eventually fill the entire page. As they grow, Max's room transforms into a dark forest, the forest of the night familiar from Blake's poem and from so many fairy tales dealing with the fallen senses.

Max then finds his own private boat floating on a wide sea. The boat is another of the book's archetypal images, recalling the many boats taken by mythic heroes on their quests for identity: Telemachus and his father Odysseus in *The Odyssey* travel by boat, Jason commands the *Argo*; Aeneas moves from adventure to adventure in a succession of boats. The boat also transports souls; this is especially apparent in the figure of Charon, the ferryman to Hades, in Greek mythology. English literature offers us the Ancient Mariner's boat, the many boats of the soul in Shelley's poetry, or the ship that sails to Byzantium in Yeats. As a final example, we have a work that seems clearly in evidence in *Where the Wild Things Are*, George MacDonald's *Phantastes* (1858). At one point in the action, the hero of this work, Anodos (whose room also transforms into a forest at the beginning of the story), finds a small shallop, which takes him to a place where he meets a maternal presence who teaches and strengthens him. Sendak inverts this movement.

Max's boat takes him to a world of monsters, a world of disguised identities, the land of the Wild Things. The Wild Things are a motley crew of rearranged mothers and fathers conquered by Max, who stares "into all their yellow eyes without blinking once" (n.p.). He becomes their king and leads them in a wild midnight dance. The creatures, including Max, cavort until dawn, completing the reversal of the human version of nature. This is a ritual dance, as it turns out, a demonic ritual. As in all such rituals, sacrifice rears its not so pleasant head, and again as in many such rituals, it is the king who is to be the sacrificial victim. The Wild Things eye Max closely as the dance takes place, and shortly after it is over they are asking him to stay with them so they can show their love for him by eating him up. Sacrifice, as Frye shows in his study of William Blake, "is the most eloquently symbolic act which the dreaming Selfhood is capable of performing" (*Fearful Symmetry*, 397). Sacrifice is a sign of a fallen society that exists on the death impulse, exerting its power over individuals by eating them up. It presents a perverse desire to stop the natural cycle by putting a stay to change. It attempts to consume the power of its members. Max's refusal to grant the Wild Things' wish to eat him up is a refusal of the dream—or at least a disembarkation from the dream. This refusal is also a form of self-sacrifice. Max sacrifices his position of power, his kingship, to return home and to reassume his position of sonship.

Sendak explains his mythic story through the psychology of emotions. Max's anger at his mother prompts him to have this dream; his fantasy is therapeutic and safely releases his anger (see Hentoff, 344). That Sendak is interested in the therapeutic power of dreams is clear. It is evident in the first book he both wrote and illustrated, *Kenny's Window* (1956), in which Kenny dreams of a garden with a tree and the sun and moon shining together. Kenny's desire is to live in the dream garden. He does not exactly get what he desires at the beginning of the story; instead he receives seven questions from a four-legged rooster. If he answers these questions, he hopes he can live in the garden. He does answer the questions, with a little help from his friends, but his reward is not exactly as he had expected. He learns that wishing for something takes you halfway to having what you wish for. And you can travel the rest of the way imaginatively. By the end of the story his dreams are where his desires come true.

Sendak returns to the dream quest in *In the Night Kitchen* (1970), where Mickey dreams of trouble in the Night Kitchen. Three jolly bakers, triple replicas of Oliver Hardy, need milk if they are to complete their cake by morning. Mickey falls asleep, falls into the Night Kitchen, falls into the batter being prepared for the morning cake, and saves the night's baking. The bakers need milk and Mickey, wrapped in his plane of batter, gets it for them. This dream offers Mickey the security of the womb, and his waking is a renewal; he is born into a new day. He and the cake rise from the dream ready for the morning. The dream not only provides Mickey with the wish fulfillment of a return to the safety of the womb, but it also satisfies his sense of accomplishment.

If we apply the psychology of dreams to *In the Night Kitchen* or *Where the Wild Things Are*, our interpretations must be extraliterary or extrinsic. To see these stories as mythic, however, is to stand back from them and see how they fit the totality of imaginative possibility that has its expression in literature. *Where the Wild Things Are* is an exciting example for the young child of the structure of stories. Not surprisingly, it tells of a journey, a journey on which we encounter many familiar images: a wolf, a forest, a full moon, monsters, a cave, and the sea. These should remind us that we are in a literary landscape that may or may not be a psychological one too. The fact that Max's journey is a dream journey should lead us to other literary dreams. Lewis Carroll's Alice dreams because she is bored, Chris Van Allsburg's Ben dreams because the sound of music lulls him, and Max dreams because he is angry, but in every case falling asleep means falling. The characters enter unfamiliar worlds where threats to their identity lurk behind every false grin. Such a world remains untamed and unpredictable, until the hero either orders it or leaves it. Once he has ordered it, the story is over; if he simply leaves it, the story may continue, as in series books by such writers as C. S. Lewis, Susan Cooper, Lloyd Alexander, or Ursula LeGuin. In Lewis's *The Last Battle* (1956), the last of the Narnia books, the children reach the perfected Narnia and stay there. We learn, disconcertingly, that they are dead, having been killed in a train crash. We can explain the story through Christian eschatology, but in terms of the literary fantasy the story has ended, the struggle has been successfully completed, and the final social perfection realized. Identity is now complete. This is the story that ends with the new heaven and earth. But Revelation also contains the story of the binding of Satan; he escapes after a thousand years to keep the story going. In *Alice's Adventures in Wonderland* (1865), Alice cannot order her dream world, and she destroys it out of frustration. But the story does not end here. Alice's sister imagines a future for Alice, which she will have to struggle to attain. The story presses on.

An even more cunning example of the continuing story is Chris Van Allsburg's *Ben's Dream* (1982). The reader who has a copy with a dust jacket will find on the back cover a picture that records an incident inside Ben's dream but that does not occur in the pages of the book. The continuing of the dream onto what Genette calls the peritext (that which lies outside the text itself; for example, endpapers, title page, covers, and dedication pages) teases the reader back into the dream even though the final pages of the book apparently saw the dream come to an end. We are reminded that Ben's friend Margaret had the same dream, and that Ben saw her in his. The question arises: are they, in fact, awake at the end of the book? Romantic poetry is fond of conceiving of life after the Fall as a sleep; history is, in Stephen Dedalus's formulation, a nightmare from which we are trying to awake (Joyce, *Portrait of the Artist As a Young Man*). Van Allsburg's book implies that the dream is a reality from which we have yet to awake. All stories take us to a world in which the only reality is a dream reality. When we finally do wake from this dream, we will live in the world that literature creates (see Frye, *The Great Code*, 108).

Such a concept of story gives us a method of evaluation, but what we evaluate is less the literary world than the nonliterary world. We accept George MacDonald's fantasy worlds as imaginative constructs that transcend conventional morals. Something revolutionary in MacDonald's books keeps our eyes on human possibility (see McGillis, *For the Childlike*, 12–13). We see that this has something to do with integrating human and natural life in a single but separate relationship.

This is why Lewis's Narnia books are popular, not because of the Christian allegory, which many of my students assert they had not at first recognized in the books anyway. As for *Where the Wild Things Are*, this integration of the natural and the human is evident not in Max and his wolf suit (from which he is emerging at the end of the story), but rather in the plant standing beside Max's hot supper on the table in his room. The wolf eats raw food; the boy cooked food. Both plant and supper signify the presence of Max's mother. Although we never see her in the book, she is intensely present. She provides evidence that the natural and the human need not be set against each other. She represents a humanized nature, whereas the island of the Wild Things represents nature as alien, a force that desires to swallow us.

I have spent a considerable time on *Where the Wild Things Are* because it is a picture book and because it shows the pattern of romance so clearly. We may, however, bring this same approach to any fictional work for children, even one so apparently discontinuous as Van Allsburg's *The Mysteries of Harris Burdick*. Here, the fourteen discrete illustrations with their captions are ostensibly the germ of fourteen unrelated stories. The genre of this quirky work is probably best described as "anatomy," in Frye's terms a type of prose fiction that is free-ranging and intellectual. Frye says this type of work "is not primarily concerned with the exploits of heroes, but relies on the free play of intellectual fancy and the kind of humorous observation that produces caricature." He goes on to say that at its most concentrated, this form "presents us with a vision of the world in terms of a single intellectual pattern" (*Anatomy of Criticism*, 309–10). If there is a single intellectual pattern in *Harris Burdick*, then it is the pattern of fantasy; each of the illustrations invites the reader to construct a story that will undoubtedly stretch the laws of nature. Over and above this, however, the familiar pattern of romance uncannily appears in *Harris Burdick*. Not only do each of the illustrations point to irruptions of the marvelous into the mundane—and several provide distinct hints of romance plots, journeys into unknown territory—but the book as a totality moves from an image of sleep and its attendant dreams to one of apocalypse. The "perfect lift-off" in the final illustration might be read in the context of 1950s science fiction, but it equally suggests a departure from the known to the unknown, a journey of heroic proportions. If we read the book using the peritext again, we move from the front cover with its illustration of a mysterious quest, to this apocalyptic final illustration, to the totally black back cover. Perhaps romance turns into irony here. In any case, each of the illustrations in *Harris Burdick* continues the questioning of reality we saw in *Ben's Dream*, and which we can find in virtually all of Van Allsburg's work. Van Allsburg never tires of playing with the metaphor of sleep, so important to mythic thought.

One illustration in *Harris Burdick*, the one that also appears on the front cover, shows four people, two adults and two children, sailing on a cart that travels on rails. They move away from the viewer into a foggy distance (I am reminded of Caspar David Friedrich's painting, *Wanderer Above the Mists*). In the distance and to the right is visible a Gothic looking building. The title and caption for this illustration read: "Another Place, Another Time" and "*If there was an answer, he'd find it there.*" The hero of *Harris Burdick* is the reader, and what he or she finds in these haunting pictures is an invitation to find himself or herself by completing the stories suggested by pictures, titles, and captions. In romance, heroes go looking for something, and what they usually look for and sometimes find is themselves. Winnie-the-Pooh and Piglet stalk a Hefalump in their backyard; what they find is themselves. This is precisely what most characters in romance discover in the creatures they meet. This signifies that the landscape of romance is internal. This explains why such books lend themselves so readily to a psychological reading.

Elliott Gose, for example, sees Max's journey in *Where the Wild Things Are* as a journey into himself for the purposes of "psychic integration" (13). Perhaps this example is too pat. *Charlotte's Web*, however, appears to take place in a real—as opposed to an imaginary or purely psychological—landscape. Yet here, too, readers have found psychological comfort. Margaret and Michael Rustin, for example, see the book as a lovingly delicate evocation of mother-love and its importance in the healthy growing process of a child (146–62). Both Gose and the Rustins employ the psychological work of such object-relations theorists as D. W. Winnicott and Melanie Klein.

We could, however, apply the Jungian model of the individuation process to Wilbur's experiences to show that these experiences reflect psychic growth. As Marie von Franz describes it, the "actual processes of individuation . . . generally begin with a wounding of the personality and the suffering that accompanies it" (169). This wounding is, in effect, a separation of the unconscious inside us from the social world outside us. What usually follows is a meeting with the shadow part of the self, the unconscious self that we usually avoid. Connected to the shadow experience is a desire to break free of restrictions; the shadow serves to criticize the self for being incomplete. Another aspect of this process counters the shadow. This is the anima or animus, depending on whether the individual is male or female. The male discovers an anima figure in his unconscious, and this figure has some connection with his mother. If the person attends to his anima, growth toward an integrated personality takes place. As von Franz puts it: the anima has the role of "putting a man's mind in tune with the right inner values" (193). These right inner values have to do with both the private and social self; in other words, the individual comes to terms with himself or herself and with external nature or the world outside the self.

Jungians are wont to specify a fourfold movement in the complete individuation process: initial wholeness, alienation of the ego, struggle with shadow and anima figures, and final reintegration of the ego with the Self, "the ordering and unifying center of the total psyche" (Edinger, 3). Looked at in this way, *Charlotte's Web* tells the story of Wilbur's happy first days, followed by loneliness and fear of death when he goes to the Zuckermans. His childish behavior manifests itself in a concern for himself, and Templeton functions somewhat as a shadow figure by representing an exaggeration of Wilbur's own greedy self. Charlotte, of course, is a maternal anima figure who teaches Wilbur to accept life in all its contradictions. She not only teaches him this, but she also puts him in touch with his Self. By the book's end, Wilbur has matured. He thinks of others as well as himself. He is "radiant," and he comprehends the "glory" of all things. The book in its use of the four seasons, the cyclical round of one year, and the mandala-like barn shows the unity of both life and literature.

Whereas Frye sets out to show how the structure of an individual work fits the larger structure of the literary universe, Jungians set out to illustrate how an individual work expresses the structures of consciousness. For the Jungian, *Charlotte's Web* not only expresses the idea of wholeness, it also has the potential to accomplish wholeness for the reader.

Such archetypal criticism, as Elizabeth Wright notes, argues for the universality of literary symbols and plots (69). The tendency is to see all works of literature as examples of the same pattern. Above all, both Jung and Frye see literature as the healthy expression of humanity's desire for wholeness and unity. Consideration of the author, the historical context of a work, or the cultural milieu from which it derives are overlooked. One positive result of this for children's literature specialists is that archetypal criticism is teachable. As Jon Stott, Anita Moss, Kieran Egan, and Alvin and Hope Lee have all argued, an elementary curriculum can be created based upon Frye's critical model. Frye himself has provided a rough sketch of what such a curriculum would look like. In his essay "Elementary Teaching and Elemental Scholarship," he writes:

> As for the teaching of literature, it is obvious that a good deal of it should consist in reading and listening to stories. The stories of Biblical and Classical mythology should clearly have a central place in all elementary teaching of literature, so that the student is thoroughly familiar with them, as stories, before he embarks on the more systematic study of mythology that I have assumed would begin with high school. (*The Stubborn Structure*, 101)

Frye stresses the importance of exposing young readers to a variety of stories in the romance and comedy modes, and I have before suggested that much literature for young children falls into the category "fantasy." Such works are primitive in the sense that they demand little special education from the reader. Many commentators, including Tolkien, tell us that fantasy's importance stems from the fact that it reminds us of the wonder in life, that it freshens our contact with the world allowing us to see the world again as if for the first time. But this is not the special prerogative of fantasy, or of art. One's experience of art may do this, but so will other experiences. Fantasy (and literature in general) offers us metaphor. A Wild Thing is unique but sensible because it looks like a cuddly teddy mother or father with claws, horns, and funny barracuda teeth. The importance of metaphor, here and everywhere, is not that it reveals life's wonder, but rather that it reveals the wonder of the human imagination that can create the world it desires.

In Saint-Exupéry's *The Little Prince* (1943), the narrator sees, while he is still a child, a fascinating book called *True Stories from Nature*, which contains a picture of a boa constrictor swallowing an animal, an image that suggests what happens to the narrator (and all children) as he grows through the smiling jaws of adulthood. What the child does with the fact of the boa's eating habits is to transform them into the imaginative vision of the snake with an elephant in his gullet. He tames natural fact, absorbs it, and re-creates it in a genuinely human form. The image of a boa constrictor with an elephant inside it can only exist as an imaginative idea, not a reality in nature.

This is where the social significance of literature becomes clear. In literature language is at its most metaphoric, controlled not by laws, regulations, tables, or standards of verifiable truthfulness, but by the disciplined imagination. At the other end of the verbal spectrum we have the language of science, conceptual language that binds us to rules of logic and natural fact. The child will have to cope with both modes of discourse, and we should ensure that he or she does not lose one at the expense of the other. Conceptual language suggests an absolute external to man; it implies our life can be and has been planned. If we follow the proper path of rational discourse, the answers to all problems lie before us. We can logically prepare for the future. Contingency comes under control. Metaphor, on the other hand, reminds us that we live in the world we create. It also reminds us of the unreality of language. Burns tries to convince us that his love is "like a red red rose"; we know she is and yet she is not, and it is this space between the is and the is not that frees us. The metaphor (here a simile) trips up the supposed "reality" of what we look at or read; it keeps us aware of the conventions that surround us in life and in literature.

My students often drag up the old cliché about realism, the true to life syndrome, as a tool of evaluation for literature, but it should be clear that this demand ignores the nature of the imagination, which they also feel requires plenty of nourishment. The demand for realism indicates the desire to "believe in" something, and those same voices also demand definitive interpretations of the texts we read. Rather than seeking single meaning and Newton's sleep (an approach to the world that is scientific, rational, one-dimensional, and decidedly materialistic), readers should accept the challenge of imaginative contact with literature and its many conventions. It is these many conventions that archetypal or myth criticism sets out for us to use as propaedeutic knowledge.

The creation of a literature curriculum based on the "circle of stories" or on the quest theme or on various large metaphors such as the garden and its opposite the wilderness or the city and its opposite the ruin is quite possible, but it means educators must take seriously the notion of literature as a total structure of words rather than as a series of discrete works that deal with more or less relevant themes. Too often, we utilize literature for nonliterary ends: to keep students quiet, to supplement work in history or social studies, to encourage children in the other arts such as drawing or drama, or to inculcate improving manners and conventional moral behavior. The archetypal or mythic approach has the virtue of centripetal force. The literary universe remains central even when we turn our attention to its role in young readers' lives.

Two arguments are often brought to bear on the archetypal approach. First, the archetypal critic concentrates on the recurring patterns in a literary work to the neglect of its uniqueness. We might argue the reverse in connection with New Criticism: this approach is so intent upon the uniqueness of a work that it renders the critic myopic, and he or she cannot see what connects one work with another. However this may be, a second argument against archetypal criticism, as I noted in chapter 1, is that it is powerless to initiate political action. The important point here is that this approach does not take into account the social forces that shape and speak through works of literature. Archetypal criticism is, so the argument goes, politically naive, perhaps even reactionary. From a psychological perspective, the idea that a work of art might have something to do with the particular neuroses of an author or an age remains as irrelevant as it was for the New Critics. The attention to broad strokes, to familiar symbols, plots, and characters does not take account of nuances of language and less familiar images. Another kind of psychoanalytic criticism does.

4

Journey to the Interior:
Psychoanalytic Criticism

Psychoanalysis is a theory of interpretation which calls into question the "commonsense" facts of consciousness.

—Elizabeth Wright

A psychoanalyst interpreting a symptom, dream or verbal slip and a literary critic interpreting a poem thus share the burden of having to become conceptual rhetoricians.

—Harold Bloom

There are a wide variety of activities called psychoanalytic criticism.

—Meredith Anne Skura

But all stories—and all literature—have this basic way of meaning: they transform the unconscious fantasy discoverable through psycho-analysis into the conscious meanings discovered by conventional interpretation.

—Norman N. Holland

My epigraph from Norman Holland's *The Dynamics of Literary Response* draws attention to the role of literature as itself an analyst; it is as if, for Holland, literature has the power to make what is latent in our fantasies—that is, in the fantasies of both reader and writer—manifest. The very ambiguity of his statement situates our problem. Literature is a transforming power, but it remains fixed between the fantasies that require an analyst to decipher and those that require a literary interpreter (critic) to discover. What remains ambiguous here is whose fantasies become interpretable: the author's or the reader's. Holland sorts this out in his book by arguing that the work of literature presents the reader with disguised childhood fantasies, which the reader unconsciously compares with his own versions of these same fantasies. In other words, the psychoanalytic critic comes to understand in the light of consciousness the repressed desires that the writer has encoded in the text and that the reader has buried deep within his or her own unconscious. The question, however, does not go away: whose psyche does the text represent? And is the text itself a psyche?

The answer to the questions will depend upon which brand of psychoanalytic activity the reader practices, and as Skura notes, psychoanalytic criticism takes many forms. For our purposes, we need to ask an even more fundamental question: of what use is psychoanalytic criticism to the study of children's books? Before we can approach an answer to this question, we need to have some idea how such criticism works. Perhaps the first step in clearing some ground here is to point out that the term "psychoanalytic criticism" refers to a type of reading and interpretation based on the work of Sigmund Freud. "Analytic psychology" is the term used to describe the kind of activity associated with C. G. Jung. My review in this chapter of several forms of Freudian reading must necessarily be brief and somewhat reductive. The main point, however, is available in my first two epigraphs: whatever psychological approach one uses, one has the task of unearthing a latent meaning lying beneath a manifest one, and of finding a language in which to articulate this latent meaning.

Freudian language has achieved some familiarity in nonpsychoanalytic circles partly because of Freud's notoriety, especially in mid-century. I have already used two of Freud's terms: "manifest" and "latent." These terms refer to the obvious (conscious) level of meaning of a dream or of a literary text and to the "hidden" or "buried" (unconscious) level of meaning. The use of the word "level" suggests layers of strata, something akin to a geological formation. The interpreter must dig deep to uncover all the meaning embedded in a text. Such metaphors surface when students exhibit resistance to "digging for hidden meaning." Their resistance is understandable when we remember just how resistant we all are to uncovering facets of our own unconscious. Freudian interest in sexual implications, or at least in aspects of the psyche having to do with the comforts of desire that social forces demand we repress, meets with the very disapproval sanctioned by social forces.

Freudian readings can have wit. Randal Helms points out the Freudian implications at the beginning of Tolkien's *The Hobbit*. He directs our attention to the latent meaning of Bilbo's snug warm round home, Bag End. Bilbo lives in his comfortable "bag" without anxiety or fear. He has everything he needs to nourish himself, and he likes nothing more than sucking on his pipe. He remains in the oral stage of development, that stage in which, as Freud writes, he does "not as yet distinguish his ego from the external world as the source of the sensations flowing in upon him" (Holland, 34). Bilbo's world is akin to a womb, and he leaves this in chapter 2 when he begins the journey. We already know that this journey will prove formative for Bilbo, take him to maturity, and it should be no surprise that early in his adventure he breaks his pipe and acquires a sword, which he places in his belt. As Helms notes, the sword is a perfect little phallic symbol, and it signals the beginning of Bilbo's empowerment, his ability to stand erect and take care of himself and others (cf. Helms, 41–43).

This reading of *The Hobbit* represents the most basic form of Freudian analysis, but it also provides a paradigm for much of what the reader meets in children's literature. It might almost be an axiom that books for children are Freudian in the sense that they offer maps to the unconscious stages of psychic development. From an anthropological perspective, and perhaps from a Jungian one too, children's

books, both collectively and in each work of fiction, present a rite of
passage from dependence to maturity. The journeys they so sedulously
and insistently chronicle are versions of the internalized romantic
quest romance, which in Freudian terms becomes the "family
romance," that struggle to comprehend our origins. Children's books
and the criticism of children's books more often than not, as
Jacqueline Rose has noted (see chapter 1 of *The Case of Peter Pan*),
assume that memories of childhood are transparent rather than opaque
and mysterious. Because they are transparent, they provide clear
visions into the psychic past and into the working of the mind. They
are comforting both to the adult who writes the books and to the child
who receives them.

Take, for example, *Charlotte's Web* again. In chapter 1, Fern
saves the runt pig from death and becomes its mother. She teaches it to
suck from a bottle, and Wilbur, the pig, enters the oral stage, all his
needs and desires satisfied by Fern, who strokes him, feeds him, and
puts him to bed (8). We might argue that the day Fern and Avery go
swimming in the brook marks the day Wilbur enters the anal stage,
that stage when passivity-activity gives place to defiance-submission
(see Holland, 39). Wilbur delights in the sticky and oozy mud along
the shore; this is his first experience playing by himself. Shortly after,
Wilbur goes to live in a manure pile at the Zuckermans' farm.

Here Wilbur will, of course, enter the phallic stage; that is, he
will learn what it means to be in the world. Finding himself bored,
Wilbur expresses a weariness with life. The animals nearby encourage
him to buck up and to escape from the barnyard. He does this by
pushing through some loose boards in the fence, but he finds the freedom of the outside not to his liking. Faced with the freedom to do
what he wishes, he cannot think what to do. Instead he longs for a
return to the safety and comfort of the yard, and when Mr.
Zuckerman offers him a pail of warm slops, Wilbur gladly returns to
the barnyard. In other words, Wilbur gladly represses desire in order
to remain safe. His first desire is for safety and comfort, the things he
experienced in the oral stage of his life, and therefore he readily
accepts the slops to satisfy his oral needs. The slops are, of course, a
substitute for the original oral satisfaction of the bottle (the mother's

breast), and as substitute they should remind us that the bottle, the mother's breast, cannot be reclaimed. In other words, Wilbur transfers his desire for the bottle to the slops, but this very transference indicates removal from the mother, and removal from the mother initiates the movement toward death. *Charlotte's Web*, as everyone knows, is about death. Just how it is about death, however, remains to be seen.

From a Freudian perspective, Wilbur confronts his own instinct for death: "I'm less than two months old and I'm tired of living" (16). His attempt to escape from this death instinct proves ineffectual, for he learns that the Zuckermans are fattening him up in order to turn him into smoked bacon and ham. White attempts to bring together the two instincts, for life and for death, Eros and Thanatos, to provide his child readers with both truth and comfort, the truth that death is a reality and the comfortable fantasy that death may be overcome. Charlotte, the mother who gives Wilbur life, accepts death; Wilbur, the son who accepts the mother's sacrifice, lives with the illusion of permanency. White is subtle enough, however, to indicate that Wilbur takes the place of Charlotte; he is something of a mother to Charlotte's children tucked snugly in the egg sac Wilbur carries in his mouth. Wilbur, like Charlotte, will eventually die. Rather than emphasize this, White concentrates on Eros, on life as satisfyingly rich and pleasurable. Wilbur remains in his "warm delicious cellar" (183). This book finally refuses to leave the womb.

Another way of saying this is that *Charlotte's Web* readily accepts repression. As a postwar book, *Charlotte's Web* is sharply aware of the drastic consequences of released repression. When the id will out, death and destruction follow. White's book, then, is deeply conservative in its desire to perpetuate the stilling of desire. Repression does, after all, serve the larger social structure, and what every farmer wants is a quiet and satisfied collection of animals. What every society wants is a quiet and satisfied collection of people. Perhaps for this reason, many books for young children displace aggression and offer substitutes for desire. I think of such classics of the genre as *Winnie-the-Pooh*, Philippa Pearce's *Tom's Midnight Garden*, the Narnia series, Susan Coolidge's *What Katy Did*, *The Secret Garden*, L. M. Montgomery's *Anne of Green Gables*, and so on. These are books in which characters learn to sublimate desire, to accept repression both as a psychological and a social necessity. If we shift attention from the books' characters to their authors, we might detect a similar psychology at work: the displacement of desire into imaginative completion. To return to Wilbur for a moment, we can, I think, see in him the polymorphously perverse; in Freudian terms Wilbur's desire, his libidinal energy, is perverse precisely because it is polymorphous. Wilbur takes pleasure in many forms of sense (in Freudian terms, read "sexual") gratification without subordinating them to what Freud says the sexual life must address: "the purposes of reproduction" (*General Introduction*, 326). Wilbur's pleasure is, for the child reading the book, a forbidden pleasure because humans do not wallow in mud or manure, eat slops, or avoid responsibility and death. Children's books generally emphasize the pleasure of eating, the pleasures associated with oral gratification.

Whereas *Charlotte's Web* skirts the issues of the death drive and unconscious desires, Sendak's *Where the Wild Things Are* meets them head on. Freud's id, the pleasure principle or the instinctual drives that seek to gratify bodily needs, is apparent from the beginning of the book. Even the cover, which shows both a floating boat and a slumbering Wild Thing, prepares us for an experience of the polymorphously perverse. When we meet Max on the title page and then again on the first page, he is aggressive, even destructive as he pounds a nail into the wall. Freudians might well gaze knowingly at the nail Max hammers and the crack that it penetrates in the wall. In fact, for those who look for this sort of thing, the book is replete with images of phallic aggressiveness: the strong vertical lines of erect trees, bedposts, Max's scepter, his ship's mast, and the horns of some of the Wild Things (are these horns signs of phallic aggressiveness or of cuckoldry?). The horn turns up again in *Outside Over There* (1981), here as part of a set of images that, according to Michael D. Reed, work out in detail Freud's version of the female's Oedipal complex (see Reed).

Sendak, though, is not simply having a joke, in the manner perhaps of Tolkien. Max might be said, in words I adapt from Melanie Klein, to be mobilizing his libido against the death instinct (Klein, 250). This is why he deflects this instinct outward onto objects: the wall he hammers, the pictures he creates, his dog. The child is the site of conflicting impulses, what Freud designates the life and death instincts. Max first displaces his unconscious drive to destruction onto objects in his environment, but once his mother, acting the part of a superego, admonishes him, he transfers his aggression to her. This explains why the Wild Things of his dream are parodic of adults; again I call upon Melanie Klein to explain why Max "should form such monstrous and phantastic images of his parents." He "perceives his anxiety arising from his aggressive instincts as fear of an external object, both because he has made that object their outward goal, and because he has projected them on to it so that they seem to be initiated against himself from that quarter" (250).

A psychoanalytic reading of *Where the Wild Things Are*, then, takes account of Max's aggressive behavior as an expression of his phallic projection of the self onto the world. What he must learn is that the world cannot be brought under control; what can be brought under control is the aggressive behavior itself. Max's fantasy allows him the satisfaction of power; it is a fantasy of control and power. Like a dream, Max's fantasy maintains the repression of his desires, allowing him to return to reality quietly and in control. In other words, he learns to sublimate his instincts.

As a reward for successfully repressing his aggressions, Max's supper is waiting for him when he returns from his fantasy journey. Food, and hot food at that, is a nicely Freudian touch. The food reminds us, and Max, that his mother still loves him. Its heat warms him, just as its nutrients nourish him. Eating is pleasurable, a safe pleasure, unlike that supplied by Max's phallic aggressiveness. We might say that eating is a return to an oral stage, and that Max is regressing. But this is not the message of the story. No, Max is progressing because he has food that might derive from, but is not taken from, the mother. Max is learning independence at the same time that he is learning to curb his aggressive instincts. In addition, he displaces his desire for his mother—yes, the infamous Oedipal desire—which is apparent in his threat to eat his mother up, onto the food which he will no doubt eat now that he is back in his own room. His fantasy has shown him the lurking threat behind the apparent embrace of the words, "Oh please don't go—we'll eat you up—we love you so!" (n.p.). The desire to consume a loved one is antisocial—indeed, a taboo—and it must be sublimated for human society to function.

We note that Max is emerging from his wolf suit at the end of the book, and we might now also note that one of Freud's most famous case histories is that of the so-called Wolf-Man. Whereas Freud's patient feared animals, Max is one. In Sendak's early version of the story, however, Max does not wear a wolf suit; instead, he meets a character who claims to be his mother, but who then "turned into a terrible wolf and chased the boy out of the magic garden" (Lanes, 92). The desired object is also the feared object. The switch Sendak enacts by having Max replace his mother as the wolf reminds us of Freud's notion of "narcissism," that early stage of a child's love for the self and for the mother (or the person who nurses the child). In other words, at one time in a child's life, the child does not differentiate between himself or herself and the mother. The formation of the ego necessitates the child learning to differentiate between himself or herself and the Other (i.e., the mother, other people, the environment generally).

Freud's patient known as the Wolf-Man feared the picture of a wolf that he found in one of his early picture books. Interestingly enough, this wolf "was shown standing upright, with one foot forward, with its claws stretched out and its ears pricked" (*The Wolf-Man*, 183; see also 174). The posture of the wolf corresponds to that of Max in his wolf suit on the first full-page spread of *Where the Wild Things Are*. The tail of this wolf costume also echoes the tails of the wolves in one of Freud's patient's dreams; it is big and bushy like a fox's tail. The connection is even more intriguing when we note that the fairy tale that most disturbed the Wolf-Man when he was a child is "The Wolf and the Seven Little Goats." I think I am correct when I count seven Wild Things in Sendak's book. One of these Wild Things is clearly a child Wild Thing. We know that Freud's patient was troubled in his relationship with his sister. Is the child Wild Thing in *Where the Wild Things Are* an indication that Max, too, has a sibling and that his behavior has to do with his competitive desire for recognition?

Freud, then, can provide a model for our understanding of *Where the Wild Things Are*. But we have only scratched the surface.

Another Freudian concern—narcissism, or the "universal original condition" (*General Introduction*, 423)—might also serve to expand our reading. Note the self-portrait of Max on the second picture-page of the book. He pictures himself as a Wild Thing, thus setting us up for the Wild Things he will encounter in his fantasy. All the Wild Things are extensions of his own ego. Max's fantasy is a solipsistic fantasy out of which he is drawn by the smell of good things to eat, that is, by the smell of his mother's cooking. Max's transferral of his affection from himself to his mother is apparent in his emergence from his wolf suit in the book's final picture.

From the perspective of the revisionary Freudianism of Jacques Lacan, *Where the Wild Things Are* chronicles Max's experience of the mirror stage, or that stage in his development when he recognizes himself as Other and yet remains able to gratify his desires. The book sets out Max's crucial relationship with his mother, first by locating that moment when the child learns that his mother does not, in fact, respond positively to the child's every impulse, and then by reassuring the reader that the mother nevertheless remains as an extension of the child's desire. *Where the Wild Things Are* need not frighten young readers, because it shows the maintenance of the mirror stage in which the unity of experience gratifies desire.

According to Jacques Lacan's notions of narcissism and ego formation, however, an unpleasant truth awaits both Max and the reader. In the moment that the book explores—the moment both of the unsettling recognition of the Other and the comforting reassurance that the Other gratifies our desires—the human being's inescapable narcissism becomes apparent. The Lacanian mirror image holds within it a mirage (Bowie, 36), a false image, even an emptiness. Max's Wild Things are the stuff of dreams, but the stuff of dreams constitutes the reality with which we live. The Wild Things are figments of Max's unconscious, and as such they exist beyond the edge of comprehension, just out of sight in the cave of the mind. They are present, but absent, just the way the unconscious is, and just the way Max's mother is. In other words, Max's mother, too, is a Wild Thing. From Max's perspective, both he and his mother (as yet not distinctly differentiated in Max's mind) are Wild Things. To put this in the "derisory" manner of Lacan (Bowie, 23), Max, like all of us, is tricked by his own desires.

Freud's ideas concerning child sexuality and the mechanism of repression have proven attractive to commentators on children's literature because of Freud's fundamental moral vision. Bettelheim, for example, defends fairy tales despite their sexual content and their willingness to explore issues relating to incest, sexual desire, transgression against the authority of parents, and violence because his Freudian perspective allows him to view the tales as dream matter. That is, the tales function like dreams to sublimate and hence successfully repress desire and aggression. One reason recent ideological criticism of the tales has taken issue with Bettelheim is precisely his reading of the tales as forces for conservative social values.

Freudian readings, however, are not necessarily reactionary. As Freud learns from a case such as the Wolf-Man, childhood experiences and memories of childhood will finally escape the analyst's attempt to reduce everything to a simple allegorical meaning. To put this another way, the allegorical content of dreams and memories proves to be the dark conceit Edmund Spenser knew it was four hundred years ago. Freud himself admits the insecurity of his analysis, arguing that "it is better to perform that task [i.e., his analysis of the Wolf-Man's early phases] badly than to take flight before it" (*The Wolf-Man*, 245). I want to glance at two children's books to test the psychoanalytical approach.

First, I note how easily critics have interpreted dream books from a psychoanalytic perspective. The history of the critical reception of Lewis Carroll's two Alice books offers ample evidence of such readings. Let us look at a more recent dream book—David Wiesner's *Free Fall* (1988). Freud takes for granted that dreams and the unconscious are prior to language, and therefore it seems particularly appropriate that Wiesner should present his dream story in the form of a wordless picture book. The first images the "reader" sees on the frontispiece and on the title page are of a map. This book makes connections between books as maps for the imagination, dreams as maps, and books as dreams. The first page shows clearly that the young boy falls asleep while reading. The dream that then unfolds derives directly from the book he was reading—an atlas—and also the objects that populate his room—his goldfish, the food on his bedside table, a salt cellar, toy dinosaurs, a chess set, and white pigeons that fly outside his window. The dream is an amalgam of images drawn from these objects and from other books: Elizabethan romances, *Gulliver's Travels*, *Alice's Adventures in Wonderland* and *Through the Looking Glass*, and E. Nesbit's "The Book of Beasts," among others. The boy's unconscious has stored these images and then loosed them in this nighttime adventure. The dream contains many familiar dream motifs, including flying, changes in size, unaccountable shifts of location, and amniotic fluids. Wiesner's illustrations utilize sharp images, reinforcing the sense of clarity evident in dreams. His technique combines pencil and airbrush, giving him both clear images and a texture that is soft and dreamy. His colors are soft and clear but muted; he relies on beiges, blues, greens, and grays (my use of the plural here is to suggest varying shades of these colors).

A Formalist reading might well see this story as a heroic adventure. The dream recounts the child's wish to perform heroic deeds, to overcome great obstacles, and to visit exotic places. A Freudian reading, which the form of the story invites, will move beyond the manifest level of action to focus on the latent dream symbolism. Whatever this dream signifies in full, it has something to do with the boy's anxiety and his desire. His anxiety has something to do with authority figures; the first full-page spread of the dream shows a queen (Queen Elizabeth I?), and some ecclesiastical figures. They take the boy to their castle, which turns into a giant dragon. The boy, guided by three mysterious sidekicks (like the guides for Spenser's Redcrosse and Guyon), does not slay the dragon; instead, he escapes from it by moving from the pages of one book into another. The dragon, with its long tail dangling like a bookmark, is safely confined within the pages of its book. The boy moves on with his companions. They ride pigs, and like Hannibal or something out of a John Martin painting, they traverse a huge mountainous path until they arrive at a city, which quickly transforms into flying maps. The boy tumbles through the air but lands on a leaf, which transforms into a swan and transports him across a wide expanse of water. Swans and fishes on the ocean are the last images of the boy's dream. A Freudian reading of this dream will remind us of Freud's interpretation of maps as the human body and birds and fishes as images of the genitals. The dream is an exploration of the boy's erotic wishes. Readers of Freud's *The Interpretation of Dreams* will recall that Freud suggests that dreams of water and other fluids have erotic implications and that they are also common among bed wetters. The picture of the boy at the end of this book would suggest the former rather than the latter interpretation.

A similar reading might be brought to Van Allsburg's *The Mysteries of Harris Burdick*, which offers the reader many of the dream symbols I mentioned above: water, flying, authority figures, food, buildings (including cellars), and animals. The book might be read as a series of dream visions, each dream exploring some aspect of desire or anxiety. Each illustration offers a clue to the mind of the mysterious Harris Burdick, a person who obviously suffered from paranoia. The illustrations return again and again to images of invaded privacy. The fear of sexual violation is evident in images of humped carpets, vine-growing books, opening cellar doors, caterpillars, sailing, and so on. To read *Harris Burdick* this way is to assume the position of analyst to the book's analysand, to approach the book not as a series of discrete pictures each providing the impetus for a new story, but as the manifestation of one mind and its psychic makeup. Rather than accept Van Allsburg's invitation to investigate creatively the border between fantasy and reality, a psychoanalytic approach interprets the fantasy itself as reflective of psychic reality.

Freud provides us with several models—dream interpretation, the family romance, the id, ego, and superego triad, and so on—with which to approach literary texts. Many practicing psychoanalysts have, in fact, turned their analytical powers to the study of fairy tales: Roheim, Fromm, and Bettelheim, among others. But these are Freudians, and Freud is not, of course, the only psychoanalytical model we have for interpreting literature. I have already mentioned Melanie Klein. Her work, along with that of W. D. Winnicott, informs David Holbrook's *The Skeleton in the Wardrobe: C. S. Lewis's Fantasies: A Phenomenological Study* (1991), and Margaret and Micheal Rustin's *Narratives of Love and Loss: Studies in Modern*

Children's Fiction, which I mentioned earlier. For me, an even more fertile figure for the study of children's books is Jacques Lacan. Lacan's writing is notoriously intractable; it is difficult to assimilate to children's literature not merely because of his highly allusory writing style, but also because of his pessimistic view of human development. I want to argue, however, that Lacan can offer a useful way of reading stories that take up the fairy-tale interest in sexual and psychological maturation.

My example is less well known than the texts I have referred to until now: Harriet Childe-Pemberton's "All My Doing; or Red Riding-Hood Over Again" (1882), one of many Victorian retellings and recastings of traditional tales. This story is precisely aware of the intimate connection between the social self and the psychological self. Childe-Pemberton examines the female's entry into the social order, and what interests me here is the struggle she has with a language of social integration that is unfalteringly male. Childe-Pemberton's language is to a great extent male language, but she does offer examples of a literal language that is something of a return to what Lacan calls the Imaginary, that is, the pre-Oedipal stage in which no difference exists between signifier and signified (terms Lacan picks up from Saussure).

For example, in Childe-Pemberton's story, the fairy-tale woods are literalized in the very Victorian railroad train on which the young girl takes her journey. The train is, of course, a symbol of the masculine spirit, its aggressive and panting energy, chugging relentlessly through what was once placid (and feminine) countryside. But it is also literally true that young women and others might meet confidence men as fellow passengers on trains. My point is simply that Childe-Pemberton speaks literally to her female readers. The very form of this story, which incorporates the tradition of the motherly narrator, a tradition that dates back at least to the seventeenth century and that Mitzi Myers has studied in the late eighteenth century, creates an intimacy, a sense of experience shared.

Briefly, "All My Doing; or Red Riding-Hood Over Again" is a retelling of "Little Red Riding Hood" in a realistic late-Victorian setting. On hearing her fifteen-year-old niece complain that "Red Riding

87

Hood" is only of interest to children and that it is unbelievable because it is unrealistic, her middle-aged aunt, whom we know only as "Pussy," quickly defends the story by recounting a personal experience. This aunt, when a young woman, heedlessly chatted with a strange man on a train journey to her grandmother's house, and later, meeting this same man on the grounds of her grandmother's estate, invited him into the house. Her innocent openness and hospitality lead to the robbery of her grandmother's house late one night. During the robbery, grandmother receives a shock that permanently weakens her health, and Pussy's fiancé Herbert receives a wound that causes him to lose a leg. Worse yet, Pussy confesses that she is to blame for the robbery and its consequences because she had allowed one of the thieves to case the house prior to the robbery, and Herbert refuses to marry her because he does not wish to saddle her with a cripple. Significantly, he never again lets Pussy's name cross his lips. In short, because of Pussy's heedless and thoughtless ways, she remains "a lonely old maid," and Herbert remains "a lame old bachelor" (*Victorian Fairy Tales*, 247).

This outline might indicate, as Jack Zipes says, that the story has an "accusatory tone and moralistic message" and that it "keeps within the bounds of a male discourse" (*Trials and Tribulations*, 31). We might read the story as a crude and obvious warning to young girls not to be taken in by strange men, "crude and obvious" because what Childe-Pemberton appears to do is to take a well-known fairy tale and render both its message and its form clear. She appears to remove the magic from the tale in order to emphasize its moral message. And from the perspective of symbolic or male discourse, this is exactly what she does. She literalizes the story and in the process destroys its symbolic resonance. In fact, she goes out of her way to emphasize the literal nature of her discourse. When the niece, Margery, complains that "Red Riding Hood" "can't possibly be explained to be true in any kind of way," Aunt Pussy speaks up and asks whether she is certain "that it cannot possibly be explained to be true in any kind of way." She then proceeds to tell her a story "out of my own experience" (212). In other words, she not only speaks personally, but she also renders literal what the traditional story only communicated symbolically. In light of the story's interest in the differences between male and female education—boys go off to school, girls are educated at home; however, Margery is learning mathematics, natural philosophy, and political science, subjects traditionally reserved for the male—this female project of literalizing the fairy tale should interest us. (A modern version that literalizes "Red Riding Hood" is Sarah Moon's version in photographs of Perrault's story: *Creative Education*, 1993.)

First, we should note that Margery is receiving something of a progressive education; that is, she is learning what have traditionally been male subjects. She is learning, as Pussy says, "to set great store by whys and wherefores, causes and effects" (212). A quick glance might lead us to conclude that Margery slights the story of Red Riding Hood because it appears to her to lack a literal meaning or what she refers to as a "*true* meaning." Clearly, she does not take it seriously because it is "altogether too unlikely for anything" (211). In effect, she appeals to her aunt to make the story meaningful, to explain not the literal action of the story but the symbolic action. She is, as her aunt says, "beginning to put away childish things," and one of these childish things is the child's capacity to accept at face value the wonderful happenings of fantasy. When Margery asserts that "Red Riding Hood" cannot be explained "to be true in any kind of way," she means in a symbolic way; when her aunt demurs, she explains the story to be true in a kind of way I would call literal. The story is literally true as Pussy's personal experience illustrates. What Pussy offers her niece is a mother's language: literal, personal, direct, and heartfelt. Although Pussy has "never learnt half the things" Margery is learning, and although she knows "very little about mathematics and political economy," she has herself to offer her niece. Her experience is something Margery cannot find substitutes for in her books. In short, Margery is entering the adult or what more pertinently we might call the "father's" world, and her aunt offers her the comfort of maternal language and affection, perhaps even the hint of what Cixous calls the "impregnable language," the language that will "wreck partitions, classes, and rhetorics, regulations and codes" (256).

From a Lacanian point of view, Margery has entered the symbolic order. According to Lacan, the very young child experiences union with the mother, or what Wordsworth describes as "The gravitation and the filial bond/Of Nature that connect him to the world" (*The Prelude*, 1850: 243–44). At the age of eighteen months, however, the child begins to acquire the sense of "I," which at first, in the "mirror stage," is a "primordial" I. Later, the child begins to sense language and sexual difference, and at this stage, what amounts to Freud's Oedipal crisis, brings the father into the picture as a force that separates mother and child. In Wordsworth's version of the myth, which was well known to Victorian readers, the mother dies and the child is "left/Seeking the visible world, not knowing why" (277–78). The loss of the mother coincides with the acquisition of language and the awareness of sexual difference, the father replacing the mother. I turn to a passage from Margaret Homans's *Bearing the Word: Language and Female Experience in Nineteenth-Century Women's Writing* (1986) to explain this coming of the father:

> The father, who is discovered to have all along been in possession of the mother, intervenes in the potentially incestuous dyad of mother and child. Because what marks the father is his possession of the phallus, the phallus becomes the mark of sexual difference, that is, of difference from the mother. The phallus becomes the mark of language's difference as well, which becomes equivalent to sexual difference. Whereas in the preoedipal relation to the mother, communication required no distance or difference, now, with the intrusive entry of the phallus, "the child unconsciously learns that a sign has meaning only by dint of its difference from other signs, and learns also that a sign presupposes the absence of the object it signifies" [Lacan]. . . . Thus the child leaves behind the communication system he shared with his mother, which required no difference, and enters what Lacan calls the "Law of the Father," or the symbolic order. (6–7)

To enter the "Law of the Father" is to lose not only the mother, but also the phallus because the father prohibits its use. The child accepts with enthusiasm the symbolic order because language substitutes for what is lost; it provides something *like* what is lost. As Homans says: "Figuration, then, and the definition of all language as figuration gain their hyperbolical cultural valuation from a specifically male standpoint because they allow the son, both as erotic being and as speaker, to flee from the mother as well as the lost referent [the wholeness that attachment to the mother represents] with which she is primordially identified" (9). The child spends his, and the masculine pronoun asserts force here, time searching for the lost mother; in Romantic poetry this also takes the form of a search for a pure language, Keats's mother-tongue, that is not sadly incompetent but rather that is literally what it speaks; to end the quest, to find the mother or attain a perfect language, would be to put an end to the law of the father, to overcome the dominance or power of the male. It would be to return to Eden. This pure language, or the lost mother, cannot be reclaimed; it is necessarily only approached in a series of figures. These figures are supplied by the speaking subject. To be a subject, Lacan notes in his essay "Of Structure as an Inmixing of an Otherness Prerequisite to Any Subject Whatever," is to introduce "a loss in reality" (193). The pain of loss, then, finds compensation in figurative substitutes for that which is lost.

As may be evident in all this, the female finds herself both troped and trapped. She is the literal that symbolic discourse constantly strives for but must not and cannot achieve. She is perpetually sought after by male desire, but just the same she is perpetually absent. Lacan smugly notes: "There is no woman who is not excluded by the nature of things, which is the nature of words, and it must be said that, if there is something they complain a lot about at the moment, that is what it is—except that they don't know what they are saying, that's the whole difference between them and me" (quoted in Homans, 9). Homans suggests, however, that the female might have a different relationship with the literal from a man's. It appears, she says, "that it would be equally satisfying for women writers to rediscover the presymbolic language shared with their mothers that writing as motherhood, as opposed to writing as the search for symbolic phallic connections, might activate" (26). Childe-Pemberton's literalization of "Red Riding Hood," then, might reflect the female writer's attempt to rediscover the presymbolic language, to write as mother. The male writer substitutes figures for what he is lacking; the female writer who does not experience lack of the mother or the phallus to the same degree as the male does not need to speak figuratively. The woman writer knows what she is saying because she says it; for her, words and nature are the same thing. The male writer, cut loose from nature by the law of the father, knows less what he is saying because he constantly defers meaning by figuring it.

To come to the point, I appropriate Margaret Homans's suggestion that a daughter's psychological development differs from the one outlined by Lacan and also by, as Homans says, Wordsworth and the tradition of male discourse generally. Because a daughter's attachment to her mother is not the same as a son's, because she is less threatened by the father, she has less reason to embrace the law of the father wholeheartedly. She does accept this law, but "she does not do so exclusively" (Homans, 13). Consequently, the daughter "speaks two languages at once. Along with symbolic language, she retains the literal or presymbolic language that the son represses at the time of his renunciation of his mother" (13). Speaking two languages, the daughter experiences ambivalence. She is, of course, expected to enter the male world, yet she remains attached to the female world. A woman's proper duty, especially as conceived in the nineteenth century, is as mother and helpmate to her husband. She is not supposed to take up language and write, and when she does write she writes like a man, one who conceives of "the idea of a mother-daughter language dangerous to writing" (27). For this reason, a story such as "All My Doing; or Red Riding-Hood Over Again" ostensibly accepts the male stance. Just as the folktale "Red Riding Hood" presents its sexual warning symbolically, Childe-Pemberton's retelling presents Pussy's violation by the male through figures: the robbery of the grandmother's house and the "penetration" (this word appears in the story) of her bedroom, the loss of Herbert's leg, and Pussy's name. The ruin of Pussy results from her ignorance of the male's designs on her. Childe-Pemberton and her narrator, Pussy, draw attention to the symbolic dimension of the story when the latter remarks that "the loss of a limb implies a great, great deal more than the loss of the limb itself" (247). Yet the sexual symbolism suggested here—loss of limb equals loss of virility (castration)—has its literal aspect. The loss of a limb does imply more than simply the loss of a limb; it implies a readjustment of one's whole life. Symbolic and literal language conjoin here.

This story of a heedless girl who suffers a life of independence and loneliness and who appears to accept society's judgment of her as the cause of her male friend and lover's single and incomplete life speaks in two languages. Not only is its literalization of the traditional story significant in itself, but the apparent acceptance of the law of the father is more apparent than actual. The story of how two people who love each other fail to make a life together is an indictment of a society dominated by male values. Even Pussy remaining unmarried is not as terrible a fate as the Victorian sense of a woman's fulfillment in marriage might indicate. As early as 1792, in *Vindications of the Rights of Woman*, Mary Wollstonecraft argued that marriage renders women like children, and she urged independence for the female. Even earlier, in her children's book *Original Stories from Real Life* (1788), Wollstonecraft urged young girls to improve their minds since "it is the proper exercise of our reason that makes us in any degree independent" (386). Certainly she does not advocate the single life, but her portrait of the widow "raised to heroism by misfortunes" in the *Rights of Woman* (138) suggests that the single life need not be the unfulfilled life. And by 1845, Margaret Fuller can write: "In this regard of self-dependence, and a greater simplicity and fulness of being, we must hail as a preliminary the increase of the class contemptuously designated as 'old maids'" (Helsinger et al., 58). In light of this valuation of independence—even to the point of the female remaining single—we might examine the lesson to be derived from Herbert and Pussy remaining "a lame old bachelor, a lonely old maid."

The comma in my last sentence signifies lack. Obviously what the old bachelor lacks is the old maid; he lacks companionship, female companionship. In turn, the old maid also lacks companionship, male companionship. They lack each other. The story in which these two lonely figures live makes it abundantly clear that this lack, their lack, results from social norms that are exclusively male. In short, Childe-Pemberton presents the reader with a picture of a society that functions on lack, absence, deferral, separation, and loss. Pussy's family is constantly "in a hurry, and nobody ever attended to any one else"

(215). Her father, she says, eats his meals standing "like the hatter in 'Alice in Wonderland,' his teacup held in one hand and his slice of bread and butter in the other" (214). The reference to the hatter nicely suggests that the father is caught in a dull round, defeated by time, and perhaps overly attentive to the judicial and class system of his age. In any case, he is often absent even when he is present. For example, Pussy tells of entering the dining room one morning to find her father "hearing one of the children say the multiplication table, eating his breakfast rapidly the while, and scanning the morning paper into the bargain" (215). Her mother has told her that her father wishes to see her, but when she approaches him she finds he has no time to tell her what he wants. As my colleague Jean Perrot pointed out to me in a letter, the appearance of Pussy has lost any real meaning for the father. Deferral is the order of the day, and of most days in this family and its world.

In contrast, nothing is deferred at Pussy's grandmother's house. Here is a small world in which comfort is the order of the day, of all days. Pussy's grandmother, like so many of the grandmother figures who populate Victorian children's books, is single. She lacks a husband, but this lack is hardly felt as a lack. This is how Pussy describes her grandmother:

> She was a large, handsome, good-natured woman, who liked everything about her to be handsome and on a large scale; she habitually wore good silk dresses, and had her rooms filled with choice flowers; her cook was good, and her carriage and horses always smartly turned out. She wore handsome rings, and had her pocket-handkerchiefs scented with the best eau-de-Cologne. Yet she was hardly to be called an epicure, was my grandmother; she only liked to be comfortable and have nice things about her; and no one was more anxious that others should be comfortable too, and take their share of nice things. (225)

The word most often used to describe this grandmother and her living conditions is "comfortable." She lives with her daughter Rosa, who spends her time "worrying, and fretting, and bustling about the comfort of the house" (225). Although both grandmother and Rosa are anxious that others are well taken care of, neither of them suffers. The Victorian ideal of female self-renunciation, articulated most influentially in Ruskin's *Sesame and Lilies* (1865), does not appear to enter their heads. This is a very comfortable household indeed, and the three women manage well without men about the house. In fact, when men enter the house, disaster follows. Had Herbert not been staying the night, the robbers would not have shot him in making their escape. And obviously had Pussy not invited the strange man she first met on the train into her grandmother's house, the robbers would not have come at all. Men destroy this comfortable woman's world.

In the traditional story of Red Riding Hood, at least as the Brothers Grimm tell it, a man saves the day. The woodcutter arrives to rescue granny and Red from the belly of the wolf. Here, Herbert assumes the woodcutter's role, perhaps the wooden leg he ends with being a grim reminder of the original story. Although Herbert assists in scaring away the robbers, he is ineffectual in saving Pussy from dire consequences of the break-in; in fact, he perpetuates these consequences by renouncing his relationship with her. The story, we might say, ends for Pussy as it ended for Perrault's Red: the man's world has swallowed her. The male experiences life as lack, and the woman represents this lack. And she does so by bearing it, by carrying the blame for the necessary loss others, that is, the male, must suffer. This story's Red Riding Hood, Pussy, carries this blame because she has been hoodwinked by a man—a thief, a betrayer, and one who violates female space. Pussy judges herself heedless and thoughtless, and yet she realizes that her betrayer played upon her innocence. She accepts blame for the catastrophe, and yet she resists blame. She, like her creator, experiences ambivalence: is she perpetrator or victim?

Pussy's initial reaction to the robbery, to the shock her grandmother received and to Herbert's wound, is self-recrimination: "I realised how the blame of it all lay primarily at my door. *I* it was who heedlessly introduced the plausible stranger into the house. *I* it was who had blindly allowed him to make a plan of the rooms under pretence of sketching the oak" (239). Her locution "*I* it" neatly communicates how the experience has desexed her. She regrets not having heeded her mother's caution not to speak with strangers, and not having taken her brother's words to heart about considering consequences before she either acted or spoke. This bringing together of the mother and the eldest brother is interesting. Taken alongside the mother's education of Margery in male subjects (and we might recall that Pussy comments that she might proceed differently were she in charge of Margery's education), this parallel of the mother's advice with the son's suggests the weakness of mothering in the book. When mothers educate their daughters in male discourse, they comply with patriarchy's systematic diminishment of the female. Pussy's relationship with Margery provides a corrective to mother-daughter relationships that are in coercion with patriarchy. Instead of providing Margery with books, Pussy gives herself; she is the text Margery reads (cf. Myers, "Impeccable Governesses," 39, 49).

Unlike her niece, Pussy has no mother to comfort her, although her Aunt Rosa's capableness and control offer her a model of female ability to cope with a crisis. After hearing that the police have a good chance of apprehending the robbers, Pussy resolves to bear witness against them, especially against the one who duped her. She reasons: "after all, he, and he only, was the real cause of my grandmother's illness and Herbert's wound." She recognizes that he has violated her: "he had traded on my thoughtlessness and had taken advantage of my innocence" (242). Her sense of selfhood reemerges in her fierce indignation against the man who has deceived her: "he had made a tool of *me* . . . he had inspired *me* with confidence and belief in his perfect honesty . . . he had contrived out of my very simplicity to make *me* the accomplice of his crimes!" (242). Her identity is strong enough to withstand the "rather unpleasant remarks" passed on her conduct that she hears during the trial of the culprits.

What might have happened to Pussy were this all her story had to relate is anyone's guess. Her testimony at the trial of the felons helped gain a conviction against the man who had violated her trust and her person. This, she says, ends her story "so far as the robbery is concerned" (244). She still, however, has to tell what happened to herself, her grandmother, and Herbert. We already know the surface details here: Pussy remains a lonely old maid, grandmother never recovers her health, and Herbert lives on a lame old bachelor. If Pussy's voice as narrator of the story is any indication, she has not lived an unrewarding and empty life. She tells her tale with gusto, obviously enjoying the role of storyteller, and amused in retrospect at her youthful bustle and self-importance. But what in the final part of her telling would account for her mature sense of self-worth? Aside from recounting the effects of Herbert's wound in the last paragraphs of the story, Pussy also recalls her grandmother's reaction to the robbery. What accounts for the depth of grandmother's shock is the red cloak that Pussy so loved, and that connects her to the Red of "Red Riding Hood."

True to her realistic and literal telling, Pussy precisely describes this red cloak near the beginning of her story. But what catches us is the alteration Childe-Pemberton makes from the original, in which Red receives the cloak from her granny. In this version, Pussy herself buys the cloak using money she has received from an "old bachelor uncle" (214). This may be the clue that the young Pussy has, like Margery at fifteen, entered the symbolic order where fashion dictates identity. Clothes make the person. In Pussy's case, her scarlet cloak, "with a pair of red stockings, just showing above laced boots, the smallest of small black hats on my head, and my hair drawn back into a chenille net" make her look "not very unlike Red Riding-Hood herself." In this getup, she says, "people took me to be younger than I was" (214). And the "dapper little man" on the train whose age "was impossible to guess at" takes her for a ride (220). Because of her vanity, because of her acceptance of identity as fashion, she easily falls victim to the charms of a man who sees her only as a mark, a mark of easy money, easy gratification of his own desire for gain.

During the robbery, one of the thieves puts on Pussy's scarlet cloak, and the appearance of this cloaked figure in her room is what so deeply affects the grandmother. She repeats over and over again: "I thought it was Pussy! I thought it was Pussy! The dreadful face under the hood! The face of a murderer! The face of a murderer!" (244). As Pussy explains, what her grandmother reacted to was not the robbery, but rather an "attempt to murder." The man's face in her granddaughter's hood signifies death to her. The discovery that the person in the hood was not Pussy unhinges the grandmother's mind. The discovery that her granddaughter was really a man was too shocking to bear. Of course, Pussy is not a man. But her grandmother's experience, mistaken although she was literally, serves as a warning. The red cloak and all it represents—Red Riding Hood, fashion, male dominance, and death to female identity—must be relinquished. Pussy must put aside the cloak; she symbolically assumes her "boots" when Herbert loses his leg. The "old bachelor uncle" is replaced by the "old bachelor aunt" who gives words and not money to protect the future of a child. The red cloak speaks to us in the two languages of the daughter: symbolically and literally. As a symbol, the red cloak connects this story with the story of Red Riding Hood and with the blood that is let in the rather bloodless account of the wolf's eating of the little girl and her grandmother, but just the same it literally signifies the fashionable world of female economy that Pussy has accepted. We might say that this Victorian retelling of "Red Riding Hood" both literally and symbolically endorses the moral warning of the traditional story that cautions young girls about the dangers of trusting male strangers.

This story also appears strongly to endorse the Victorian emphasis on the efficacy of suffering. Two trials are apparent: one, the trial by jury of the thieves; the other, the psychological trial of Pussy and the others who were in the house the night of the robbery. This latter trial, although dire, brings Pussy to a realization of her love for Herbert and to an understanding of her youthful folly. Interestingly, however, when Pussy confesses her innocent complicity in the robbery, her grandmother "chuckled . . . with the comfortable chuckle that reminded me of the days of her health." Pussy is taken aback, but her grandmother "*would* persist in laughing about it" (246). The laugh of the Medusa? True, granny does speak of the value of experience and of its cost. This platitude sits well perhaps with Childe-Pemberton's epigraph from F. W. Farrar, which speaks of "manly resolution" as the ideal result of loss. But granny's laugh and Pussy's storytelling bespeak a womanly resolution, a resolution, in the words of Xaviere Gauthier, to "*make audible* that which agitates within us" (163). Motherly speech, audible speech, oral speech, woman's speech: this is what we hear in "All My Doing; or Red Riding-Hood Over Again" as opposed to written words, metaphoric speech, male speech. The power of this speech resonates beyond its sound; Pussy indicates this at the end of the story when she says, ostensibly to Margery, but since she does not name her we may assume she speaks to her audience in general, the "slightest word has an echo far beyond what you can hear" (248).

What we can hear, of course, is contradictory: symbolic language and literal language, self-deprecation and self-assertion, acceptance of Victorian norms and resistance to those norms. If, as Perry Nodelman suggests, children's literature "is a feminine literature" ("Children's Literature as Women's Writing," 33), then such contradictions are to be expected. They are the inevitable result of an ambivalence. Women and children are familiar with disenfranchisement, with, as they say, the experience of being marginalized, and the literature produced by and for them manifests a desire to revise the power structure that excludes them. This literature must be subversive. And yet this literature written, for the most part, by women for women and for children, this motherly writing, reflects social responsibility, the responsibility a mother has to teach her child the means of survival in the social world, which has been for so long the world of the father. This contradictory impulse, this ambivalence, leads to the two languages of women's writing, and if Nodelman is right, of children's literature. What would be interesting to discover is whether this same ambivalence appears in children's own writing. Also, to hear the literal and symbolic languages Homans explicates in stories such as "All My Doing; or Red Riding-Hood Over Again" is easy because of the overtly literal setting for the fairy tale. To find such a strategy of literalization, and of course to value it, in the many fantasies written by women for children might well allow us to recover much that has lain silent and unavailable from that period. It might also allow us to read those works which have survived—for example, Frances Browne's *Granny's Wonderful Chair*, Jean Ingelow's *Mopsa the Fairy*, or Frances Hodgson Burnett's *The Secret Garden*—as poignant expressions of two languages, the language of No and the language of Yes: the No of the father and the Yes of the mother. The father's No puts an end to secrets, explains everything as figuration; the mother's Yes keeps the secret intact and returns us to the humus from which we came. To be lonely is surely preferable to being lame.

This talk of language, whether the mother's or the father's, is useful for our reading of children's books. We might adapt, as Lacan does, the concepts of metaphor (one thing standing for another) and metonymy (a part standing for a whole) to language, and suggest that the language of the father is metaphoric, always striving to state the desired thing by stating something else, and the language of the mother is metonymic, always reaching out and pointing the larger aspects of the same thing. John Stephens has nicely argued that fantasy is a metaphoric mode and realism a metonymic one (248 ff.), but from a psychoanalytic point of view fantasy might have a metonymic aspect; for example, the figures that fill the boy's dream in Wiesner's *Free Fall* do not so much stand in for aspects of his desire as they are literally aspects of his desire. Something similar might be said of *Charlotte's Web*, where the web with words in it is not a metaphor for the miraculous; it is a miracle. Or the barnyard is not so much a metaphor for the healthy psyche as it is an extension of the healthy psyches of its inhabitants. I suspect, however, that we could argue that both metaphor and metonymy apply to children's books. Children's literature might well speak the double language I outlined above; it reveals a tension between the language of Yes and the language of No.

I return to the question with which I began. What does psychoanalytic criticism have to offer the study of children's books? Unlike the Formalist and archetypal approaches, psychoanalysis is not a subject we would immediately think of as pedagogically useful with children themselves. I cannot imagine using a psychoanalytic method of reading in the schools. On the other hand, this approach does offer adult readers a glimpse of the child mind, of a child's anxieties, fears, desires, and dependencies. If we accept the idea that psychic health depends upon confronting, ordering, and understanding the unconscious, then a psychoanalytic approach allows us to defend certain aspects of children's books that might offend or disturb some adult readers. I think of those readers who complained of (and successfully censored) Sendak's *Where the Wild Things Are*. Bettelheim himself warned parents that this book might frighten young readers, but he changed his mind once he came to study fairy tales. His final assessment of such material for children is that it provides comfort for young children whose unconscious minds seethe with anxieties and aggressive instincts. Fairy tales comfort because they sublimate certain instincts, and they provide reassuring messages that all will be well in time.

Certain psychoanalytical readings stay close to the individual psyche, but as my treatment of "All My Doing; or Red Riding-Hood Over Again" should indicate, psychoanalysis does have its social significance. Those critics, however, who champion an openly political criticism argue that psychoanalysis is overly cautious, perhaps even stodgily conservative, in its treatment of the individual in his or her social and political environment. In other words, most overtly political reading of literature comes from the left. It is time we looked more closely at how political approaches to children's books work.

5

Class Action: Politics and Critical Practice

The freedom of the bourgeois writer is only masked dependence on the money bag! . . . Down with non-partisan writers.

—Lenin

Art is nothing if not social.

—Christopher Caudwell

Art is first of all a social practice rather than an object to be academically dissected.

—Terry Eagleton

The political perspective [is] the absolute horizon of all reading and all interpretation.

—Fredric Jameson

Class Action: Politics and Critical Practice

In this chapter I hope to illustrate how approaches to children's books as products of our social and economic system might work. I say "approaches" because political readings of literature can come from either the left or the right, and they can take a sociological, activist, feminist, political, or purely intellectual form. What unites the several kinds of political reading is the critic's interest in and awareness of ideology, both the ideology manifested in works of literature and that which guides the critic herself or himself. In other words, a political criticism works in two ways: (1) to set out clearly the political or ideological position of the text one is reading, and (2) to clarify one's own ideological position. Political readings ought to be clear concerning their designs upon the reader. In the course of considering the political aspects of reading, I will slip from examining literary texts as reflections of historically bound ideologies, to questions of how we read and how we might read. The chapter takes an unusual (at least for this book) form, consisting as it does of some fifteen sections, each concluding with one or more questions for the reader to reflect on.

My main concern in this chapter is concern itself. As readers and critics, we have a primary and a secondary concern with the texts we read. The one focuses on the texts themselves (their structure and language; what I have called earlier the "intrinsic" approach); the other focuses on the social environment of which the texts form a part. Which of these we give primary status will depend on our own predispositions, training, and values. My own predisposition is for a radical reading, that is, one which gets to the root of things. What does the text signify? Where does the text come from? What motivates our reading? How does a text fit with other texts? How does the act of reading a text allow us an opportunity to stand aside from political contingencies? In what way is reading a democratic activity? These are questions that float in and out of my meditation on politics and literature.

Later in this chapter I will look at chapter 8 of Lewis Carroll's *Through the Looking Glass.* I suppose I could have chosen any passage or any book; I assume my choice has to do with personal preference (I like Carroll's book and this passage) and timing (as part of another project, I was working with parodies of Romantic poetry while writing this chapter). But as many of my academic colleagues will be quick to point out, my choice has political implications whether I consciously know this or not. So: what are these political implications? And what is political about the passage from *Through the Looking Glass*? Indeed, why even concern myself with political questions?

CONCERN

I begin with a word about concern. In an essay titled "Literary and Linguistic Scholarship in a Postliterate World," Northrop Frye posits a primary and a secondary concern. Primary concern, as Frye explains it, is akin to Wordsworth's notion of the "primary laws of our nature," which are the "essential passions of the heart," the desire to live comfortably, with food, shelter, and companionship. Primary concern is something shared by all people in all places. Secondary concern, on the other hand, "includes loyalty to one's own society, to one's religious or political beliefs, to one's place in the class structure, and in short to everything that comes under the general heading of ideology" (*Myth and Metaphor*, 21). This seems clear enough, and it goes some way to explain why literature may be both universal and local in its appeal. Everyone can understand a mother's desire to protect her child from starvation, or a family's fear of separation or even annihilation; but not everyone can appreciate or understand cultural practices such as the Sun Dance of the Blackfoot peoples or the initiation rituals of North American fraternities and sororities.

Concern, whether primary or secondary, has something to do with desire. But as we have seen in our discussion of psychoanalysis, desire itself is complex; its basis in instinct is quickly affected by its existence within culture. In other words, desire as it relates to primary and secondary concerns serves to keep these concerns contiguous. They function somewhat in the way Blake's innocence and experience function: they are inseparable. Just as Blake's categories are states of being existing simultaneously, so a work of literature is never "wholly primary or secondary: it is invariably both at once" (*Myth and Metaphor*, 23).

Take, for example, *Charlotte's Web*. From one perspective, this book reflects the most primary of concerns: life is preferable to death.

I am not sure the desire to live is ideologically charged. Nor is the desire to have the comfort of a friend. But these desires for life and friendship quickly become caught up in the web of ideology. In order for the pig Wilbur to live, a sacrifice is necessary; in order for him to have a friend, privilege and care come into play. Wilbur's life of relative ease and prestige is produced by the anonymous labor of Charlotte; in effect, she gives her life for Wilbur, or at least she devotes her energy and time to him. She is the one who puts out; she toils with no other reward than the feeling that she has done something honorable. Has she? From whose perspective has she done an honorable thing in keeping alive a pig whose destiny was to have been served up as *jambon*? Wilbur becomes an old ham; Charlotte fades away. This placing on the female of values associated with nurturing, self-sacrifice, and cunning is culturally loaded, as Mary Daly has noted. In *Gyn/Ecology: The Metaethics of Radical Feminism*, Daly warns her female readers that in patriarchal myth, "the energies of the spider are drained off in the enterprise of guiding and protecting males" (397). Young female readers of *Charlotte's Web* are not invited to ask such questions as, is Wilbur worth Charlotte's sacrifice? What if the pig had been named Wilma or Wilhelmina (399)? They are not invited to ask such questions precisely because such questions are forbidden in a culture controlled by men. Women are asked to be content with the knowledge that they are the powers behind the scenes.

The question is, should we and can we, as readers, not only aspire to the condition of a politically free reading, but also achieve such a reading? Or as Frye puts it, clearly the removal of "the ideological cataracts from our social vision" (*Myth and Metaphor*, 24) is a noble enterprise. Is such a removal possible?

CHILDREN, LITERATURE, CONCERN

What does any of this have to do with children and their literature? My students often quarrel with me over the issues raised in the previous section, arguing that children themselves are innocent of the political motives of their elders. They go on to say that anything overtly political in children's books will pass over young heads simply because young children have no interest in such adult notions as politics. Children are prior to politics. Children, the argument might continue, share with adults primary concern; they desire comfort, shelter, food, and companionship. They do not, however, experience secondary concern.

Such an argument is naively romantic. The child envisaged in this picture is the child of joy, one whose whole world consists of delight and liberty. Readers of Wordsworth's great ode, "Intimations of Immortality," from which I crib here, will recall that Wordsworth placed this poem among works he classified as "Epitaphs and Elegiac Pieces." Epitaph and elegy: both speak of that which is no more, and that which has never been. Both speak of an ideal devoutly to be wished; both idealize. In other words, the sage and seer blest Wordsworth writes about never did exist as material reality, unless we accept Louis Althusser's conception of ideology as material reality in that it governs the way we live in the material world. Indeed, the nineteenth century is testimony to how powerful verbal constructions can be in shaping material reality; Wordsworth's idealized construction of the child, synchronized with that of Rousseau from which it derives, held sway for the hundred years following publication of "Intimations of Immortality." I return, then, to the notion that children and their books are ideological constructs. If we wish to remain with a literary discourse, then the child is a metaphor; if we use social and political discourse, then the child is an ideological construct. From the latter perspective, the child becomes part of the complex network within a social unit that Althusser labels Ideological State Apparatus.

Real children, that is, persons who have not long lived and breathed the air of social action, can no more avoid the politics of experience than adults can. I might add that, in *The Political Life of Children* (1986), Robert Coles has compellingly detailed just how politically aware, in the sense of being attuned to national and international events, children are. How could children avoid being in some sense political? From the beginning of their lives they must learn how to deal with the moods and inconsistencies of their parents. Even before a child attends school, she or he begins to learn the politics of a pecking order. One of this century's more enduring children's books clearly presents this necessary experience with hierarchy, power, authority, and manipulation. I refer to *Winnie-the-Pooh*. Just as Christopher Robin's father exerts his authority over his son, so Christopher Robin exerts authority over his toys, and the toy characters play the same imperial game. Perhaps the whole idea comes to full expression in the "expotition" to the North Pole where the group of adventurers lay claim to new territory.

Every children's book participates in some way in political maneuvering, and many in what I have just referred to as the "imperial game." *Where the Wild Things Are*, for example, implicitly equates the relationship between child and parent with colonizer and colonized. Just as Max's mother exerts her power over Max by stemming his wild energies, his uncivilized behavior, so too does Max exert control over the Wild Things he finds across his wide seas of thought. Max sees himself as King, a trope that recalls both literary sources from folk- and fairy tales and imperial sources from the ages of political colonization. I am reminded of Prospero's taming of Caliban in *The Tempest* and of postcolonial readings of Shakespeare's play.

My point is simply that children and children's books are not free from concern. The question is, how free from politics is this concern? Is this concern strictly primary, or does it manifest secondary qualities? Are children's concerns prior to politics?

CHILDREN AND THE POLITICS OF EXPERIENCE

Psychologists have taught us that children deal with serious emotional matters in their drawings and stories, and we know that many school-aged children over the past several decades have articulated their fears concerning such things as nuclear war, environmental waste, and racial prejudice. Schools often bring to the surface such concerns. But even preschool children reveal qualities of mind that we might usefully call "political." Many of the stories collected in Brian Sutton-Smith's *The Folkstories of Children* (1981) reveal the children's awareness of and

interest in human waste, human violence, and the possibility of humanity's self-destruction. I offer only one example: four-year-old Ingbert,
whose eighteen brief stories all deal with the end of humanity (110–15).

The stories I receive from children as a result of my visits to
schools, in the capacity of storyteller, confirm my sense of the children's political awareness. Again, I offer only one example: among a
batch of formalized thank-yous that I received from a grade two class
in 1992, I found one brief story addressed to "Mr. McGillis," by
Bobby. The story's title is "The Lion and the Tiger," and the plot is
pretty simple and very familiar: the lion eats a series of other animals
and things, beginning with the tiger. After the narrator recounts the
lion's eating a beaver, he continues this way:

> The Lion went a little farther and he met Patrick Roy. He said,
> "Out of my way! I've got a game to play!" "No!," said the Lion.
> "I don't take orders from anyone!" So Roy took out his hockey
> stick and hit the Lion aside and ran to the stadium. The Lion
> broke the roof and grabbed Patrick and ate him. He went a little
> farther and he bumped into Mr. Young and Miss Hodgson. "Do
> you know Patrick Roy," "Yes want to meet him again yeah O.K.
> in you go and ate them! Soon he took a rocket into space. He
> jumped off the rocket and ate earth. Inside him the Beaver bit
> through the Lion and everybody jumped on earth. But the Lion
> kept on falling in space and soon he died by hunger. The End.

What you might not know is that Patrick Roy is the goalie for
the Montreal Canadiens professional hockey club, and during my visit
to Bobby's class, which took place in April, the month when the hockey playoffs begin, a discussion of our favorite teams and players took
place. I also tell a story about my lifelong passion for the Montreal
hockey team. Bobby's story clearly alludes to the discussion we had,
and it sends me a message concerning what Bobby thinks of Patrick
Roy and his team. The story is a means of exerting power. Following
from this, you will have little difficulty figuring out that Mr. Young
and Miss Hodgson are teachers in Bobby's school. Bobby's lion eats

them too! We could do much more with this story, but my point is that Bobby, like most children, understands in his own way that human interaction involves the negotiation of power. At times diplomacy is necessary; at times blunt confrontation is appropriate.

What concerns me about this politically charged situation in the schools is that, in a general sense and in a literary sense, what children learn best is cynicism. They learn that the best way to survive the institutional forces that press upon them is to assimilate the rules as quickly as possible. They are as eager as Alice in Lewis Carroll's books to learn and then to show off their mastery of rules. I have no expertise here, only intuition. By the time the students reach my classroom at the university, the majority of them have learned that the best way to deal with the world is through accommodation. Rather than question the system in which they find themselves, they register a desire to comply with institutional authority in hope that by doing so the good life awaits them. For many of my students, the fulfillment of their desire is through acceptance of the repressions our social apparatuses set upon us. We quiet down our students, just as we quiet down our citizens, with what Marcuse, thirty years ago, termed "repressive satisfaction" (114).

The questions: is it fair to say that children's own stories reflect a political consciousness? How do we stain the pellucid surfaces of our children's minds clear? How do we disabuse but not disaffect our students?

POLITICAL IMPLICATIONS

One impetus for this chapter was Gerald Graff's recent book, *Beyond* ✓ *the Culture Wars* (1992). Graff's book is one of the many to appear over the past few years dealing with the politicization of education and the conflict over curricula in our schools and colleges. At one point he asks: "Is literature a realm of universal experience that transcends politics, or is it inevitably political, and in what sense of 'political,' a word too often brandished today without being defined?" (31). Graff's remark that the word "political" is too often undefined caught my attention. I have for years scolded my students for using certain words

as if they were self-explanatory, words such as "evil," "good," "innocence," "experience," "imagination," and "magic." My students too
often use these words as if the words themselves explained difficult
concepts; they fail to see that the words themselves *are* difficult concepts that require explanation. But reading Graff, I realized that I, too,
am guilty of glib speech. I use the word "political" whenever I want to
speak of a writer as anti-institutional or as critical of government. But,
as the title of a book I read twenty-five years ago reminds me (I refer
to R. D. Laing's *The Politics of Experience*, 1967), politics does not
refer exclusively to institutions; everything we do in social situations is
political.

Saying everything is political is not, however, very helpful to our
understanding of children's books. In what sense are children's books
political? Well, we know that books for children have for centuries
had a pedagogical function, and we know this pedagogical function
served (and serves) the state. The title of a British publication dating
from 1817 serves to remind us of this pedagogical function: *The
Juvenile Review; or, Moral and Critical Observations on Children's
Books; Intended as a Guide to Parents and Teachers in Their Choice of
Books of Instruction and Amusement*. Note the connection between
instruction, amusement, and morality. In 1817, as now, hundreds of
books appeared annually on the children's lists, and inevitably guides
as to their utility and worth appeared. These guides are not without
their agendas, their sense of what children should be. More often than
not, what children should be is docile citizens, productive and unquestioning members of a nation-state. Take, for instance, *Michele
Landsberg's Guide to Children's Books* (1985). This, too, is a guide to
parents and teachers, and Landsberg does not write without a political
design: her crusade is against television, and she presents it as strongly
as Sarah Trimmer, Priscilla Wakefield, and others presented their criticism of fairy tales and romance at the beginning of the nineteenth century. Landsberg promotes what she calls "the humane values we
cherish" and "our conventional moralities" (2, 3), while she warns
against transgressive themes. The absence in her *Guide* of both Roald
Dahl (whose books delight in dealing with the gross, the crude, and
the absurd) and Harry Allard (author of the books about the Stupid

family) is surely no accident. The "humane values" Landsberg refers to might have something to do with primary concern (providing all people with food, shelter, and a safe environment), but "conventional moralities" probably have to do with secondary concern. Just what a "conventional morality" might be remains vague. Landsberg, of course, expects her reader to share her particular ideological position without question.

But the books themselves must find their place on publisher's lists, and this means that editors and publishers have first crack at ensuring the books they publish follow a certain agenda, a certain sense of what children should be. Jacqueline Rose has written persuasively about this in *The Case of Peter Pan, or the Impossibility of Children's Fiction.* And many other contemporary writers have pointed out the role of children's books in socializing the child: for example, Jack Zipes, John Stephens, Bob Dixon, Peter Hunt, Peter Hollindale, Robert Leeson, Donnarae McCann, and Perry Nodelman. What few question is the institutionalizing of children's books. Book production, as John Newbery knew in the eighteenth century, is intimately a part of the capitalist modes of production. "Trade and Plum Cake for Ever" was the Newbery slogan, nicely encapsulating the economic motive with its recipe for success: give the buyer something sweet for the mental palate, something to calm the reader. The publisher publishes books not as a civic duty, but as an economic necessity. And to ensure success in the marketplace, the publisher needs to produce that which the purchaser wants. Books that are unsettling or socially subversive are unlikely to do well. Witness the failure of Harlin Quist's short-lived publishing venture in France and the United States in the 1970s (Harlin Quist produced a series of avant-garde books for children; the most notable are those by Eugene Ionesco, *Story Number 1, Story Number 2,* and *Story Number 3*), or William Blake's anonymity in his own day. Blake's patron, Dr. Trusler, who complained about the obscurity of the artist's work, is by no means unique among book buyers or patrons of the arts in his own day or in ours.

The question is, Do children's books unavoidably carry the stamp of state approval because of the institutional nature of publishing?

Why, too, have publishers recently taken to publishing so-called postmodern books, works such as the Ahlbergs' *The Jolly Postman* (1986) and Jon Scieszka's *The Stinky Cheese Man and Other Fairly Stupid Tales* (1992; illustrated by Lane Smith)? Are these books in any political sense radical, or do they too put to rest the transgressive instincts of their readers?

CHILDREN'S BOOKS AS POLITICAL

Clearly, we can speak of politics in the context of publishing books for children, and also in the context of reviewing these books. Publishers, reviewers, and university professors have reasons for publishing, reviewing, and teaching what and how they do. These reasons are unlikely to be free of ideological intent. Even if the publisher's sole conscious intent is to make money, he or she cannot be free of ideological entanglement. In order to make money, the publisher must keep on selling books. Althusser points out, in this context, the necessity for "the reproduction of the conditions of production" (127–86). To ensure the conditions of production (and hence the condition of financial solvency), the publisher must ensure nothing in the books he or she publishes alienates prospective book buyers. One way to do this is to perpetuate the values and cultural conceptions of the ruling group within the pages of the books turned out by the publisher's production line. We might also point out that reviewers work for publishers; they, like the writers whose books they review, are the labor force working for the production bosses. Reviewers have a stake in perpetuating the whole process of book production and purchase. Something similar might be said of university professors of literature or of librarians: the production of books and the valuing of books are necessary for the perpetuation of jobs dependent upon books. As I tell my students, nothing and no one in this chain is innocent.

Of course, we tell ourselves and those to whom we speak in our professional capacities as publishers, reviewers, teachers, or librarians that reading books is vital to a strong society. We go even further. We tell ourselves and other readers, actual or prospective, that reading is the one activity that keeps us from becoming mentally passive and lazy. Reading is the best way to keep us free of the hectoring of the marketplace and to allow us to understand the rhetoric of politicians and others who wish to impose a quiescence on us. The irony is that much that passes as innocent fiction designed for entertainment is what A. P. Foulkes, following Jacques Ellul, terms "propaganda of 'integration'" (10). In other words, much of the literature we say detaches and liberates us may do just the opposite—it may silently prompt us to conform to certain social modes of behavior and to accept certain cultural and political values. Perry Nodelman puts it this way: "Because writers assume that their specific view of reality is universal, texts act as a subtle kind of propaganda, and tend to manipulate unwary readers into an unconscious acceptance of their values" (*The Pleasures of Children's Literature*, 94).

This, though, has only limited relevance to the question: in what ways are books for children political? Obviously, the question has several answers, at least one of which we have already seen: texts reproduce the dominant values of a culture at a particular time. In other words, a text's politics are historically specific. Even the simplest books for the young reflect not only the climate of their age, the zeitgeist, but also ideological concerns. Take, for example, something as simple as one of Renate Kozikowski's series of Titus Bear board books, *Titus Bear Goes to School* (1984). The book clearly sets out to put to rest a preschool child's anxiety about going to school. Titus Bear rides his bicycle to school, meets some friends, engages in familiar nonstressful activities such as painting, building a model, singing, and listening to his teacher read a story. Then he hops on his bike and rides home again. The images in the book show food, clean and bright rooms painted in nonthreatening pastel shades, playground activity, and a smiling Titus. Surely this book is innocent of an ideological design on its young reader.

But we might note that Titus's friends at school, if we accept the conventions of picture book art in designating gender, are all male. His teacher is the only female we see in the book. The message is, boys play with boys, and teachers are invariably female. We might also notice that when Titus builds a model, he constructs a large truck. The equation truck = boyish activity is notoriously gender specific in North American culture. In other words, this little book perpetuates cultural stereotypes, at least in terms of gender roles. Its message is "school as a place of learning, socialization, and regimentation is good." We might argue that such a message is hardly specific to the time and place in which the book was published, the early 1980s, and I agree that the picture of school here is one that has been familiar to Anglo-American culture for one hundred and fifty years and more. The school Titus Bear attends fits neatly into Althusser's description of the modern school that has replaced the Church as a major Ideological State Apparatus: Titus, like all children, learns the rules of good behavior, the "rules of respect for the socitechnical division of labour" (132).

Assuming that all children's books, just like all books, are culturally coded, what do we as teachers and professionals do to make certain we know the ideological designs that the books we promote have on both us and the young readers we interact with? An even more difficult question is this: how do we make certain that young readers do not unconsciously assimilate the messages encoded in these books?

A POLITICAL READING

I want now to turn to an instance of politics in a children's book. My choice of text is chapter 8 of Lewis Carroll's *Through the Looking Glass* (1872). I expect some of my colleagues will be quick to point out that my choice of text is redolent of ideological implication. To choose a passage from Lewis Carroll is to choose a canonical text. I suppose I am open to the charge of perpetuating a canon, which itself has come under repeated fire in the past decade and more. Children's literature specialists are fond of splitting the subject into what are called "book people" (those such as "authors, publishers, a great many reviewers, and public librarians," whose main interest is in the quality and meaning of books), and "child people" (those such as "parents, teachers, and—in England at any rate—most school librarians," whose main interest is in the welfare of the child) (see Townsend, "Standards of Criticism for Children's Literature," 199). From this perspective I have come down on the side of the book people. Another way of putting this is to define "book people" and "child people" as those interested in what Barthes, in *S/Z*, calls "readerly texts" and "writerly texts" (4 and elsewhere). I find comfort in the fact that Barthes places children among those readers who reread. Children, old people, and professors—these are the "marginal categories of readers" for whom rereading is "play" (16).

I may find comfort in Barthes's privileging of readers who reread, but this is cold comfort. I have little doubt that my choice of text—Carroll's *Through the Looking Glass*—finds few readers among the young these days. But I remain undaunted. My reasons for choosing this book include my belief that it need not remain unread by children. A second reason is that I find Carroll's book politically useful. Rather than promote unconscious acceptance of social norms, *Through the Looking Glass* questions these norms. The reader of this book confronts questions that demand thoughtful reviewing of conventional social institutions and behavior. The very discourse of children's literature receives parodic, and hence political, treatment. Note, for example, how the book takes many of its characters and much of its structure from traditional nursery rhymes. But Carroll also pokes fun at the British judicial system and the military complex. At a more basic level, Carroll questions the English language and its relationship to reality. At the very least, readers of this book experience a discourse that questions what Marcuse calls "the syntax of abridgement" (89), a language that claims to do away with ambiguities and to speak transparently of reality, as if reality was not itself problematic.

Some questions: Is it our reading that makes a text political? Or does something political actually inhere to texts themselves? When is a text political?

THE WHITE KNIGHT AS *BRICOLEUR*

Whatever the answer to the last question, I suspect most readers would find nothing overtly political about Alice's meeting with the White Knight in chapter 8 of *Through the Looking Glass*. We might agree, however, that the very necessity of interaction between Alice and the White Knight involves the politics of experience. Both characters must negotiate their relationship to each other. But I defer this discussion for now, and turn instead to what I take to be the political interpretation that Gilles Deleuze and Felix Guattari bring to Lévi-Strauss's notion of the *bricoleur*. The *bricoleur* is a handyman who makes do with "whatever is at hand" to produce objects of his or her invention (see Lévi-Strauss, *The Savage Mind*, 17). The White Knight nicely characterizes this somewhat random inventiveness. When Alice informs him that the little box fastened upside down across his shoulders is open and consequently empty, the Knight quickly proceeds to throw the useless thing away, but before he does, he pauses in thought, and then carefully hangs the box in a tree. He proudly tells Alice that he does this so that bees can come and use the box as a hive, thus producing for him honey. Everything about the Knight smacks of the *bricoleur*'s creative energy. His horse is laden with inventions and materials useful for making inventions: anklets to guard against shark bites, a mousetrap to prevent mice from running all about the horse's back, a horsehead helmet, fire irons, and carrots. The Knight is constantly thinking of new inventions: ways to keep the hair from falling out, recipes for blotting paper pudding, new ways of getting over a gate, a sugar-loaf helmet (an invention already tried), and a tune for the song "A-Sitting on a Gate."

In what way is this bricolage political? Deleuze and Guattari, authors of *Anti-Oedipus*, point out that Lévi-Strauss's *bricoleur* exhibits "an indifference toward the act of producing and toward the product, toward the set of instruments to be used and toward the overall result to be achieved" (7). As I see it, the desire is for production itself, not for the power that production can confer on those who control it. Lurking here is the spirit of Georges Bataille and his notion of heterology, a resistance to systematization. The White Knight is more concerned with the play of his own inventiveness than he is with ordering the world. His concern, to return to the word I began with, is not based on some ideological design, but rather on an enthusiasm for inventive play. He invents a pudding that will likely never be cooked, yet he argues that despite this "it was a very clever pudding to invent"

(217). The song he sings either brings tears to those who hear it, or it does not. He seems not to care whether the beehive attached to his saddle attracts bees or not.

This spirit of nonchalance even appears in the Rules of Battle which the White Knight seems anxious that his rival the Red Knight follow in the struggle for Alice. What these Rules are remains a mystery. What's more, once the battle is over, the victorious White Knight takes no prisoner. Instead, he informs Alice that she will be Queen. For Alice, the desire to be Queen has something to do with her sense of herself as a person of position and power, but the Knight knows just how meaningless the designation "Queen" really is. The Knight follows the rules established for his moves on the chessboard, but his real passion is for invention. If Alice can learn anything from him, then what she can learn has something to do with transcending secondary concern.

Is the impetus to play or to invent as exemplified in the White Knight politically loaded? Or does a form of play exist that is prepolitical?

ALICE AND CONCERN

I have stated, perhaps rashly, that the White Knight has something to teach Alice about concern. That she needs such a lesson is clear to me. Throughout both of the Alice books, this little girl, fictional creation of a fictional author ("Lewis Carroll" is, after all, a pseudonym), strives to show off what she has assimilated in school and to understand and follow the rules of the society in which she finds herself. Alice's concern is decidedly secondary; she actively seeks to function as a good citizen, one who follows all the rules and who looks forward to the rewards that follow from such compliance. She wants to be a queen!

The world Alice enters on her quest for social fulfillment offers her many warnings that the world of her desire is fraught with danger, the danger of tyranny and determinism. The rule Victorian society holds out to its members, especially its women and its workers, is "jam to-morrow and jam yesterday—but never jam *to-day*" (174). Or to put it another way, in this world "it takes all the running *you* can do, to keep in the same place" (145). Alice is prepared to run twice as fast as that because she has not grasped the first rule about the jam. She insists: "It *must* come sometimes to 'jam to-day'" (175). For her, the desire to be a queen prevents her from overcoming the ideological pressures of her time. Her model, besides the obvious one within her dream worlds—the Queen of Hearts, the Red and White queens—is Victoria, she whose skirts encompass the empire. I think it no exaggeration to suggest that Alice's desire has an empirical/imperial edge to it. She enters her wonderland and looking-glass worlds with the spirit of the colonialist. Note, for example, her experience in the garden of live flowers. She assumes the flowers need taking care of and she threatens to pick the daisies if they do not keep quiet. Then she leaves the flowers when the Red Queen arrives; Alice thinks "it would be far grander to have a talk with a real Queen" than to chat with the flowers (141). Alice is ever aware of the class system.

But before I chastise Alice's colonial attitude too severely, I ought to point out that similar attitudes are apparent in many of the people she meets, including the flowers, who first assume that Alice herself is a flower. Then they remark on her color, her lack of sense, and her awkward shape. Clearly, this episode introduces readers to the subject of "otherness." Rather than learn from each other, however, both Alice and the flowers maintain their sense of superiority. Indeed, this desire for prominence and position fills the Alice books. Characters regularly refuse to accept others for themselves. Solipsism threatens to become xenophobia, even under the guise of kindness as evident in "The Walrus and the Carpenter." The clearest instance of the colonial mentality is Humpty Dumpty, whose views on language are well known. Humpty uses words as if their meanings were his to fashion. He tells Alice, "When *I* use a word . . . it means just what I choose it to mean— neither more nor less" (190). When Alice asks whether a speaker can do this with words, implying that speakers come to a language that already has meaning attached to words, Humpty replies: "The question is . . . which is to be master—that's all." Humpty approaches language the way a colonist approaches a new land; he imposes his own shape on it. Humpty wants the creatures he meets to speak his language. This is largely true of all the characters in the Alice books. Alice is constantly being catechized by others who want her to accept their reality, and she in turn constantly strives to gain control of situations by imposing her own will on others.

If we look for a moment at Alice's experience in the wood "where things have no names," we might conclude that secondary concern in the way I have organized this notion in the past few paragraphs is inescapable. Identity is something everyone desires, but the forging of identity necessitates viewing oneself in relation to an Other, usually to the diminishment of that Other. Alice experiences a sense of harmony with the fawn she meets in the wood of no names precisely because neither she nor the fawn can remember who and what they are. The "who" has to do with their names (e.g., Alice); the "what" has to do with their biological natures. Once out of the wood, the fawn shakes itself free of Alice's embrace and notices that Alice is a "human child" (136–37). Fright comes into its eyes, and it bounds away, instinctively reacting to Alice as Other, in this case a threatening Other.

It occurs to me that many of the classic children's books express a colonizing ideology. And I recall Jacqueline Rose's treatment of children's fiction as, in effect, a colonial discourse? The colonizers are the publishers, writers, teachers, librarians, and parents who write, print, and disseminate these books. The primitives are our children, still defined in Lockean fashion as impressionable slates upon which we inscribe correct cultural practice. Do children's books express a colonizing ideology? Is it possible to write a book that does not express such an ideology?

THE WHITE KNIGHT AND CONCERN

The White Knight is one of the few characters in the Alice books who actually converses with Alice. Most of the characters Alice meets speak as if she were not there or as if she had no independent selfhood. Alice, too, is guilty of conversing with herself while ostensibly conversing with others. Simply put, characters fail to communicate in

Alice's dream worlds. One reason for this is their assumption of superiority; Alice and most of the characters she meets assume that they
know proper behavior or that they know what is real and what is unre-
al. Alice strives to put into practice what she has learned as a docile
and receptive upper-middle-class Victorian child, never for a moment
thinking any other cultural practice might be possible. We could say
the same about the creatures she meets in respect to their unfamiliar
behavior.

The White Knight, however, learns immediately Alice's aspiration to be Queen, and he sets about assisting her in fulfilling her desire.
As soon as he rescues her from the Red Knight, the White Knight
offers to accompany Alice to the end of the wood. She too offers him
assistance, asking him if she can help him off with his helmet. Their
time together is agreeable and friendly. He shows concern for her, and
she shows interest in him. On more than one occasion Alice and the
White Knight cooperate to accomplish some task: removing his helmet, getting the plum-cake dish into a bag, and placing the White
Knight upright and on his horse after he has tumbled off. Alice
remains polite, but amused by the Knight's awkwardness and eccen-
tricity. He talks continually about his inventions, absorbed with his
bricolage. Yet he is not unaware of Alice's changes in mood, and while
they talk of his blotting paper pudding, he thinks she must be sad. To
comfort her, he suggests that he sing a song. His concern is for Alice.
He is concerned that she successfully become Queen, that she not be
sad, that she appreciate his inventiveness, and that she understand the
logic of calling a song names. He is unconcerned about his own moves.

The White Knight, like the Lion and the Unicorn, Tweedledum
and Tweedledee, and the beamish boy earlier in the book, engages in
battle. But he does so as an act of chivalry; he fights not for himself,
but for Alice. He rescues her from the Red Knight. He really has no
prize to gain in rescuing Alice, and he does not appear to glory in his
victory. What's more, he is much more of a vorpal blade than a gay
blade. His first words to Alice after he dispenses with the Red Knight
are: "It was a glorious victory, wasn't it?" (211). But these words are
less a glorying in victory than they are an irony; the White Knight's
words parody a repeated line in Robert Southey's "Battle of

Blenheim." The White Knight's words are also a form of bricolage: parody delights in creating something new from something old. The Knight likes to chatter, and he likes to sing; he likes verbal invention as much as he likes other forms of invention. Yet to suggest the White Knight is without political significance is disingenuous. Parodies, as David Kent and D. R. Ewen point out in relation to parodies of the Romantic period, "record struggles for power" (20). The politics of the White Knight are to be found in his song, "A-Sitting on a Gate."

Carroll's Knights and Queens reflect his use of the chessboard as a structural device for *Through the Looking Glass*. Is the chess game itself politically loaded? Is the White Knight's move an indication of his acceptance of control? Does the deterministic framework of the chess game indicate Carroll's belief in strict social control?

PARODY AND POWER

The White Knight's song is perhaps the best-known parody in the Alice books. Most of the writers parodied by Carroll have receded into history—Isaac Watts, Southey, Jane Taylor, William Mee, Thomas Moore, Norman McLeod, and so on—but not Wordsworth, whose "Resolution and Independence" lies behind "A-Sitting on a Gate." Wordsworth was often parodied in the nineteenth century. As Kent and Ewen note, parodists drew attention to Wordsworth's "particularities of description," his humble characters, and his "child-like expressions of faith" (17); the point was to denigrate Wordsworth's egalitarian sensibilities. The poems that received the most attention from parodists are from Wordsworth's early career, up to 1805. In other words, parodies of Wordsworth are often conservative attacks on a radical poet.

But as Linda Hutcheon points out in her foreword to Kent and Ewen's *Romantic Parodies, 1797–1831*, parody need not be a conservative force; it also functions as "a form of oppositional discourse against a dominant cultural, social, or political force" (7). In the White Knight's case, we have a character who strains against his position in a game with predetermined rules. He acquiesces to Alice's desire to be Queen; he accepts his knightly position in the game. His inventive turn and his parodic discourse, however, read against the grain. To read against the grain is, at the very least, to rough the surface of dominant ideological forces. Dominating Victorian attitudes toward Wordsworth are Matthew Arnold's construction of Wordsworth the healer, the poet who speaks the true voice of feelings. For the Victorians, Wordsworth is the poet to read when we need to repair the tear in our psyche caused by alienating modern and urban life. Wordsworth puts the reader in touch with those bracing and healthy impulses from vernal woods. This, however, is not the Wordsworth the White Knight calls on for his parody.

The Wordsworth we meet in the White Knight's song is Wordsworth the leveler, the person speaking to persons, the people's poet. Rock and defense of human nature, this figure reminds us of our commonality. The Goody Blakes of this world are as important as the Harry Gills to this person. The precise allusion is, of course, to the Leech Gatherer, the aged man whose endurance and independence in the face of age and hardship are a lesson to the petty bourgeois poet. Carroll no doubt had Wordsworth's Laureateship and Civil List Pension in mind when he gave this song to the White Knight, but the reverberations are complex. The White Knight, with his lack of concern for power, nicely suggests the nobility of the rustic poet. And the often-made connection between the White Knight and Carroll himself reminds us of a kinship he must have felt with Wordsworth.

If my remarks sound to you as if I do not take Carroll's parody as a comic criticism of Wordsworth's poem, then you are right. Some parodies serve as homage rather than devaluation, and in keeping with the White Knight's lack of concern for power, his parody of Wordsworth does not assume a position of dominance over "Resolution and Independence." No, "A-Sitting on a Gate"—albeit in a comic manner—highlights ("foregrounds" our discourse now prompts us to say) Wordsworth's sympathy for the proletariat. Just as Wordsworth's speaker shows little real concern for the Leech Gatherer, so too does the speaker in "A-Sitting on a Gate" show little interest in the old man. This parody voice reminds us of the White Knight himself, preoccupied with his many inventions. Tenniel's illustration clearly shows the speaker in the poem to be none other than the White Knight himself. The conclusion to the poem, however, returns us to Wordsworth's poem and the moral chastening the young poet receives from his encounter with the Leech Gatherer. The parody speaker, too, receives thought for future years. He often recalls the gentle, bright-eyed, cunning, wanderer of an old man. The old man lives on meager fare, and so too does the White Knight, who by implication has learned the relative worth of things partly from his encounter with this aged man.

The lesson about power, then, is its illusory nature. The only real power is the power to invent things. Story is power; language is power. The White Knight and his song remind us that the power of language and story need not be a coercive power. The White Knight takes no captives, although, perhaps, he makes a friend. How does "A-Sitting on a Gate" affect our reading of "Resolution and Independence"? Does the reader of Carroll's text need to know what texts receive parodic treatment? What does the use of parody in children's books suggest about children's books?

CHILDREN'S BOOKS AND PARODY

At first, parody may seem at odds with literature for children. The same may be said for a variant of parody: satire. Young children, so the argument might go, cannot appreciate parody and satire because their experience is too limited. For example, children who know little about adult society or about the conventions of book publishing may simply not notice parodic elements in *Winnie-the-Pooh*. Allusions to and parodies of René Magritte (who himself used parody extensively) pop up regularly in the work of Anthony Browne. An even more obvious example is the one before us. How many seven- or eight-year-olds have read Wordsworth's "Resolution and Independence"? Perhaps in Carroll's day seven- to ten-year-olds did know this poem, but I own a copy of Wordsworth's *Poems for the Young*, published in 1866

(Alexander Strahan), and "Resolution and Independence" is not one of the poems collected. But the point is that writers and illustrators who employ parody show a respect for the young reader. The sense of empowerment arising from a recognition of parody is political in the sense of passing authority to the reader. This is one aspect of overtly parodic texts such as *The Stinky Cheese Man and Other Fairly Stupid Tales* that makes them politically important.

Children's books are chock full of parody and other forms of intertextual allusion. Rather than existing as a parasitical discourse feeding on previous works, parody such as we see in Carroll and in much children's literature serves to maintain contact with history. It reminds us of the past, while at the same time it re-creates or transforms the past. It is no accident that much of Carroll's satire is directed at earlier children's books, books from the age of instruction, the kind of books written by Anna Laetitia Barbauld and her brother John Aikin or by Sarah Trimmer. Carroll's book maintains contact with, even a dialogue with, the past; it situates itself vis-à-vis the past. And in doing this, it respects the intelligence of children. Children, too, are part of history, just as the books they read are part of history. With this in mind, I may be permitted a digressive observation: historical fiction is one of the most enduringly popular forms of writing for the young, and even this form itself is parodied in Joan Aiken's wonderful series of books about the irrepressible Dido Twite.

Parody's eye on the past is important for political reasons. The reader of parody must confront questions of change, meaning, and significance. How does the parodied text differ from the parody of it? How does the present cultural moment reflect itself differently from the earlier cultural moment? The presence of parody has an estranging effect. I take the idea from the Russian Formalists, but the estrangement I speak of has a political edge. The reader of parody cannot be drawn into the text in the sense of being carried away or rendered passive. The reader of parody must be active. The active reader is the reader on the alert for designs, both designs in a purely literary sense and designs on the reader herself. Reading parody, children receive one of their first lessons in criticism and critical detachment.

Is parody a conservative or a subversive force in books for the young? Why is parody so insistent in children's books? Does it matter whether the child reader understands the parody?

PARODY, CONCERN, CHILDREN

The discussion of parody might seem to have taken us away from questions of concern and children. I say this because parody is, in its most obvious sense, literary, or, more bluntly, bookish. My interest in parody might place me in the camp of the "book people" I spoke of earlier. Now according to Peter Hollindale, the book people, those interested in the literary quality of books for children, "have become linked with a broadly conservative and 'reactionary' ideological position" (5). This implies some kind of Leavisiste belief in a great tradition that must be conserved if we are to maintain social stability. To be interested in literature is, so the argument goes, not only to be indifferent to the child reader, but also to be indifferent to such political concerns as classism, racism, and sexism. Such concerns pale under the sun of aesthetic beauty. The book person's concern is for an aesthetic quality that transcends local politics. Most of my students fall into this attitude when they speak of a book's appeal to the imagination or its power to enchant its reader. Hollindale posits this politically incorrect "book person" as a "caricature," an exaggeration (9).

Yet even those of us who remain inveterate book people (mea culpa) realize that what we might wish to think of as a primary concern, the reading of books for their own sake, cannot be separated from secondary concern, the need to accommodate oneself to an environment, a social group. The reader who reads for pleasure does not read without a context. Or as Hollindale puts it: "ideology is not something which is transferred to children as if they were empty receptacles. It is something which they already possess, having drawn it from a mass of experiences far more powerful than literature" (17). In other words, child readers, like adult readers, use literature just as much as literature uses them. And also like adult readers, child readers come to books through a medium; no reading is unmediated (see Jameson, *The Political Unconscious*, 9).

And we as adult readers of children's literature are part of a large social structure that stands between children and their books. We do not simply teach children how to read; we are ourselves reading models. The way we read—not simply what or how we read—serves to introduce children to the politics of reading. By way of reading, I mean both the delight in language admired by the book people and the attention to books as experience admired by the child people. By way of reading, I mean keeping the questions coming. By way of reading, I mean delighting in rereading. As Benjamin Barber notes, in *An Aristocracy of Everyone: The Politics of Education and the Future of America*, children are born "neither wise nor literate nor responsible— nor are they born free." Paraphrasing Rousseau, Barber argues that we, as teachers, must "force our students to be free" (210). This speaks to me both as a reader and teacher.

Let me not leave Barber just yet. He points out that many kids we think of as failed readers, street kids who might even be "illiterate," are adept readers of "the social signals emanating from the world in which they have to make a living." For teachers these young persons have television, advertising, movies, videos, pop stars, politics, and popular culture generally. As Barber has it: "The first lesson these kids learn is that it is much more important to heed what society teaches implicitly than what school teaches explicitly" (216). In my experience, students do not really care what Lewis Carroll might have to say about William Wordsworth. They do not even care to read a funny book that is now so old-fashioned as to contain Queens, Knights, and Anglo-Saxon Messengers. Not that they have anything against Queens and Knights, but they want them in high romance rather than in parody and satire. They want books, if they have to have them, written at least in the last forty-five years. They want books that reflect the interactive passivity of video games.

In whatever way we look at this question of reading, our young people are learning (and want to learn) to read with the grain. Whatever smooths their way to success and a comfortable place in the economic network is what they look for. They read what they read for the messages concerning survival. They are cunning readers, but their cunning is our cunning; they want what we have implicitly said they should want: lives of material ease and social conformity. If all read the same way, perhaps this ease and this conformity will be theirs.

It is, however, this reading for the message, for the path of least resistance, that we must refuse to accept. My choice of text, then, is deliberate, not to signal my belief in canonical texts, not to provide a finished interpretation, but to indicate my belief that the past informs the present and that books remain open. To read and reread a text such as *Through the Looking Glass* is to offer encouragement to inventiveness. My hope, like Alice's as she departs for the eighth and last square, is that I have offered some encouragement.

In What Sense Political?

I began with a series of epigraphs that might indicate that the ideology of this chapter reflects a leftist belief, and it may seem as if most of the recent work done on ideology and literature comes from left-leaning critics. But as the rest of this book should indicate, I do not subscribe to the notion that a Marxist criticism is that "untranscendable horizon" embracing all critical operations that Fredric Jameson announces it is (*The Political Unconscious*, 10). I do, however, accept that "in the last analysis" everything we read has its political dimension (20). Indeed, I have argued that not only do the books we read communicate political "messages," but that reading itself is fraught with political implications. We choose to read what we read for a reason, and we choose books for our children for a reason. One need only look to the history of book censorship in North America to understand just how political the act of reading is. A glance through Joan DelFattore's *What Johnny Shouldn't Read* gives a disturbing account of just how political reading and the world of children's books are.

Recently in Canada, a book by one of the country's most popular children's authors, Robert Munsch, received much criticism and

some censorship for its presentation of that greatest of authority figures: God. The book is *Giant or Waiting for the Thursday Boat* (1989),
and in it, the giant McKeon says he will pound God until he looks like
applesauce. This disrespect for God offended adult readers, or at least
this is the claim. I suspect that the real reason this book offended adult
readers is the depiction of God as a child and a female. This, apparently, is much more offensive than presenting "good families" with farts
in their bedrooms; I refer to Munsch's *Good Families Don't* (1990),
which seems to have created less of a stir than his book about the giant
McKeon.

Our question must be, once again, of what use is a political reading of children's books? Obviously, reading for the ideological assumptions of any book is important if we believe in knowing how our
culture works upon us. And as difficult as it may be, teaching children
to read for the ideological messages in books (or in any other manifestation of their culture—videos, advertisements, and so on) is important
if we wish them to be informed and independent citizens. Training
politically astute young readers may be difficult in any direct way, but
we can introduce even the very young to the political implications of
the books they read simply by providing a range of books. For example, feminists criticize fairy tales for their sexual stereotyping, citing
such stories as "Cinderella," "Sleeping Beauty," and "Snow White" as
culprits in perpetuating the beauty myth and promoting the ideal of
the passive woman. To counter this, we need only offer a wider range
of fairy tales; for example, from the Brothers Grimm we might choose
to expose children to "The Robber Bridegroom," "The Rabbit's
Bride," "Fred and Kate," or "The Glass Coffin" to give them visions of
women and marriage that sharply differ from those in the more
famous stories.

At the very least, we might introduce our students to notions of
culture and the construction of culture. To speak of the construction
of culture brings me to notions pertinent to semiotics and structuralism, our next topic.

6

Constructivist Reading: The Structuralist Activity

Structures are self-sufficient . . . to grasp them, we do not have to make reference to all sorts of extraneous elements.

—Jean Piaget

Form is defined by opposition to material other than itself. But *structure* has no distinct content; it is content itself, apprehended in a logical organization conceived as property of the real.

—Claude Lévi-Strauss

The goal of all structuralist activity, whether reflexive or poetic, is to reconstruct an "object" in such a way as to manifest thereby the rules of functioning (the "functions") of this object. Structure is therefore actually a *simulacrum* of the object, but a directed, *interested* simulacrum, since the imitated object makes something appear which remained invisible, or if one prefers, unintelligible in the natural object.

—Roland Barthes

> At the heart of the idea of structuralism is the idea of system: a complete self-regulating entity that adapts to new conditions by transforming its features while retaining its systematic structure.
>
> —Robert Scholes

Like every other method of reading we have looked at, the structuralist method takes several shapes depending on the theoretical and disciplinary background of the particular structuralist. For example, the taxonomies of fairy- and folktale plots outlined by such scholars as Vladimir Propp and Stith Thompson differ from the genre speculations of someone like Eric Rabkin or the breakdown of narrative by such writers as Gerard Genette, Gerald Prince, Mieke Bal, and other narratologists or the study of image clusters and patterns in such writers as Frye. What unites most of these various structuralist activities is an interest in how things work, in the thingness of objects, whether those "objects" are organisms, constructed machines, literary texts, or cultural practices. The structuralist is as interested in the object as the formalist, but as my epigraph from Lévi-Strauss hints, without the Formalist's idealizing tendencies. Structuralism does not look beyond the structure for meaning, and it finds in each structure a coherent and self-contained system. Unlike Formalism, however, structuralism does not isolate its structures from other structures. At some level, the structure under scrutiny—let us say a literary text—is connected to other similar structures—other literary works—and these other literary works form parts of a larger structure—literature itself—which is in turn related to an even larger structural context—the society that produces the literature.

Perhaps the most influential aspect of structuralist thought on children's literature is in the area of narratology, and for this reason I shall not offer a detailed narratological reading of a children's book here. For those who wish to pursue the subject, I suggest Joanne M. Golden's *The Narrative Symbol in Childhood Literature* (1990) and John Stephens's provocative and highly readable *Language and Ideology in Children's Fiction* (1992).

I will, however, offer a simple and extreme structuralist analysis of a book I have worked on several times, George MacDonald's *The*

Constructivist Reading

Princess and the Goblin (1872). My contention is that the book is a complete self-contained system of opposites. We do not have to interpret the book's symbols to fit our extraliterary biases. We need only see that everything in the book makes sense in a pattern of opposites reconciled. The reader's experience, her education, consists in isolating the parts and then fitting them together again. The book presents us with a dialectic. Its images reflect each other, rather than concepts outside the book. The characters and images do not represent anything but what they are; each one is part of a structural pattern that shows opposites reconciled. For example, in chapter 10, "The Princess's King-papa," MacDonald describes the garden of the king's house:

> The garden was a very lovely place. Being upon a mountain side there were parts in it where the rocks came through in great masses, and all immediately about them remained quite wild. Tufts of heather grew upon them, and other hardy mountain plants and flowers, while near them would be lovely roses and lilies, and all pleasant garden flowers. This mingling of the wild mountain with the civilized garden was very quaint, and it was impossible for any number of gardeners to make such a garden look formal and stiff. (57)

This describes an unusual garden, a fairy-tale garden. The castle and garden together represent an ideal, the ideal presented in the 21st and 22nd chapters of Revelation. False distinctions have no place here; all is unity. This explains why the description of the garden is replete with opposites: rocks (wasteland) and vegetation, natural plants (heather, etc.) and "symbolic" plants (roses and lilies), wildness and civilization. Even the gardeners are but partially in control. The opposites somehow synthesize into the garden, which in its very blend of opposites expresses the structural pattern of the book. The rocks, heather, and wildness constitute the phenomenal; the vegetation, roses and lilies, and art manifest the noumenal. The two, phenomenal and noumenal, are reconciled; they exist together, informing each other. This is what the book is about: the reconciliation of opposites. The book does not offer easily identifiable "meanings" or "messages"; rather, it instructs us in the nature of metaphor, symbol, and image. Their significance is multifold, but what matters is whether they are united. Their unity means MacDonald's book is successful as a work of art; what they unify—opposites—explains the creative potential of the human imagination.

Blake's word for opposites is "contraries." Without contraries humanity cannot progress, yet the marriage of contraries suggests an end to progress, a completed realization or entelechy; what Blake refers to as "The Last Judgment." The imagination that can envisage a blending of opposites not only perceives that perfect society, but also moves toward it. In the process of moving toward this new society, the imaginative person transforms the present world. We see this in Irene, whose "good moments" are her visits to the grandmother, that grand reconciler of opposites. Irene's visionary experience changes her mundane experience; she has an intuitive grasp of nature which those who do not experience the grandmother lack. She perceives the interpenetration of what I have called the noumenal and the phenomenal, and what MacDonald calls "fairyland" and the "world of shadows" (see the final chapter of *Phantastes*). Virtually every detail in *The Princess and the Goblin* serves this pattern of opposites.

Everything serves the larger pattern that we see in miniature in MacDonald's description of the garden. Even the title of the book, which appears odd in that it mentions only one goblin (presumably Prince Harelip, who has only a minor role in the action), alerts us to the pattern of opposites that threads its way through the book. This pattern operates in all facets of the book, as Figure 3, a partial list, shows (see next page).

The left side of each of these columns roughly corresponds to what I have called the noumenal, and the right corresponds to the phenomenal. For example, Irene, whose name suggests "peace," represents "princess" in its metaphorical suggestiveness. MacDonald insists throughout the book that "the truest princess is just the one who loves all her brothers and sisters best" (137); she "never forgets her debts until they are paid" (54); and she is obedient. In short, she is an ideal. Her relationship with nature penetrates the phenomenal; she communicates with flowers and hillside. The animistic quality of nature prevalent in fairy tales here expresses Irene's harmony with that sense sublime which rolls through all things. She remains unaffected by adult sarcasm, and she need fear no harm from the goblins. On the other hand, the goblins are obviously of the earth, chthonic. They live underground "in cold and wet and dark places" (6). They are grotesque and possibly cannibalistic. Their heads are hard and their feet soft. They are remnants of a fallen nature that is still falling.

Of course this distinction between Irene as noumenal and the goblins as phenomenal is not entirely satisfactory. More accurately these opposites are two facets of the phenomenal. So are "castle" and "cottage." This works in the noumenal as well: "fire" and "water," "red" and "white" are pairs identified in the book with the noumenal

Princess	Goblin	dream	reality
mountains	caves	natural	unnatural
moon	sun	child	adult
female	male	light	dark
Queen	King	castle	cottage
royalty	miners	Irene	Curdie
pigeons	cob's creatures	oval bath	goblin Hall
spider's thread	string	white	red
silver	gold	sound	sight
young	old	poverty	wealth
human society	goblin society	cleanliness	dirt
rest	work	imagination	reason
poetry	political discourse	soul (sole)	Head
fire	water		

Figure 3.

world of the grandmother and her tower. And finally, certain pairs explicitly juxtapose phenomenal and noumenal: "King" and "Queen," "dream" and "reality," for example. Such flexibility illustrates the vitality of MacDonald's structural pattern. It is not mechanical. It is consistent, yet dynamic, substantiating both his dislike of "sharp-edged systems" (Greville MacDonald, *George MacDonald and His Wife*, 155) and his belief, following Novalis, that the fairy tale "is like a dream work without coherence. An assembly of wonderful things and happenings, e.g. a musical fantasy, the harmony of an Aeolian harp, nature itself" (epigraph to *Phantastes*). The phrase "without coherence" is misleading because a fairy tale such as *The Princess and the Goblin* is a rich and complex harmony of opposites, which are either negations (in Blake's sense) like "dirt" and "cleanliness," "poetry" and "political discourse," or they are contraries like "male" and "female," "castle" and "cottage." The garden clearly shows the contraries at work; opposites synthesize to form a third entity, in this case the garden itself. This embracing of opposites is the message of the book.

Such a reading focuses, as a glance back at the list of words will show, on the book's images or on what we might refer to as its "signs." This interest in image and symbol as communicative signs indicates the intersection of structuralism and semiology. Although semiology and structuralism are not the same, semiological analysis is a familiar feature of structuralist analysis. So what is semiology? Simply: the science of signs. The semiologist is interested in any system of signs, and it has its roots in the philosophical work of Charles Sanders Peirce and in the linguistic theorizing of Ferdinand de Saussure. A literary critic who employs a structuralist method will most likely gravitate to what traditional literary scholarship thinks of as symbols, characters, images, recurring events in fiction, and so on, but a more embracing semiological approach is brought to children's literature in the work of Zohar Shavit, who studies what she refers to as the "literary polysystem" (*Poetics of Children's Literature,* x and passim; cf. with Culler, who says literature is "a second order semiotic system," *Structuralist Poetics*, 114). The study of signs is brilliantly brought to bear on the study of children's picture books in Perry Nodelman's *Words About Pictures*.

Constructivist Reading

Indeed, the method is particularly fruitful for the study of illustrations. Take, for example, the complete title page of *Where the Wild Things Are*. The title, and author's and publisher's names appear on the recto as we would expect, but the illustrations on both verso and recto communicate, effectively connecting both left and right pages. To make the connection emphatic, Sendak has the tail of one of the Wild Things trail across the gutter. Clearly Max's posture and gesture, depicted on the extreme right and lower half of the recto, are meant to threaten the two Wild Things who occupy most of the opposite page. Between Max and the two Wild Things lie not only the gutter, but also the title and author's name; from the way Max flails his arms, we might conclude that he flings these words at the Wild Things. At the very least, this conjunction of illustration and printed words prepares the reader to look for the relationship between the two forms of discourse, the verbal and the graphic. The conjunction between words and illustration here should tell us that where the Wild Things are is on both pages. Max, whether he tosses the words or not, is as much a Wild Thing as the two large figures on the verso.

This connection between Max and the Wild Things, strengthened by the strong horizontal line of the two tails—one on a large Wild Thing and the other on Max's wolf suit, is clearly evident in the eyes of the three figures. The two figures on the left look at Max (or perhaps at the words he throws), who, in turn, looks at them. Max looks impish, confident, in control; the Wild Things look hesitant, insecure, perhaps fearful. Looking more closely, we note that Max's posture and gesture are imitated by the two Wild Things, as if they are attempting to follow his movements. This is especially clear in the figure closest to the inner margin. Whatever this illustration depicts, one thing seems clear: the Wild Things pose no threat to Max. Although the illustration contains several sharp lines—the horns, the spikes of Max's crown, the claws on hands and toes, and the Wild Things' teeth—the texture of the drawing likewise works to mitigate fear. Sendak's cross-hatching and his use of open lines and soft colors do not create a threatening mood.

Another sign for the reader is clothing. What the figures "wear" is important in preparing the reader for the story to follow. I place the word "wear" in quotation marks because it remains questionable whether the Wild Things wear anything or whether their bodies have clothlike fur. In any case, that Max wears a costume is clear from the buttons on the front of his wolf jumpsuit and from the way the suit frames his face. If Max wears a costume, then why might not the Wild Things? Perhaps we have here some fanciful costumes reminiscent of those ape costumes so prevalent in the inexpensive horror films associated with Universal Studios in the 1930s and 1940s. The male Wild Thing—convention tells us that one is male, the other female because of the one's horns, beard, and short hair and the other's long hair and dainty feet—appears to "wear" a striped T-shirt and plain checked trousers, or perhaps the whole outfit is a jumpsuit. Whether the Wild Thing wears clothes or has fur designed to look like clothes, his appearance might remind us of young boys. But these Wild Things are clearly larger than Max, and their size, too, is a sign. A sign of what? Given the whole configuration—young boy wearing a wolf suit in a position of power vis-à-vis these large figures, whose appearance is "wild" but nonthreatening and who "wear" clothes—could we not have communicated here that delightful child fantasy: control of one's elders, perhaps even of one's parents? The hint that all these figures are in costume suggests the playful nature of this book; it is, after all, a fantasy.

Before we leave this analysis of the title pages as a sign (consisting of several signs), we might notice that the movement implied by the characters' actions goes from right to left. This may not seem unusual, but it is. This is a book, and the normal procedure in Western culture is to read a book from left to right and from top to bottom. Here, however, the eye catches the title and Max as one would expect and then must take in the large figures to their left. The outstretched tails indicate movement away from the extreme right-hand outer margin, or in other words, against the grain. The reader reads backward. (We might mount an argument for a backward reading of the book as a whole, too.) That this is appropriate will become evident once we have read the book and learn that it is about Max's transgressive, perhaps subversive, behavior. The book is about the formative function of such behavior, and about the formative nature of signs themselves.

Constructivist Reading

You can see that my analysis has strained to remain within the title page, but that hints of the larger design of the book creep in. We might ask, then, what a structuralist would make of *Where the Wild Things Are* in its totality. What the structuralist does is to order what he or she perceives into segments (see Leach's *Claude Lévi-Strauss*, 15–32). This ordering process characteristically takes the form of paired opposites, or binary opposites, and these may be neatly listed. I illustrated the method earlier in my glance at *The Princess and the Goblin*. The structure of binaries in *Where the Wild Things Are* might look something like this:

child	adult
wild	civilized
animal	human
food (raw)	food (cooked)
bedroom	forest (and sea)
pictures	printed words
dream	reality
powerlessness	power
night (moon)	day (sun)
son	mother

Figure 4.

This list might be extended; James McGavran, for example, notes the pairs "friend-foe, joy-fear, self-other" in *Wild Things* (173). But we have enough to work with in the list I offer. The column on the left is regressive, but as it turns out, regressive in a useful because psychologically strengthening way. Max's dream is a reaction to his experience of powerlessness; his mother has the authority to send him to bed without his supper. Max's only recourse to his mother's disapproval of his behavior is first to threaten to eat his mother up (presumably raw), and then to allow his fantasy life to take over. In his dream, Max releases his wild or uncivilized energies by leaving (in his dream world, at least) his room for a journey to the land of the Wild Things. He lives his dream life under the aegis of the moon, that ancient image of the unconscious and its desires. The moon is also a feminine symbol, perhaps reminding us that Max never does leave behind the protective influence of his mother. As he moves deeper into his dream of travel and power, the pictures become larger and the printed words begin to retreat, until, at the time of the wild rumpus, they disappear altogether. Max has regressed to a stage prior to language, or as McGavran says, "Max's imaginative interaction with his creatures takes him beyond words—or before words" (173). Language is a sign of civilization, of order and clarity. It is surely no accident that what the reader first meets and last sees within the pages of this book are printed words on white pages empty of illustration. The very first page of the book contains only the words of the title, and the final page contains only the words, "and it was still hot." These final words reinforce the emerging order signified by the words themselves and by what the words signify: cooked food prepared by mother. The son returns to his room, but the room, as the final illustration on the penultimate page shows, is a little larger than it was. This is a book about growing.

This analysis of the structural pattern and its "meaning" in *Where the Wild Things Are* is repeatable with any book; I suggest you might look at Jean Perrot's use of Lévi-Strauss to complicate Sendak's play with meaning in *In the Night Kitchen* (see Perrot). For our purposes, however, we can turn again to *Charlotte's Web*. The central image of the web might indicate a book that tries to overcome the structuralist view of the world as based on binary oppositions. As Rushdy eloquently argues, as an image for relationships, the web is more integrative than the mirror. Whereas the mirror sets up reflections, doubles, binaries, the web connects and embraces several things. It breaks down simple oppositions. This is, however, only partially true. In the book the web itself introduces the opposition spider's web–web as text, or the web as something natural and as something unnatural. This binary set implicates the entire novel:

spider's web	web as text
spider	pig
writer	written
reality	fantasy
death	life
////	////
child	adult
female	male
nature	civilization
summer	winter
spring	fall

Figure 5.

As with the list for *Where the Wild Things Are*, this list could well be extended, but it will suffice. The break after the first five pairs draws attention to a shift in consistency; the pairs below the break show the positive half of the binary pair on the left, but those above are not so easily separated into positive and negative. The reason for this is simple: the structuring principle in this book is more complex than that in *Where the Wild Things Are*. This is perhaps clear in the pattern shown in Figure 6.

This diagram articulates the book's main concerns. First, the axis Charlotte/spider–Web-as-death: Charlotte is a spider, and her nature demands that she prey on insects in order to live. Her web is a trap to capture the insects she will put to death. Along this axis, then, we have reality, nature red in tooth and claw. Following counterclockwise, we have the axis Web-as-death–Wilbur/pig. When he first meets Charlotte, Wilbur learns just what and how she eats. He learns that her web is a death trap. This cold wind of reality chills Wilbur and reminds us that all things in nature die and that some of them die prematurely, that is, not of old age. The reality is that Wilbur, too, will die, and if the sheep is correct, he will not die of old age. This is the left axis, but as we begin to mount the right axis we see Wilbur/pig–Web-as-writing. The connection between these, too, has to do with Wilbur's life. The writing in the web prolongs Wilbur's life indefinitely. Here Wilbur the pig is inscribed onto the world as something too valuable to do away with. We enter here a fantasy, one that becomes clear when we draw a contrast between Web-as-death and Web-as-writing. This fantasy grows fuller when we complete our trip along the axes: Web-as-writing–Charlotte/spider. Here the idea of a spider who is also a good writer is clearly the stuff of fantasy.

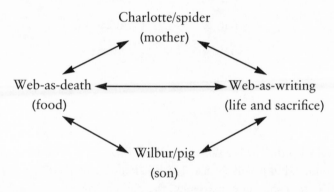

Figure 6.

Before we leave the diagram we ought also to connect top and bottom: Charlotte/spider–Wilbur/pig. These two are friends, and even more than friends, since Charlotte serves as a maternal figure for Wilbur. It is natural and realistic for mothers to wish to protect their sons. In order to do this, Charlotte becomes a writer (shades of so many nineteenth-century women who wrote to feed their families). It is unnatural for spiders to become writers, just as it is unnatural for spiders to befriend pigs. The diagram, then, points out just how complementary fantasy and reality are in this book. They form a circle, rather than being two discrete forms of experience. The circular form of the diagram serves also to remind us of the book's insistence on nature's cycles: the four seasons, life and death, and so on. We might

even integrate the bracketed words "(food)" and "(life and sacrifice)."
The Web-as-death provides the spider with food and thus is necessary
for the spider's life; the Web-as-writing keeps Wilbur alive even as it
signals Charlotte's sacrifice and death. In other words, death and life
are intimately connected here; they go together like the horse and car-
riage. The myth inherent in *Charlotte's Web* is that art (writing; note
also Dr. Dorian's name) puts a stay to death; it is life affirming, and it
does affect society directly and is not simply an entertaining frill.

Once we have located a structural pattern, everything else in the
columns falls into place within this pattern:

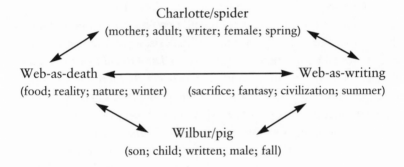

Figure 7.

We need not stop here. Other combinations come to mind such
as animal/human, the individual/the community, enclosure/freedom,
self/other, selfishness/selflessness, the miraculous/the mundane, pub-
lic/private, and change/permanence. The important thing is to look on
the book as a system or code of signification. It communicates through
patterns, whether these patterns are thematic or linguistic. Ultimately,
the structuralist is interested in language not only as a lexical phenom-
enon, but as any form of human communication. How does
Charlotte's Web communicate? The structuralist's answer is that it
communicates through its codes, and as Jonathan Culler argues in
Structuralist Poetics, the reader needs to understand the nature of literary codes if he or she is to read competently. Culler states: "The [lit-
erary] work has structure and meaning because it is read in a particular

way, because these potential properties, latent in the object itself, are actualized by the theory of discourse applied in the act of reading" (113). The question, which we will return to later, is whether the patterns that we find in a text are there as patterns or whether we create these patterns through our own method of reading.

Before going on, however, we need to bring two more concepts into play: paradigm and syntagm. These words derive from Saussure's linguistic theories, and they refer, respectively, to a word's "vertical" relationship to other words not present within a sentence and to its "horizontal" relationship to the words that are present within a sentence. The paradigmatic, or vertical, relations are, then, not necessarily spread out in time or space; the syntagmatic are. This is why these terms are sometimes used in conjunction with two other terms: synchronic and diachronic. For purposes of literary analysis, a paradigmatic approach might work like the one taken above to *The Princess and the Goblin*, *Where the Wild Things Are*, and *Charlotte's Web*. Here the attempt was to locate and examine the system of binary opposites in these books. At its most extreme, this paradigmatic approach keeps us within the text. The text's meaning is simply the interplay of binary structures.

To approach these texts syntagmatically would result in a somewhat different emphasis. For example, we might locate the most important binary opposition in *Charlotte's Web* in the opposition between human and animal (including insect). This produces the following chain: animal = dominated creatures—turn tricksters/human = dominating species—become tricked: result == dominated become dominating and vice versa. The point of this structural chain is to reveal what is, perhaps not surprisingly, at the center of the book. The central chapter—number 11 out of 22—is the one in which the focus is on the human reaction to the appearance of the first words in the web. This is the most satirical chapter in the book, and it threatens to take us outside the fantasy to examine human gullibility and pride. When the local minister remarks in his Sunday sermon that "the words on the spider's web proved that human beings must always be on the watch for the coming of wonders" (85), the irony has to do with human failure to locate the real source of "wonders." Everyone focuses on Wilbur and fails to notice the spider. Some readers might remember the bad press the spider sometimes receives for its associations with dark forces.

The reader might also recall that the book first appeared in 1952, only seven years after the end of World War II and in the midst of the early cold war scare in the United States. The fear that democracy might be in jeopardy from skilled and subtle tricks of communist infiltration does not lie far removed from *Charlotte's Web*, although just what stance this book takes to the climate of the early 1950s might be debatable. One thing is certain: a focus on the relation between animal and human must result in a focus on the dialectic of master and servant. In other words, our analysis has moved beyond the literary system to speculative commentary on the historical moment of this book's creation. The enclosed world of the farm in *Charlotte's Web* is only as enclosed as the world in which the book itself exists. Just as farmer Zuckerman (the Germanic name may or may not have significance here) can have his normal routine altered by a spider, a small and apparently insignificant creature who has, possibly, arrived here on her air balloon (cf. Charlotte's children at the end of the book), so too might small and seemingly insignificant things alter the life of America in the postwar days. Because the reader's sympathies lie with Wilbur, Charlotte, and their friends, we might conclude that American populism is alive and well, with its source in the transcendentalism of Thoreau, or more immediately in the American small-town democracy of someone like Frank Capra. A reading of *Charlotte's Web* along these lines must conclude that it is, indeed, a wonderful life.

To return to our original terminology, I want to equate "syntagmatic" with "extrinsic." The equation is wobbly, but once again, it serves to make clear just how our readings always move along an axis: extrinsic/intrinsic or syntagmatic/paradigmatic. The reading I gave earlier in this chapter to *Where the Wild Things Are* is paradigmatic, but a syntagmatic reading is also possible. We might read the book as the triumph of "No." Max's refusal to accept his mother's scolding and then his refusal to accede to the Wild Things' desire for him to stay with them is the triumph of the child's instinct for refusal. We might, in other words, have here an early version of what Mordecai Richler's *Jacob Two-Two Meets the Hooded Fang* (1975) refers to as "Child

Power," the phrase deliberately resonant of other slogans of the 1960s, "Black Power," "Flower Power," and so on. *Where the Wild Things Are* produces this chain:Max–mischief–reprimand–resistance–punishment–retreat–refusal to accede–return and reward. True, Max does desire to return to "where someone loved him best of all," but the point is, he achieves his desire. Published in 1963, *Where the Wild Things Are* coincides neatly with the beginning of the period of youth rebellion of the 1960s and early 1970s. Another product of American culture of the same year serves as nifty chorus for the sensibility apparent in Sendak's book:

> Come mothers and fathers
> Throughout the land
> And don't criticize
> What you can't understand
> Your sons and your daughters
> Are beyond your command
> For the times they are a-changin'.

> (Dylan, 91)

The structuralist approach, then, offers an easily repeatable method for studying children's books (or anything else, for that matter). The prevalence of fantasy and of animals in children's books sets up the binaries fantasy/reality and animal/human. Many children's books invite an analysis of binaries in their very titles: for example, *The Day Boy and the Night Girl* (George MacDonald), *Lily and the Lost Boy* (Paula Fox), *The Grey Lady and the Strawberry Snatcher* (Molly Bang), *Shadow Play* (Paul Fleischman), *Black and White* (David Macaulay), "Snow White and the Seven Dwarfs" (Brothers Grimm), *Outside Over There* (Maurice Sendak), *The Five Children and It* (E. Nesbit), *Yellow and Pink* (William Steig), *Amos and Boris* (William Steig), *The Princess and the Musician* (Fiona French), *Willy and Hugh* (Anthony Browne), and *Fast-Slow/High-Low* (Peter Spier). I offer this list only to suggest how readily books and stories for the young set up a binary pattern. But of course we have examples of books that appear to resist such systematizing, and one just happens to be familiar from my earlier discussions: *The Mysteries of Harris Burdick.*

Constructivist Reading

As I noted in chapter 2, *Harris Burdick* appears not to have the formalist's prerequisite: unity. Its fourteen discrete drawings do not participate in a single narrative, and therefore the book does not have the unity supplied by plot. As Van Allsburg's introduction points out, the drawings may, and ought to, give rise to as many stories as there are readers. The structuralist, however, looks for some self-regulating principle in the book, and such a principle is not difficult for the intrepid hunter after structures to find. Anyone who has read Tzvetan Todorov's book, *The Fantastic: A Structural Approach to a Literary Genre* (1975), will find ready-made a structuralist approach to this picture book.

Todorov suggests that the fantastic occurs when an event takes place in our familiar and mundane world that we cannot explain "by the laws of this same familiar world" (25). When faced with such an event, we either find a rational explanation for it, accept it as inexplicable, or remain in uncertainty as to whether the event is explainable or unexplainable. Should we find a rational explanation, then the event is no longer fantastic; instead it is, according to Todorov, "uncanny" (Todorov's use of this word differs from Freud's, where it has something to do with the strangeness of the unconscious and hence is familiar yet unfamiliar). The opposite, that is, when we cannot find an explanation and yield to the impossibility of explanation, is the "marvelous." Todorov posits three "genres": the fantastic, the uncanny, and the marvelous. To show their relationship, he sets out the following diagram.

uncanny	fantastic–uncanny	fantastic–marvelous	marvelous

Figure 8.

Todorov glosses this diagram: "The fantastic in its pure state is represented here by the median line separating the fantastic-uncanny from the fantastic-marvelous. This line corresponds perfectly to the nature of the fantastic, a frontier between two adjacent realms" (44).

The pictures in Van Allsburg's book fit neatly into this scheme. His visual style might almost be termed photographic in its clarity of representation, and what he represents is mostly the familiar features of the world we live in: suburban houses with their suburban bedrooms and basements, woods with streams, a canal in Venice, the nave of a Gothic cathedral. Invariably, however, something in the picture casts everything into an unfamiliar light. Most of the pictures present a world situated on the frontier between Todorov's uncanny and marvelous, and they invite the reader to complete the investigation as to whether what the pictures present is fantastic, uncanny, or marvelous. Most of the pictures suggest the marvelous, but some—the one with the small basement door or the one with the harp in the woods, for example—might have plausible explanations and therefore be representative of the uncanny. As we have them, however, all the pictures illustrate the fantastic.

I mentioned in parentheses Freud's definition of the uncanny, and this may provide us with another structuralist perspective on *The Mysteries of Harris Burdick*. Whereas for Todorov the uncanny is an explainable mystery, for Freud it is precisely that which is unexplainable. More important for our discussion of *Harris Burdick*, however, is Freud's brilliant connection between the uncanny and the canny. The German words are *unheimlich* (unhomely, unfamiliar) and *heimlich* (homely, familiar) (see "The Uncanny," 339–47). The homely, even the house we inhabit, can be both canny (known and familiar) and uncanny (unknown and unfamiliar). This sets up the binary canny/uncanny. Seven of the fourteen pictures in *Harris Burdick* contain images of homes, homes decidedly under the spell of the uncanny. Many of the other pictures are of scenes in nature that contain some mysterious element, and these set up the binary natural/supernatural. What connects these—canny/uncanny and natural/supernatural—is the emergence of an "animistic conception of the universe" ("The Uncanny," 362). Van Allsburg's world is alive with suggestions of spirits and other forces or even beings ready to erupt into our normal reality at any time.

The uncanny takes us into the inner world of the unconscious, and the pictures in *Harris Burdick* likewise take us to the inner world of dreams and night visions. Four of the pictures clearly depict strange events at night or sleeping persons, and the other ten are redolent of neuroses and paranoia. Here such common objects as books or wallpaper can come alive, creating a sinister or wonderful sense of the uncanny. Something from the deep well of unconscious desire and anxiety appears in each picture. If, as Lacan says, the unconscious is structured like a language, then Van Allsburg's book speaks the language of the unconscious. Let us look at one example, the second picture in the book, the one accompanied by the words, "UNDER THE RUG: Two weeks passed and it happened again."

At the center of the picture stands a man holding a wooden chair above his head. The man wears a cardigan, pressed trousers, white shirt, slippers, bow tie, and spectacles. He is also bald. Behind him, to the left side of the picture, stands a bookcase filled with hardbacked books. In the extreme right foreground, a bump under the carpet rises, knocking over a small table with a lamp on it. Framed paintings on the wall appear to be conventional landscapes, perhaps reminiscent of the Impressionists. Whatever is under the rug creates terror in the man whose eyes and mouth express his distress. From the point of view of our structural reading, we need not know precisely what is under the rug, because its significance resides in the bump's presence rather than its form. Whatever it is, it does not belong there and it unsettles the man. The man, associated with books, a light, and spectacles, is rational man, here confronted with the irrational. Neurosis erupts in this picture. Rational/irrational, known/unknown, dream/reality, and authority/subservience: all these binaries form the mysteries of Harris Burdick. This picture sounds one theme in the fugue that is *The Mysteries of Harris Burdick*.

This search for the patterns of binary opposites in texts leads us back to my earlier question regarding the existence of patterns: are patterns *in* texts, or do readers find them because they impose them *upon* texts? Our answer to this question will reflect a philosophical and political bias. If we argue that structural patterns are *in* texts, just as they are *in* nature, then we argue for a closure imposed upon us as readers. We must accede to the demands of the text. If, on the other hand, we argue that the reader brings a model (set of patterns) to and places it on the agreeably yielding text, then we argue for a closure imposed by the reader on the text. Whichever position we take, the result is closure, the belief that a text is knowable in its construction; its meaning yields to structural analysis.

I mentioned earlier in my list of titles that indicates a predilection in children's books for binaries, Peter Spier's *Fast-Slow/High-Low* (1972), but I did not give the book's subtitle: "A Book of Opposites." Perhaps the subtitle goes without saying, but it underlines this whole discussion of binaries, and it points to what might appear to be a naturalness in approaching the world in this way. At least one commentator on early childhood education, Kieran Egan, argues strenuously that this pattern of binary opposites conforms neatly with young children's thinking. In *Primary Understanding*, Egan notes that the term "binary opposites" is somewhat misleading since "most of the binary discriminations" referred to in Lévi-Strauss's work "are strictly neither empirical nor logical opposites" (131). He, however, retains the term because "it draws attention to the way we generate oppositions in the construction of thought" (132). He then asserts that the "prominence of such binary opposites in young children's thinking is evident to the most casual observation" (132). What's more, binary thinking appears to be the common principle in all human thought, and its usefulness for the young child attempting to sort out his or her difference from others and from other things in the world is "easy to see" (133). For this reason, Egan advises teachers to cast their lessons in the form of stories, stories in which binary opposites are the structuring feature (232).

As a pedagogical device, stories that contain binary opposites (and Egan suggests teachers "create" stories that contain binaries) may indeed be useful for imparting information, the kind of information Peter Spier includes in *Fast-Slow/High-Low*. As an interpretive method in the reading of literature, however, the concept of binaries is problematic. For one thing, this method seeks closure. Once we have found or created the structural principle of a work of literature, its system of binary opposites, then we have cracked its code, unlocked its meaning by understanding how it works. We have the illusion of transparency; that is, we have taken authority over the book by closing it with the belief that it has nothing more to offer in the way of new information or significance.

A second problem with this search for binaries is less linguistic than it is~~ethi~~cal. Despite Egan's care in pointing out that the term "binary opposites" is misleading because the binary pairs are not strictly speaking "opposites," a sense of hierarchy remains. We find it difficult not to privilege one of the two opposites. Even in the title of Spier's book we have opposites that our culture differentiates evaluatively; wouldn't we all, despite such famous stories of our culture as "The Tortoise and the Hare" and *The Little Engine that Could*, rather be fast than slow and high than low? Egan's examples of human nature's tendency to form binaries is equally loaded: "big/little, love/hate, brave/cowardly, good/bad, fear/security, dominance/submission" (132). We are not far from self/other, we/them, I/it, and so on. The notion of binaries depends on a reflective figure, and we might recall from Lacan that the reflective moment is also the moment of separation. In a different discourse, reflection brings a fall; it marks the entrance into the world—again I turn to Lacanian language—of the father. This is the world in which "No" triumphs, in which "Thou shalt" implies a "Thou shalt not."

Much of what I have presented in this chapter might remind you of my discussion of Formalism and the New Criticism in chapter 2. And a structuralist approach to works of literature often does result in a close and an intrinsic reading of a text. One difference between Formalism and structuralism, however, is their respective attitudes toward literary texts. The Formalist sees the literary text as estranging; it remains "literary" precisely because of its difference from real life. Our experience of literature "defamiliarizes" us, alters our sense of reality. The structuralist, on the other hand, does not conceive of the text as any different from other aspects of real life. Everything we perceive and experience is text; that is, everything participates in structuring the world. Even nature functions on the basis of binary opposites: summer/winter, prey/predator, fish/fowl, land/water, plant/animal, and so on.

We are still, however, left with the nagging question: who creates the structures the reader discerns in texts? Is the search for binary opposites an intrinsic or an extrinsic approach to texts? And what motivates the reader to utilize a structuralist method in the first place? One thing is clear: structuralism as the dominant form of literary analysis did not last long, and one reason for its short time at the top is its implicit conception of the text as transparent, as graspable. Whether the critic investigates structures inherent in texts or brings structures to texts, he or she engages in a rational activity, one with some claim to scientific rigor.

The irony here is that the very basis of structuralism in Saussurian linguistic thought easily turns against structuralism, or better yet, easily transforms structuralism into poststructuralism. Lacan says that the unconscious is structured like a language, but his acceptance of the notion of the arbitrariness of language and of the slipperiness that exists between signified and signifier opens the door to notions of language and its meanings as opaque, unknowable, and untraceable. In other words, it did not take long before the seemingly rational discoveries of structuralism were turned upside down. What is knowable in a literary text (or in life) is only what is available to each reader's (or each person's) limited, if expanding, knowledge, and all knowledge is limited no matter how much it expands. Even if we could have all the knowledge in our heads that is embedded in a text, bringing the two sites of knowledge together would be a never-ending task. Michael Ende's well-known fantasy speaks of a "never-ending story," and the critic's task is equally never-ending since to trace through one story all its allusions, implied meanings, and contingent stories plus all the associations we bring to it is beyond even the most recondite and dexterous readers.

Thus, our reading of *Charlotte's Web*, for example, does not even begin to take account of the possibility that all motive in the book might have something to do with positions of power. Our binary "life/death," with Fern and Charlotte representing the life force as opposed to the death drive inherent in change, in the use of barnyard animals, and in male aggression (typified by Avery with his toy knife and rifle) might well find a counter in the notion of "power/subservience." Fern's desire to save the pig is a desire to have her own way, to have a pet, to have something to control and nurture. The same might be said of Charlotte, who takes a position at the center of things by extending, through writing, her web into the community. In other words, we might pursue a reading of the book that takes into account conflicting images of the mother as both benign and terrible. Or we might argue that, in *Where the Wild Things Are*, the fact that Max has a wolf suit reminds us of the myth of the lycanthrope. Under the power and influence of the moon, the child's wild energies will inevitably break out again. The fantasy of the Wild Things, rather than putting these destructive energies to rest in a psychologically therapeutic way, merely reminds us that these energies lie within, ready to reemerge at the appropriate time in their cycle. Humans, child or adult, *are* wild things, and the desire for control and power is inherent in every child (or at least every male child).

Such counterinterpretations reveal cracks in our texts' unity. Faced with such obviously fragmented and disunified texts as *The Mysteries of Harris Burdick* or, say, Ellen Raskin's *Figs and Phantoms* (1974), or David Macaulay's *Black and White* (1990), the critic both accepts disunity as a virtue and decides that fragmentariness is indeed the condition of texts. All texts, or at least all traditional texts, might aspire to the condition of unity, but given the nature of language as arbitrary and polysemous, given language's relation to the unconscious, this aspiration is doomed to failure. My point is to move us on to the myriad forms of critical activity that go under the name of poststructuralism. We have arrived at the fin de siècle intricacies of "postness," postmodernism, poststructuralism, postindustrialism, postliteracy, and so on. We have arrived at the end of things.

7

Criticism at Work and at Play: Poststructuralism

A postmodern artist or writer is in the position of a philosopher: the text he writes, the work he produces, are not in principle governed by preestablished rules, and they cannot be judged according to a determining judgement, by applying familiar categories to the text or to the work.

—Jean-Francois Lyotard

Our own recent criticism, from Macherey on, has been concerned to stress the heterogeneity and profound discontinuities of the work of art, no longer unified or organic, but now a virtual grab bag or lumber room of disjoined subsystems and random raw materials and impulses of all kinds.

—Fredric Jameson

I would want to argue for the powerful impact of feminist practices on postmodernism—though not for the conflation of the two.

—Linda Hutcheon

Criticism at Work and at Play

I am trying, precisely, to put myself at a point so that I do not know any longer where I am going.

—Jacques Derrida

I have a photograph of myself and my daughter Kyla taken by my second daughter Kate while the three of us were on a trip to South Dakota in 1991. In the photograph you can see Kyla standing at the edge of a precipice in the Badlands. She is taking a photograph. To the right of her and closer to the camera that takes the picture of her stands her father—me. I too am taking a picture, only I am taking a picture of Kyla taking a picture. Absent from the photograph is Kate; she is, however, present by virtue of the fact that she takes the picture of her sister and father. So: we have a photograph in which the two people being photographed are taking photographs. The result is that everyone looks *through* a camera; no one looks *at* a camera. All of us are taking pictures, and as a consequence no one is simply *in* a picture.

What is the subject of this picture? Is this a picture of Kate's sister and father? Is this a parody of the vacation photograph? Is this a study of figures in a landscape—here, a particularly spectacular landscape? Is this simply a joke? Why has Kate taken this picture; why am I taking Kyla's picture in this picture; and what exactly is it that Kyla wants to record? It would be possible to assemble a series of pictures something akin to Chinese boxes: Kyla's picture of the Badlands, my picture of Kyla taking a picture of the Badlands, and Kate's picture of me taking a picture of Kyla taking a picture of the Badlands. Each photograph would record the same geographical place, but from differing perspectives. Would the three photographs complete a picture of this particular place in South Dakota? The answer is no. The three photographs would merely complicate an already complicated situation.

Admittedly, my example is not momentous, but it does allow me to surface interpretive issues directly related to what is commonly referred to now as the postmodern condition. This family photograph displays the art of coincidence, even happenstance. It records a moment of a moment's recording of a moment's recording, and in its little series of regressions it manages to play out a deconstruction of vacation recording moments. Everyone has become a camera in this picture, and no one is a personality, a subject. Perhaps we have here what Jameson refers to as "the liberation, in contemporary society, from the older *anomie* of the centered subject" (*Postmodernism*, 15). Kate's playful capturing of her sister and parent reflects the estranging sense of the photograph even as it displaces her relatives as subjects.

As I mentioned at the end of the last chapter, *The Mysteries of Harris Burdick*, one of the books I have concentrated on in this study, is a good example of a postmodern book. It lacks the unity of a plot; we know nothing about the people who inhabit this book; no single subject is evident in the pages of this book; the setting appears historical, but this is constructed history, history imaginatively created, not factually presented (see Hutcheon, 62–92); we know nothing about the purported "author," Harris Burdick; and his "disappearance" serves to remind us of the supposed "death of the author" in postmodern art. Like Kate's photograph, *Harris Burdick* offers the reader/viewer an opportunity for performance, an opportunity to participate in the creation of the meaning of the images. Both photograph and book disrupt the reader/viewer's expectations, expectations based on genre (the vacation photograph and the "mystery" story), and they disclose their meaning. By "disclose," I mean they do not open up a single meaning, rather they refuse to close, they "unclose" their meaning, keeping it always mysterious and relative. Neither text totalizes in the sense Linda Hutcheon uses the term: "totalizing" points "to the process . . . by which writers of history, fiction, or even theory render their materials coherent, continuous, unified" (62).

"Postmodern" as literary descriptive term applies to many recent works for children, some of which I have already mentioned: Macaulay's *Black and White*, Ellen Raskin's work (for example, *The Westing Game*, 1978), the Ahlbergs' *The Jolly Postman or Other People's Letters* (1986), Briggs's *Fungus the Bogeyman* (1977), the work of Jon Scieszka and Lane Smith (for example, *The Stinky Cheese Man and Other Fairly Stupid Tales*, 1992), Aidan Chambers's *Breaktime* (1978), or Peter Hunt's *Backtrack* (1986). Such books are playful and fundamentally mysterious. When we enter William Steig's *The Zabajaba Jungle* (1977), for example, we find ourselves following

Leonard, who hacks his way through vines and creepers. How he got in this jungle and why he is journeying through it remain undisclosed. The text itself asks and answers this question: "Why is he there? He himself doesn't know. He just has to push on" (n.p.). After a series of adventures, with the help of an "ungainly bird," Flora, Leonard comes across his mother and father sitting inside "an enormous bottle." He rescues them and leads them from the jungle. How his parents got inside the jar is never explained. The whole experience remains a mystery.

A longer consideration of postmodern books for the young is possible, but I want to turn away from samples of the postmodern and toward strategies of reading that we more usefully label "poststructuralist." As the label clearly indicates, poststructuralist interpretive strategies are the varied forms of critical reading that displaced structuralism, including feminism (a form of criticism aimed at exposing the workings of patriarchal society), deconstruction (a disruption of "centered" or transparent thinking that focuses on the disunity inherent in all verbal constructs), the new historicism (a form of history writing that takes account of all aspects of culture and cultural production), postcolonialism (an examination of cultures and emergent cultures following in the wake of imperialism), reception theory (pays attention to the way texts are received), and varied forms of linguistic-centered reading (e.g., speech-act theory, which examines verbal performances, and stylistics, which examines an author's style by paying close attention to linguistic patterns). As my epigraphs should indicate, my focus in this chapter is on two forms of poststructural reading: deconstruction and feminism. These two interpretive approaches to texts might appear incompatible, but my hope is that their similar revisionary tendency will become apparent.

Let us begin with feminist criticism. A few years ago, Perry Nodelman noticed that many, if not most, of the well-known children's writers are (and were) women. Taking this as his starting point, he examined children's books to see whether anything in them suggested the presence of female influence; in other words, he argued that children's books exhibit values and approaches to the world that he perceived to be distinctly feminine. His prime example was Virginia

155

Hamilton's *M. C. Higgins the Great* (1974), a book that presents, despite M. C.'s giant phallic pole, values associated with passivity and gentleness rather than aggression and force. Nodelman concluded that all children's literature might well be termed "women's writing." Recently, Claudia Nelson posits something of a similar argument with regard to nineteenth-century British writing for the young in her book, *Boys Will Be Girls* (1991).

The nice thing about such approaches to children's books is their renewal of our sense of literature and its traditions. For example, feminist literary criticism has opened up the previously slim canon of children's books. Even ten or twelve years ago, the history of children's literature in the nineteenth century included Grimm, Andersen, Ruskin, Thackeray, Carroll, MacDonald, Kingsley, Kipling, Twain, Wilde, and not much else. That "not much else" included Alcott, F. H. Burnett, and perhaps Catherine Sinclair. Now, however, we have available in paperback such women writers as Frances Browne, Diana Mulock, Mary Molesworth, Jean Ingelow, Juliana Horatia Ewing, Evelyn Sharp, Susan Coolidge, Kate Douglas Wiggin, and, of course, E. Nesbit. Scholars such as Mitzi Myers and Alan Richardson take seriously the once forgotten writers of the early century such as Laetitia Barbauld, Maria Edgeworth, Mary Wollstonecraft (forgotten as a children's writer), and Sarah Trimmer.

We have much to be grateful for in this enlargening of the canon of children's literature. But just how does a feminist reading of a children's book proceed? Well, it proceeds along one of several possible paths: an examination of the presentation of the female in literature, a reading of archetypes from a feminine perspective, an examination of feminine values and community, a focus on patriarchal modes of subject construction and ways of resistance. In other words, no one feminist approach to literary texts exists. For children's literature, however, perhaps the most important use of feminist criticism is in its ability to articulate the gender bias of books for the young. For example, we might ask, is it happenstance that makes the main character of *Where the Wild Things Are* a male child? What difference would it make were Max, Maxine? As we have it, the book presents a young male child in all his phallo-aggressive glory. Max, the resourceful *bricoleur,* uses a hammer to construct a makeshift tent; he stands on books instead of reading them; he molests the dog; he journeys away from home; he confronts and controls wild creatures; he learns the language of "No." A feminist reading of this story might well ask whether Sendak perpetuates and condones Max's phallic-aggressiveness. Max behaves mischievously, and his mother does punish him. The punishment—she sends Max to bed without his supper—is, however, overturned when she brings to Max's room his supper, hot and smelling good. Does this gesture negate the punishment and reinforce Max's earlier behavior? Just what message do readers of this book receive concerning gender?

Questions like the ones in the previous paragraph appear, with unequivocal answers, in much recent criticism of the traditional fairy tale, especially those tales associated with the Brothers Grimm. I want now to offer a reading of the Grimms' tales that takes up a feminist approach, while at the same time it takes issue with more familiar feminist readings of the tales. My contention is that many of the Grimm Brothers' tales are not expressions of a patriarchy perpetuating itself; rather, they express a female's fear of derangement, her fear unto hysteria of death: that is, loss of life, self, independence, identity. This fear derives from the female's sense of her function in the world; she is, both in the fairy-tale world and in the preindustrial economy, chattel. Decorative, passive, and domestic—females must cook but not be heard. They must follow instructions, but father forbid that they think for themselves. Inevitably, when independent (and private) thought is methodically, even forcefully, denied to a person, loss of reality results. The tales that confront this derangement of the female psyche are perhaps less well known than "Snow White," "Sleeping Beauty," and other tales of domestic success because they disturb our sense of the fairy tale's happy ending and because they reveal that all is not well in the kitchen.

"The Hare's Bride" is a short and very powerful example of the female fear of diminishment through marriage, of marriage as death. A woman and her daughter live "in a pretty garden with cabbages," but a rabbit arrives and eats "all the cabbages" (*The Complete Grimm's Fairy Tales*, 332). The mother tells her daughter to "chase the hare away"; this she attempts to do three times. Each time she shoos the hare, he exhorts her to sit on his tail and go with him to his hutch. Third time unlucky; she seats herself on the hare's tail and goes to his hutch, where she receives orders from the hare to get into the kitchen and cook. Meanwhile, the hare leaves to gather the wedding guests. Wedding guests? It seems the hare's invitation was a proposal. However the young girl interpreted the invitation when she sat on the hare's tail, she is not pleased with the results of her trip to the hutch. She is lonely and sad. In desperation, she makes from straw an effigy of herself, dresses it in her clothes, and then goes home to mother. The rabbit returns, thumps what he thinks is his bride on the head, sees her tumble to the floor, and thinks he has killed her. He is very sad. The story ends on this lugubrious note.

The allegory here is not difficult, but it is doleful. Rabbits with marriage on their minds destroy beautiful gardens. Wives are drudges, headpieces filled with straw. The marriage, the narrator informs us, is to take place "under the rainbow" (333), but the only pot found there is a cooking pot, not a pot of gold. The straw girl left behind by the bride signifies the girl's fear of male domination and her fear of life-lessness. She has nowhere to go except back to her mother. She has no room to roam in this fairy-tale world.

Had the girl remained with the hare-husband, she may well have passed from loneliness into hysteria. Few tales depict married life, but those that do rarely offer much to flatter patriarchy's version of angel-ic femininity warming the hearth. According to "Frederick and Catherine," one of the most amusing yet terrifying of the tales, the madwoman does not reside in the attic, but in the kitchen. In this story, Catherine ruins her husband's supper and loses his gold coins because his instructions have not been clear enough. It is easy to dis-miss Catherine as simpleminded, but surely her foolishness is a func-tion of her position as wife, a person worthy of instruction but not of trust. Frederick tells his wife that his gold coins are "yellow counters for playing games" (*The Complete Grimm's Fairy Tales*, 284); he does not mention gold. Catherine, later in the story, suggests following the rogues who make off with this gold, and she accomplishes the regain-ing of the money. In this first part of the story, Catherine appears foolish, platitudinous, and impractical; she also appears compassionate, compliant, and instinctive.

The brief second part of the story, significantly omitted in some translations, begins with Frederick instructing his wife to "be industrious and work" (288). She goes into the field to cut corn, falls into a doze, and inadvertently cuts her clothes. The tearing of her clothes is both a rending of her sense of self, of reality, and (as in "The Hare's Bride") a cutting loose from her role as wife. Catherine returns home where she knocks on the door and asks Frederick if she—Catherine— is inside. He replies: "she must be in and asleep" (289). Hearing this, Catherine runs away until she takes up with some robbers who quickly decide she will not be of use to them, and who tell her to fetch some turnips from the parson's field. There she stoops to pick turnips. A man sees her; thinks she is a demon; runs for the parson, who claims to have a lame foot and who agrees to have the man carry him to the field. When they arrive, Catherine stands upright and frightens the parson and the man. The parson cries: "Ah, the devil" as he sprints away, his lame foot no longer a hindrance. Here the story ends, its silliness displaced by a dire sense of loss. Loss of reality and identity are Catherine's gifts from patriarchy. Once lost from, or cut from, her role as obedient wife, she becomes a demon to men. She is a terror, identified only as a demon.

Where can she go? Who is she? How can she define herself? In short, Catherine is trapped; she is either wife and adjunct to her husband, or she is a demon. The metaphor of entrapment is clearly articulated in a story similar to "Frederick and Catherine," "Clever Elsie." In this tale, everyone agrees that Elsie "has plenty of good sense" (*The Complete Grimm's Fairy Tales*, 171), and so Hans marries her. Once married, Elsie follows instructions and goes, like Catherine, to cut corn. She, too, falls asleep. Hans comes to look for her, sees her sleeping, and hangs "a fowler's net with little bells" around her (174). When she wakes, Elsie hears the jingle of bells, grows frightened, and wonders who she is. Like Catherine, she goes home to ask if she is who she thinks she is. Hans has locked the door and replies from within that Elsie is with him. In fright, Elsie cries, "Then it is not I" (174). I prefer the Lucy Crane translation, which has Elsie say, "Oh dear, then I am not I" (*Household Stories*). She runs beyond the village, and since then no one has seen her. Truly, the sweet bells are jangled.

These are stories of fear and disintegration. We might conclude that these stories are patriarchal warnings to women, showing them what they have to expect if they defy patriarchal norms. If, however, the stories in their oral form derive from female tellers such as the Grimms' informant, Dorothea Viehmann, then it is not difficult to imagine why they should reveal such anxiety (see Marina Warner, *From the Beast to the Blonde*, 21). The female sense of self is trapped in male expectations. The female in these stories has no power to speak for herself or to voice her concerns. She has no place beyond the kitchen or the garden; she is a domestic animal. For a woman to hit the road is to be crazy. Men may travel from their homes and villages to gain fortunes, kingdoms, or brides, but the woman's journey beyond home and village is to lunacy or death. When, in "The Robber Bridegroom," the young woman journeys into the woods, it is to seek her husband-to-be, who is not only a thief in the conventional sense, but who also robs females of life. To marry is to be robbed of life.

"I am not I." Elsie, Catherine, and the hare's bride are not who they are because they have no interiority, no voice. The woman without a voice is common in the Grimm Brothers' tales, as Ruth Bottigheimer has noticed (see *Grimms' Bad Girls and Bold Boys*). Bottigheimer argues that "*Grimms' Tales* demonstrates a . . . persistent pattern of silencing and silence" (72) enforced upon female characters. "The Twelve Brothers" and "The Six Swans" show women suffering, respectively, seven and six years of silence. Disobedience to the Virgin Mother brings speechlessness to the main character in "Our Lady's Child." In "The Iron Stove," silence is the female's reward for delivering the male from enchantment. Without a voice, these females are powerless, like the Goose Girl who suffers passively and quietly. Sleeping Beauty spends one hundred years in silence. Snow White, too, lies in deathly silence.

Stories, however, do exist that show the female acquiring a voice and beginning to narrate her own story. The most powerful of these is "The Robber Bridegroom." Here, the girl escapes from the robber's house with the aid of an old woman, a mother surrogate. On the wedding day a feast precedes the marriage ceremony, and all the guests tell stories. The bridegroom asks his bride whether she has a story, and she replies that she will relate a dream she has had. What she tells is a masterful recounting of her nightmare trip to the woods and to the robber's house, where she had learned of his cannibalistic habits and where she had witnessed the brutal murder of a young girl. The result of this telling is panic on the part of the robber, followed by his apprehension and execution. The female passes from silent fright in the woods to narrative and into power over her would-be ravisher. Once she has a story, she is free from menace.

In "The Brother and Sister," the sister marries a king only to fall victim to her stepmother's envious design to replace her with the stepmother's one-eyed daughter. Suffocated while in her bath, the young queen, who is also a mother, returns in silence at midnight to see her son and brother. Although she comes for many nights, she "never spoke a word" (*The Complete Grimm's Fairy Tales*, 72). It comes to pass, however, "the Queen began to speak in the night" (72). (Lucy Crane renders the passage this way: "the Queen seemed to find a voice.") Only now does the truth of the stepmother's wicked plot come out; the queen tells her story and regains her family.

The Complete Grimm's Fairy Tales offers many examples of tales that contain females without voice and those with voice, passive females and active ones. At one extreme we have the girl in "The Spindle, the Shuttle, and the Needle" whose only voice is the voice of her homely industry; her voice is truly the voice of the shuttle. She never utters a word in the story, even when she accepts the prince's proposal. Then there is the clever and vocal female in "The Peasant's Wise Daughter" who wins her way with wise words and intelligent stratagems. Her ability both to answer the king's riddle and to point out his error suggests her confident sense of self. She survives in her marriage because she knows her worth and because mutual affection exists between her and her husband, the king. In fairy-tale terms, this female is worthy to be a queen.

What I am trying to convey is the fairy tale's sensitivity to female fears. Although the tales form a corpus that we learn how to read by reading many of the individual tales, we should not assume a unity of theme or focus in this body of material. Generalizations are reductive and even unfair to the richness these stories manifest. They present females from many perspectives. Not all tales prepare females to be passive, self-sacrificing, obedient, and self-denying. Not all tales present marriage, in Karen Rowe's words, as "an *enchantment* which will shield her [either the female character or reader] against harsh realities outside the domestic realm and guarantee everlasting happiness" (220). But to point out the variousness of the tales is not only obvious, it is also somewhat unfair to feminist criticism of the fairy tale. Critics such as Marcia Lieberman, Karen Rowe, Rosemary Minard, Jennifer Waelti-Walters, Kay Stone, and Ruth Bottigheimer concentrate on what they point out are the best-known tales: "Snow White," "Sleeping Beauty," and "Cinderella" receive much scrutiny for their sexist treatment of the female. For example, according to Waelti-Walters, "Snow White" is "an overt commercial for marriage" (3); according to Lieberman, "Cinderella" reveals that the female who meekly accepts "rejection and bad treatment" will, if not inherit the earth, at least receive a "special compensatory destiny" (194); and according to Rowe, "Sleeping Beauty" contains a "double enchantment," the enchantment of the malevolent wise woman and that of the "guardian spirit" that ensures that a king's son will wake her (219–20). Each of these stories has a princess, a much misunderstood character in the tales. Waelti-Walters asserts that "Nobody in her right mind could possibly want to be a fairy tale princess" because princesses do nothing "except play dead across the path of some young man who has been led to believe that he rules the world" (1).

Invariably, feminist readings of the tales take them literally. The messages of the tales are meant, Jack Zipes has argued, "to indoctrinate children so that they will conform to dominant social standards which are not necessarily established in their behalf" (*Fairy Tales and the Art of Subversion*, 18). Fairy tales, like all children's literature, "were written with the purpose of socializing children to meet definitive normative expectations at home and in the public sphere" (9). Little girls who read or hear tales such as "Sleeping Beauty" will be content to wait passively and quietly for Prince Charming; they will, as Kay Stone puts it, believe that "nice and pretty girls have the problems of life worked out once they have attracted and held Prince Charming" (142). Power truly resides in the word, and in fairy-tale discourse the word serves patriarchy. To liberate the reader from a traditional male-dominated and capitalist society, the tales must undergo "reutilization" (*Fairy Tales and the Art of Subversion*, 46 and passim).

The so-called reutilized tales are often interesting. Snow White, it turns out in a version by Margaret Switzer, was an actor who married a house painter, had four children in seven years, died at sixty-two, and "was reincarnated as a brine shrimp" (*Existential Folktales*, 125). Sleeping Beauty was the daughter of a Polish immigrant who owned a vacuum cleaner repair shop in New York City, and her problem was ennui, not somnambulence. Such wit has its pleasures. Fiona French's art deco version of Snow White (*Snow White in New York*, 1986) is both clever and beautifully done, and Raymond Briggs's *Jim and the Beanstock* (1970) presents a gentle and subtle relationship between a boy and an elderly person who happens to be a giant (the book is something of a preparation for Briggs's recent, and more ambitious, *The Man*, 1992). These and other reutilized tales are often brilliant, but surely this is no reason to reject the traditional tales; we can read them as symbolic acts and not merely as blueprints for behavior. To say, for example, that in "Sleeping Beauty" the head of the family "is an authoritarian male, who makes most of the decisions" is misleading because, although early in the story the king does make all the decisions, these are wrong every time. The king knows there are thirteen wise women in his kingdom, yet he provides only twelve gold plates, not inviting the one wise woman who will take the slight meanly. After hearing the unpleasant gift of the uninvited wise woman, the king commands that all the spindles in his kingdom be burned. This merely takes livelihood from his people and ensures that his daughter will be ignorant of spindles and their use when she reaches her fifteenth year. When the princess is fifteen, her mother and father leave her alone in the castle, conveniently allowing the nasty wise woman's prophecy to come to pass. Sleeping Beauty pricks her finger and falls asleep, thereby falling into what Lieberman calls "the ultimate state of passivity, waiting for a brave prince to awaken and save her" (191). But it is worth asking: why does everyone (including the king and queen) and everything fall asleep at the same time as the princess? Why overlook details such as this in a rush to establish an ideological significance in the plot?

When we establish that the series of actions in a story results in marriage or presents us with a contemplative, beautiful princess, we can happily consign the story to the dustheap of a powerful but expendable socializing process. Indeed, in their eagerness for female autonomy some readings reject the tales precisely because they speak of community (see Rowe). Independence is much preferable to conformity. But do these tales really ask the reader to conform to anything? Do they suggest all girls should be princesses and get married to the handsomest, wealthiest, and most powerful man available? Can we reduce the stories to "sermons" (*Fairy Tales and the Art of Subversion*, 41) and leave it at that? We can, but what does it mean to be liberated in this way? It means to refuse the authority of the text, its author, and the social norms that inform both author and text. To read the fairy tales in the way many feminist critics do is to pierce them; to accept the authority of the text is to get the point. Whichever way we perceive the act of reading, to get the point or to pierce the text is to explain the text. Whether we have mastered it or submitted to it is an open question, although the two amount to much the same thing here.

If we read "Snow White" as the story of a girl's maturation and socialization, we either assimilate the values it places on a female's passive goodness and domestic worth or we perceive these same values as binding and suffocating. A girl's world is the safe world of home, quietness, and service, or the closed world of coffin, silence, and "submissive femininity" (Gilbert and Gubar, 205). But why accept this either/or? Is the story about maturation or liberation? The queen is, as Gilbert and Gubar note, imprisoned in her mirror, her obsession with her own beauty as defined by the patriarchal voice she hears. She seeks, however, freedom from the voice in the mirror, freedom from fear of displacement. She seeks stability, a permanent state of beauty and power. Thus she tries to eat Snow White. Her desire is to assimilate Snow White's beauty and energy. Failing this, she tries to kill her by offering her false femininity, fashion's beauty (the lace and the comb). Her final assault on Snow White's life is with an apple. What better way to end innocence and beauty than with the poison of an apple? The irony is that the apple must awaken Snow White to the facts of generation and labor, whereas the queen's idea is that it will permanently close Snow White's growth and activity. In short, the queen desires to assimilate Snow White into the diurnal round in which she will have no motion, no force.

We may interpret the tale as an exploration of nature. By this I mean that the world in which we live may enclose us, draw us into it and thereby control our actions, or we may create the world by releasing ourselves from its enclosing structures. In fairy-tale terms, we may become queens and kings. Snow White rises from her glass coffin, the beautifully transparent enclosure in which she may be admired, but in which she cannot move. She wakes, throws open the coffin lid, and sits up "and was once more alive" (*The Complete Grimm's Fairy Tales*, 257–58). Immediately the prince proposes marriage, and the tale informs us that "Snow-white was willing" (258) (Lucy Crane's translation has, "Snow White was kind"), and she accepts the prince. That she "was willing" suggests choice; she chooses to marry, rather than accepting the proposal without willing to. The marriage is, in effect, an act of liberation, a release from the confines of a dull round. This is a romantic reading in which marriage is a sign of apocalypse, that is, the replacing of an old world by a new and better world. The old world is one of desolation and barrenness; the new one of celebration and fertility. The pattern is perhaps most succinctly and clearly apparent in the Grimms' "Sleeping Beauty," but it recurs in many tales. In the new world, false desires are no more. The perversions of witchcraft are no more. Secret chambers are open. The desire to destroy others, even to self-destruction, is no more. Mirrors, towers, glass coffins, glass mountains, iron ovens, iron bands, and caged birds are no more.

The female fear with which I began this account of the Grimms' fairy tales is a dread that such a possibility for renovation, for a new world, does not exist. The dread is that the dull round of labor and loveless coupling will continue, that females will have no independence from father, mother, brother, husband, or house. The hope for independence resides in the many metaphors of release in the tales. Perhaps this is the reason that tales such as "Frederick and Catherine" are less well known than tales such as "Snow White." To assume that the popularity of "Snow White" depends on its powerful social message, to conjecture that it, and the other "best-known stories . . . have affected masses of children in our culture" (Lieberman, 186) is to focus on both the "realism" of the tales and on their content, their messages. I suggest that the tales may liberate the reader from existing social structures by transforming those social structures into metaphor. The fairy-tale world is a metaphor of a possible reality, not an imitation of reality or a blueprint for reality. I think of Dickens's ironic depiction of the factories in Coketown as fairy palaces; the point is that the human imagination can transform these ugly factories if only it has the will to do so. Like all metaphor, fairy tales direct our attention to the play of language and convention. Their words are things to which we need to cock an ear, and over which we need to cast an eye in a lively dance of the imagination.

Kay Stone, in her study "The Misuses of Enchantment: Controversies on the Significance of Fairy Tales," provides evidence from interviews she held with many females from the ages of seven to thirty-six that indicates that some women are indeed affected in their lives by reading fairy tales in childhood. Because this is so, she argues, it matters "how and why readers, male or female, interpret and reinterpret fairy tales that they feel were significant to them as children" (140). She suggests that through reinterpretation of the tales "women can eventually free themselves from the bonds of fairy tale magic" (143). And she concludes by asserting that "while fairy tales are not inherently sexist, many readers receive them as such" (144). To me, this is sensible. All depends on how we receive the tales. If we are open to the possibility of language as endlessly meaningful, if we accept story as a symbolic projection of the endlessly meaningful, if we listen to the tales' many voices, we will have an endless pleasure, the pleasure of reading and rereading, of interpreting and reinterpreting.

The mention of language as endlessly meaningful neatly brings me to the subject of deconstruction. Where deconstructive reading differs from feminist reading is in the direct or openly political commitment of the latter. Feminist readings have a basis in action; they set out to alter the way we perceive the world and hence the way we behave in the world. Deconstruction, on the other hand, pretends to eschew politics for play, the free play of a mind making its way through the tangle of an ungrounded, decentered world. The two approaches— feminism and deconstruction—come together in their search for moments within texts in which apparent meanings are reversed. In other words, both deconstruction and feminism are interested in moments of reversal, or at least the possibility of reversal in a textual sense and hence in a social and political sense too. For example, let us take another look at *Charlotte's Web*. I glanced at the book from a feminist perspective in chapter 5, when I suggested that E. B. White presents a staunchly patriarchal version of women's place in the power structure, anonymous and behind the scenes. We might, however, relook at this idea in the light of the book's ending.

Charlotte dies, of course. But Wilbur brings her egg sac safely back to the barn, where in the spring the new little spiders, Charlotte's children, are born. It might be worth asking how these tiny creatures came into being in the first place since not only does Charlotte not have a mate, but no male spiders are even mentioned in the book. Apparently Charlotte's conception of the egg sac is immaculate. As soon as the tiny spiders emerge from the sac, they begin to fill the air, floating under their clouds of fine spider silk. This is, one of the small spiders says, their "moment for setting forth" (179). This spider names all the floating spiders "aeronauts," a word signifying these small bal- loonists. Earlier in the text Charlotte had told Wilbur a story about one of her cousins who was an intrepid aeronaut. The word contains traces of "argonaut," a reminder of the Greek sailors who adventured for the Golden Fleece, and "aeranth," a word coined by George MacDonald in his mysterious story, "The Golden Key." "Argonaut" and "aeranth" bring into play ideas relating to heroic quests and sacri- fice and rebirth. These ideas now take on subtle displacements from earlier in the text. This text's hero is, ostensibly, Wilbur; he it is who has an auspicious beginning, and he it is who quests for life. But in reality it is Charlotte who is the argonaut; she is the heroic adventurer into the web of meaning that transforms the world. She, too, is the aeranth, the character prepared to offer her services for another, ask- ing for nothing in return; something like MacDonald's fish characters in "The Golden Key," Charlotte is reborn in her hundreds of children and grandchildren who then take on the role of heroic travelers.

But the crux of the ending is this: the only children of Charlotte's we know by gender are female. Three of Charlotte's daughters, each allowing Wilbur the power to name her, remain in the barn; they are Joy, Aranea, and Nellie. The reader has the distinct impression that *all* Charlotte's children are female. Never is a male spider mentioned. We might notice that when Charlotte tells Wilbur the story of an epic battle, it is about her female cousin who captures a fish in a "never-to-be-forgotten battle" (102). This female takes on the role of male hero; Charlotte's story effectively deconstructs male hero stories. And she also tells Wilbur about the other female cousin who was an aeronaut. We are reminded that the female spider hoodwinks all the humans (except perhaps Dr. Dorian) in the story. Does the end posit a sky full of tiny female Charlottes scattering to the four winds, about to make an assault on the deeply ingrained male hegemony?

To read the end this way is to take a step toward revising the way we might have read other parts of the book. For example, I have always found Fern's interest in Henry Fussy troublesome, although something about Henry's name kept telling me to look for that deconstructive moment. What troubles me about Fern and Henry is the way White appears to condone, through Dr. Dorian and Mrs. Arable, Fern's entry into typically gendered adolescence. Early in the book Fern plays with dolls and assumes a domestic role; then she takes up with Henry and loses interest in the world of the animals. Her mother is comforted because she can see Fern developing in a "normal" way. Once they reach puberty, so the book appears to say, girls will turn away from childish things such as farm animals and take up with their proper mates—boys.

We remember that ending, though, with the sky full of tiny female spiders all carrying something of Charlotte in them, and we look for something about Fern that suggests strength and difference. We have, of course, the opening chapter of the book, in which Fern audaciously quarrels with her father and bests him at the adult game of rational argument. From the outset, then, White depicts Fern as independent minded. She may wish to play mother to a little pig, but to do so she must stand against the conventions of farm life that say that a runt must die. When the family reaches the Fair near the end of the book, White makes it clear that the Fair represents change, and one change that is taking place is the growing independence of both Fern and Avery. Fern delights in riding the Ferris wheel with Henry, especially when it stops at the top and she can "see everything for miles and miles and miles" (173). The Ferris wheel serves as Fern's ferry carrying her from one stage of her life to another, except here the ferry does not cross anything. This is not a typical rite of passage; instead, the wheel goes round and round suggesting perhaps that Fern does not really leave anything behind. What's more, the Ferris wheel is part of the Fair, and we are reminded of carnival. Indeed, much of what happens at the Fair has a carnivalesque feel to it, and this reminds us of a counterdevelopment to the conventional. Perhaps, as Mr. Arable remarks, a Fair is as good a place as any to start growing up, for a fair disrupts normal expectations, overturns rules and norms of everyday life. If we pursue this reading, we are apt to find that *Charlotte's Web* is a feminist book after all.

But is it? Is anything really different at the Fair? The one thing that finally matters here is money. Both children ask for money, and Fern asks at least three times. Also, winning is important at the Fair, whether the winning takes place at the beano booth or in the pig judging ring. We might also recall Mrs. Arable's conversation with Dr. Dorian earlier in the book where it is clear that girls will settle on boys, but boys will continue to get into poison ivy, be stung by wasps and bees, bring frogs into the house, and break everything they can lay their hands on (111–12). My point is that *Charlotte's Web* is a deeply uncertain book. Take the book's most famous theme, for example. I refer to the book's handling of death. First, we have Charlotte's "hour of triumph": her death. Nothing could be more final. White presents her death clearly and without euphemism. Children are to know that death is a fact of life. And yet, children also learn that nothing "can harm [Wilbur] now" (163); he will live on and Zuckerman "will not harm [him], ever" (164). Reality is Charlotte's lot; fantasy is Wilbur's. Nothing is certain in life but death, and yet nothing is more certain than that Wilbur will continue to live. Is the message for children really clear? Put another way, we might conclude that this book is split between the impulse to fantasy and a counterimpulse to realism. It cannot, by very definition, bring these two impulses into coherence.

All of this playing with the text that is *Charlotte's Web* is what occupies a deconstructive reading. The point is not to find a total reading, but many partial ones. We used to think that one thing differentiating literature from life was the completeness of the work of literature, its coherence. Deconstruction highlights the literary text's similarity to life; they are similar in that the text is no more unified or coherent than life is. At one moment *Charlotte's Web* argues that humans are credulous, simpleminded creatures not only prepared to believe anything, but also quick to pass over the obvious for the less obvious. The next moment, we have characters such as Fern and Dr. Dorian, sensitive, imaginative, and wise. The wisdom of both Fern and Dr. Dorian comes under question when Fern turns to Henry Fussy and when Dorian accepts gender stereotyping. The foolishness of other humans is countered by their simple humanity, the pride that Lurvy and the Zuckermans take in their prize pig. The reader is faced in this novel with the stuff of life, its vagaries and changes. The only stability is instability, passings from one state of being to another. This is why Wilbur's apparent fixedness fails to convince. He, too, must surely pass away.

Another aspect of this book that deserves comment in the context of deconstruction and poststructuralism generally is its invitation to the reader to participate in working through the text. Admittedly, this aspect does not compare with more recent examples of postmodern texts such as the choose-your-own-adventure books or such interactive books as Van Allsburg's *The Mysteries of Harris Burdick* or Macaulay's *Black and White*, which solicit reader participation in the creation not only of meaning, but also of story. But in its own way, *Charlotte's Web* nudges the reader into activity. An obvious example appears in the following passage, in which Mr. Arable gives Fern and Avery money for the Fair: "Mr. Arable gave Fern two quarters and two dimes. He gave Avery five dimes and four nickels" (131). The careful reader will want to be certain how much each child receives. This learning device in children's books dates back at least as far as *Little Goody Two-Shoes* in the eighteenth century.

What such moments in the text—and we might include here the several other "teaching" moments when the text introduces the reader to new words or to aspects of zoology—deconstruct is the drive of what Kermode, in *The Genesis of Secrecy*, refers to as "sequence" in narrative. I offer one other such moment as the prime example of the deconstructive imperative. When Charlotte first meets Wilbur, she greets him with the word "Salutations" (35). Wilbur replies: "Salu-*what?*" To explain herself, Charlotte tells Wilbur: "Salutations are greetings. . . . When I say 'salutations,' it's just my fancy way of saying hello or good morning. Actually, it's a silly expression, and I am surprised that I used it at all" (35–36). Now how does this short passage deconstruct the text?

First, we have a moment of word play. "Salu-*what*" reflects Wilbur's linguistic innocence, yet his breaking of the word draws attention, at least on the printed page, to the closeness of "salu" to "sale." To find the sense in this transposition of the "u" into an "e" we need only recall (a recollection available only on rereading) that to save Wilbur's life, Charlotte must "sell" him to the Zuckermans. She is as much an ad-person as a writer: "We must advertise Wilbur's noble qualities, not his tastiness," she says (98). Moreover, the linguistic play does not stop here. Charlotte says her expression is silly, but she does not say why. We might assume the word is silly because it is long, latinate, and pretentious—hardly the appropriate word for a barnyard greeting. But we cannot be certain of this. In any case, if the expression is silly, then its silliness is sufficient reason for using the word. Children's books delight in language for its own sake, as such famous examples as Lewis Carroll's "Jabberwocky" or Spike Milligan's "On the Ning Nang Nong" indicate.

But this is not all word play. Surely, this moment, like others concerning words such as "tenuous," "sedentary," and "aeronaut," serves a pedagogic function. The reader finds lessons in vocabulary in this book. Words are put to work, so to speak. "Salutations" is hardly silly in its relevance to the plot. Wilbur suffers from angst, from a fear of loneliness and mortality. How fitting, then, that Charlotte should greet him with a word that carries in it both an acknowledgment of its recipient's status and a hope for his good health: "salutary," "salubrious," and "salute" all relate to "salutations." Charlotte's greeting indicates in advance that she will have Wilbur's well-being in her spinners and that she considers him someone special.

This in itself leads to another aspect of the passage: its traces. When Charlotte announces that she does not know why she uses the word "salutations," she admits that she is not fully in control of her own words. In this book, words control those who use them, and not vice versa. We find the words we use to construct the world already in existence before us. We find our existence *in* language; we do not create our language *out of* the world we exist in. The echo here is not to postmodern theories of language, but to that most famous of word controllers, Humpty Dumpty. Humpty, we remember, makes words mean just exactly what he wants them to mean. In Humpty's view of things, words have no power to manipulate their user; the world and the language used to describe it are fully in control. Alice's confusion derives from her failure to assume Humpty's self-confident position vis-à-vis language; on the contrary, she is forever finding words slip away from her. Alice is used and sometimes abused by language, although she never ceases to try and overcome the sad incompetency of language to say precisely, once and for all, what she means. The passage from *Charlotte's Web* ought to tell us that Charlotte, too, cannot control every nuance of her language.

Charlotte's fallibility in her control of language might suggest a larger fallibility. We took it for granted earlier that Charlotte's writing in the web accomplishes a miracle of wish fulfillment in that it determines Wilbur's future comfort, his freedom from harm. Maybe, just maybe, the fallibility we discern here in Charlotte's use of language will color her other language performance: her writing. We know that she does not think up the words she spins by herself; she takes them from old newspapers and such. We know that these words exert control over the humans who read them. But is anything certain in this uncertain world? The book contains many instances of failure, of changes both in nature and in people's minds, of decomposition, of ends and beginnings joined. Might not we conclude that in the final analysis Charlotte cannot save Wilbur from death any more than she can save herself from death? The words she spins—"some pig," "terrific," "radiant"—might finally prove as ineffectual and as arbitrary as her first greeting to Wilbur, "salutations."

I have written elsewhere something of a deconstructionist/feminist reading of one of the more popular of the Brothers Grimm's fairy tales: "The Fisherman and His Wife" ("Repetitions"). One of my points was that the story raises unanswerable questions regarding gender; the reader may find the story either a misogynist statement or a challenge to patriarchy's insistence on power, position, and exclusion as desirable modes of behavior. I also noticed that the folktale form offers a prime example of a textuality that is never complete. A story such as "The Fisherman and His Wife" is a deconstructionist's delight because of its link to a continuing condition of orality; it is forever being re-created by both artists and translators, and by critics. The meaning of the story can never be closed. I suggested that what we have in such a story is a dramatic example of what pertains to every text, and that each re-creation is a performance. Performance, as Henry Sayre argues, "has come to refer to a kind of work from which the authority of the text has been wrested. The concept of the 'original,' the self-contained and transcendent masterwork, containing certain discernable intentions, has been undermined, and a plurality of possible performative gestures has supplanted it" (93–94).

The situation is nicely presented in yet another recent retelling of "The Fisherman and His Wife," this one by Mitsumasa Anno in his book *Anno's Twice Told Tales: by The Brothers Grimm and Mr. Fox* (1993). The book contains two of the Brothers Grimm's stories, but I shall concentrate only on "The Fisherman and His Wife." Before I discuss the story, I must note the book's title because of its explicit problematizing of the concept of "author." Three "authors" appear on the cover and title page: Anno, the Brothers Grimm, and Mr. Fox. The inclusion of Mr. Fox, a character in the book, should remind us that he is no more "real" than the other two named authors. All three are constructs, and the story they tell belongs to all three. But this notion of "belonging" already complicates the issue: if the stories belong to these three authors, then is not the idea of belonging compromised? Can one thing belong to three people? And if one thing can belong to three people, then cannot it belong to more than three people? The implication is, I think, that the story belongs to anyone who reads it (or who illustrates it).

The title—in English anyway—serves up another author. The title *Twice Told Tales* invokes two volumes (1837 and 1845) of short stories by Nathaniel Hawthorne. Not only does this bring another author into consideration, but it also brings into focus the notion of literature and nationality: Anno is Japanese, the Grimms are German, Hawthorne is American, and Mr. Fox is from the imaginary country of the folk mind. The idea is, perhaps, that literature transcends national boundaries; we have here a postcolonial book. The invocation of Hawthorne, however, alerts us to something paradoxical. The title tells us that these are "Anno's" twice told tales, not Hawthorne's. Even more perplexing, these are Anno's tales by the Brothers Grimm and Mr. Fox. In other words, just as Anno complicates the idea of an author by multiplying the authors of these stories, he also lays claim to his own status as author.

The cover of the book is no less playful. Pictured on the cover are the farmer and his four sons from the story "The Four Clever Brothers," one of the stories Anno performs in this book. We might expect some evidence of the other story on the cover. None is evident. Instead, the reader notices four animals—rooster, cat, dog, and donkey—one on top of the other. The allusion here is to another famous Grimm story, "The Bremen Town Musicians." This story is not told in Anno's (or the Brothers Grimm's or Mr. Fox's) book. The detail serves merely to take the reader to the whole context of Grimms' fairy tales. Anno's cover, then, directs the reader to stories by Hawthorne and to stories by Grimm not included in Anno's book. At the very least, the reader might ask why these allusions occur and what connection might exist between the fairy tales and Hawthorne's allegorical romances such as "Young Goodman Brown" or "Rappacini's Daughter."

I have perhaps adequately shown how this book moves us outward from the stories themselves to other stories and other authors—and I might add, other illustrators, since the depiction of the four animals on the cover alludes to the familiar manner in which illustrators depict these animals (see, for example, the illustration by Joseph Scharl in *The Complete Grimm's Fairy Tales*, 145). But Anno ingeniously shows how one story contains many meanings when he presents three versions of "The Fisherman and His Wife" simultaneously. First, he gives us a translation of the original story by the Brothers Grimm; then, he illustrates this story with his own artwork; and finally, he creates a second written version of the story based on a reading of his illustrations. This second written version is Mr. Fox's. Mr. Fox cannot read the printed words of the translation from Grimm, and so he invents a story based on what he sees in Anno's illustrations to the Grimm story. Here we have a written story prompting translation into illustration, and in turn the illustrated version prompting translation into a simulation of oral discourse.

I have struck upon a word that constitutes a main idea of the postmodern: simulation. Every version of "The Fisherman and His Wife" is a simulacrum, a substitution of the real story for the real story itself (see Baudrillard's *Simulations*, 1983). The real story existed in some oral and hence unfixable form. Every attempt to fix it is a simulation of the oral event, until we have Anno's clear simulation of the oral event in the illiterate Mr. Fox's telling of the story to his son. Here the postmodern serves deconstruction's playful dip into disunity. The reader has three versions of one story. These versions are so different that in one we have a fish and in another we have a turtle. As far as I can see, Mr. Fox's turtle serves just as well as the Grimms' fish. The point is that one good simulation leads to another and to another.

The situation is splendidly rendered in a double-page spread near the end of William Steig's *Shrek!* (1990). The title character finds himself in a hall of mirrors surrounded by "hundreds of hideous creatures" (n.p.), each of which is, of course, himself. The trick is that some of these reflected figures are turned sideways, others are face forward, and still others have their backs turned. Each figure is a simulation of Shrek, and the whole illustration simulates moments in many famous films: Buster Keaton's *Balloonatics* (1923), Charlie Chaplin's *The Circus* (1928), Orson Welles's *The Lady from Shanghai* (1949), and Tonino Valerii's *My Name Is Nobody* (1974) to name a few. Shrek is happy because all of these simulations are him; given all these images, he can choose to be what he is. The choice to perform is now entrusted to the viewer, or in the case of *Anno's Twice Told Tales*, to the reader. To put this another way, postmodern approaches to literary interpretation entrust authority in the reader. We appear to have come full circle from our opening forays into New Criticism with its homage to the work of literature and its refusal to accede to an author's intentions. The homage here, however, is not to the work of literature, but rather to the reader, whose task it is to make his or her way through the web of associations and disparate meanings inherent in any literary text. The next logical step is to focus more clearly on this reader-oriented criticism.

8

Investigating the Reading Subject:
Response Criticism

The reader's creation of a poem out of a text must be an active, self-ordering, and self-corrective process.

—Louise Rosenblatt

A literary text must therefore be conceived in such a way that it will engage the reader's imagination in the task of working things out for himself, for reading is only a pleasure when it is active and creative.

—Wolfgang Iser

The wisest of the Ancients considered what is not too Explicit as the fittest for Instruction because it rouzes the faculties to act.

—William Blake

When knowledge is no longer conceived as objective, the purpose of pedagogical institutions from the nursery through the university is to synthesize knowledge rather than to pass it along: schools become the regular agency of subjective initiative.

—David Bleich

We have not, then, come full circle. The New Critical approach we began with depends upon a view of the world that still retains absolutes; the responsibility of the reader and critic is to the work of literature in all its numinous glory. The postmodern approaches to literature rest on shifting ground, on a relativism at least as regards what is knowable through the senses; the responsibility of the reader and critic is to his or her own intellectual and emotional clarity. The text is a means of activating the reader's mind, and the pleasure the reader takes in reading is to a great extent the pleasure of discovering just what it is the reader knows and feels. Reading offers self-knowledge, the only knowledge that is possible. Self-knowledge, however, entails the knowledge of all those forces—social and cultural—that constitute the self. The question of extrinsic and intrinsic approaches evaporates because the transaction that takes place between reader and text always involves both extrinsic and intrinsic matters. The reader reads what the text says, but she does so in the context of everything outside the text that she carries in her mind. Even to look at the title of a book activates thoughts and feelings extraneous to the text itself; some of these thoughts and feelings will prove fertile in the developing relationship between a text and the reader, and some will not.

The main thing is that a reader-based approach to literary study recognizes a fundamental subjectivity in our ways of reading. Each reader interprets texts in ways that are peculiar to this reader. The reader who has gone through years of literary training does not learn to read objectively in the sense that he reads what is really there or what a text really means; rather, he learns to read, as Stanley Fish has repeatedly reminded us, as part of a community of readers whose reading appears "objective" simply because so many readers share assumptions and values associated with reading. But can so many communities of readers all be objectively correct? Can all approaches be equally valid? For a critic such as E. D. Hirsch, the answer will be "no." But the response critic accepts a plurality of responses and encourages the formation of communities of readers sharing their subjective reactions to texts. The plurality I speak of here is not the plurality of a critic such as Wayne Booth, which accepts more than one position on a text; it accepts as valuable each reader's avowedly subjective response to any text. Insight comes from readers delving into their own reactions to the texts they read.

Just as other methods of reading and interpretation such as the psychological, the formal, or the structural take several directions, so too does a response-based method. The study of response might investigate the ways in which a text has been received over the years; this carries the label "reception theory" and is most often associated with the work of Hans Robert Jauss (see *Toward an Aesthetic of Reception*, 1982). Jauss argues that we ought to study the way a contemporary audience receives a literary work and to pay attention to the way the attitude toward a work alters over time. An interesting project for the reception theorist today might be a study of some of the books written for children by women in the later nineteenth century. For example, the work of such writers as Mary Molesworth, Mary DeMorgan, or L. T. Meade, popular in its day, disappeared not long after the writers died, only to resurface in the 1990s. What made the books popular, the reasons for their disappearance, and their current revival (at least in the academy) are areas of much interest in informing us how readers are formed and how trends change.

Another aspect of response criticism involves an analysis of the text as a repository of psychological meaning activated by and in the reader; this is an approach that sees the text as always in touch with and as expressing the reader's deepest psychological anxieties and desires, and one of its most impressive proponents is Norman Holland (see, for example, *Dynamics of Literary Response*, 1968). Literature for Holland is an exchange (cf. with Louise Rosenblatt, for whom the relation between text and reader is a "transaction"): "we absorb and become absorbed into the literary experience" (79). Literature, then, is like dream: a storehouse of fantasy. It is also therapeutic because it manages our fantasies. It keeps repression working by managing our deepest fears and desires. For example, a work such as *Where the Wild Things Are* (which Holland does not discuss) touches on each reader's Oedipal experience; the desire to assume power over the father and to find reassurance and love in the mother finds powerful expression here. Max's phallic aggressiveness finally works itself out and results in the mother's approval. Perhaps this goes some way to explaining why adults admire this book as much as children do. The experience of reading this book gives us the pleasure of having our fantasies taken care of. We are complicit with the literary text. Thus Holland describes the virtues of naive reading: "To paraphrase, except ye become as little children, ye shall not enter the kingdom of literature. And we do—we become infants prior even to an awareness of ourselves as such, quite unable to disbelieve [in the literary text]" (80).

This return to infancy takes place for the reader when the texts he or she reads contain "formal or defensive techniques" that match those of the reader. Once we know what kind of works readers like, we should "be able to correlate different readers' preferences among a collection of more or less equally good short stories with the different readers' characteristic patterns of fantasy and defense, discovered by interview or projective test" (317). This implies a sensible notion of evaluation: that which matches and manages our fantasies we think "good." Also lurking here is a possible argument for bibliotherapy, but Holland swings back to the text: "One could, for example, ask readers to explain their preferences for one or two versions of the same line of poetry to get at the way the sound of the line manages the fantasy" (317). Holland is not arguing that any interpretation of a literary work will be acceptable. On the contrary, he urges teachers to understand their students' characteristic patterns of fantasy and defense, and then to get their students "to accept more complex or exotic works within [their] established pattern of preferences" (332). Implicitly Holland speaks of college students, but what he says might apply to children as well.

Holland's approach to bibliotherapy is evident in his understanding that a text might be a pretext for a therapeutic delving into the reader's feelings; this is an approach that subordinates the text to the emotional life of the reader, as in the work of David Bleich (see *Subjective Criticism*, 1978). Bleich is ready to allow the reader his or her interpretation, no matter how subjective (i.e., removed from the primary level of a text) this may be. What is important to Bleich is "whether the child will like the book or not" (154). We all know the student who feels interpretation is an inviolable part of the interpreter. Whatever one feels, that is right. Bleich would add, right for him or her who feels, and after feeling must come a discovery of the motivation for feeling. Rather than direct his attention to traditional areas of investigation—the author in the book, style and tone, thematic integrity, form, and so on—Bleich concentrates on the reader and his or her feelings. He makes this switch in focus for two reasons: since all knowledge is subjective, we will be better off understanding ourselves rather than accepting someone else's view of the world, and such a freeing of readers from the authority of critics opens literature to a wide public. To accept subjectivity in literary response is a democratic gesture. For Bleich, knowledge is made by people; it is not found.

The danger in this approach is, of course, solipsism. But Bleich argues that to "understand the existence of an object as subjective is not the same as to understand it as imaginary" (295). Instead, subjective perception such as "The earth is flat" must be accompanied by "an intervening intersubjective negotiation—such as 'Does it seem flat to you?'" (295). Subjectivity is necessarily relational. Any relationship, Bleich says, must be subjective and consequently involves responsibility. Moreover, relationship and responsibility exist by virtue of language; the more articulate we become, the better able we will be to fulfill our responsibility by sharing subjective knowledge. Ultimately, however, this responsibility is to ourselves. "Rather than raising human beings out of nature, language is part of the human means of adaptation in nature. When this part is cancelled by violence or other destructive and nonsymbolic behavior, we lose our only natural means of survival" (28–29). We must strengthen our own "language systems," and we can do this by studying our response to other language systems.

Much of this is attractive, and especially so to teachers of both children and children's literature. After all, most agree that children should learn about themselves and their relation to the world, and that they should mature their understanding and use of language; it is comforting to have an authoritative statement as to literature's place in this developmental process. The irony is that Bleich's authoritative statement sets out to destroy all authority outside the self. A truly subjective response to texts ought, in Bleich's view, to undergo two scrutinies: one is continuous analysis of our previous responses in order that we acquire knowledge of ourselves, and the second, which is in fact a function of the first, is negotiation of response within a group in order that that knowledge have a definition or at least a sanction. The problem is that if knowledge is purely subjective, then the subject contains it; if, however, a community of two or more share the knowledge (accept it or sanction it), then it inevitably will take on the status of objectivity or at least authority. Another way of looking at this is to point out that if all knowledge is subjective, then Bleich's parade of learning and his authoritative statements rest on subjective ground, thus making them no more correct than any other set of authoritative statements or displays of learning.

Even without these problems, the turning away from texts to readers in Bleich's manner strikes me as dubious. When he argues that interpretations of *Hamlet* "which *say* Hamlet is a woman" contain "truth value" when "seriously" presented, I can agree if the italicized word "say" means that Hamlet is himself a metaphor for female traits; but I suspect such an understanding of Bleich is hasty, since he quickly reminds us that "the text cannot . . . be understood as constraining, except in a trivial sense" (112). Surely our responsibility must take in the self as experienced and perhaps changed by another (even a text). Hermeneutics circles neither within the self nor within the text; it circles between the two.

Recently, in the work of Michael Steig (see *Stories of Reading*, 1989), we have seen an attempt to overcome the extreme subjectivism of Bleich; Steig's desire is to bring objective and subjective approaches together. Like Bleich, he sees the value of intersubjectivity. He takes seriously "personal modes of understanding literary texts based on individual experience." The sharing of such personal modes of understanding "can enrich others' understanding and can move from the state of subjectivity for the individual to that of a gained, rather than prior, intersubjectivity for the social group" (xiii). He also sees the value of "objective" knowledge, knowledge of an author's life and time, to a subjective response to literature. Readers, he argues, inevitably "construct" an author, and any biographical or historical information available helps the reader build this construct.

Steig's intention in *Stories of Reading* is to account for his responses to several texts that are literary in both a primary and a secondary sense. He offers his response to the writing of critics (including himself) and students, as well as to familiar and less familiar works of literature. The intention behind this acceptance of student writing (something Bleich, and response literature generally, shows) as equal to professional academic writing and of children's books as equal to canonized works of literature is a healthy subversion of hierarchies. Steig states that he hopes to "offend against both the traditional canon of English literature and the concept of 'great' literature." Many concerned with the study of children's literature will perk up when he adds: "the distinction between children's and adults' books [is] merely a matter of intellectual snobbery" (xvii).

In other words, the distinctions we make concerning literature and its value are deeply and unavoidably personal. Our account of what we read must take the form of what Steig refers to as "stories of reading." Each of us who reads has such a story to pass on. Let me recount a story of reading passed on to me from one of my students, whom I shall refer to as Helen. A few years ago, Helen handed me a remarkable essay on C. S. Lewis's *The Lion, the Witch and the Wardrobe*. I must say right away that I knew something of this student's personal background; she was and had been a victim of child abuse, and she began around the time I write about to edit a newsletter for other incest victims. Still I was not prepared for the long and intensely felt essay she handed in. Over some eighteen single-spaced typed pages, this student expressed her revulsion toward Lewis's fantasy. She was candid and courageous in setting forth her feeling that this book presented in a thinly veiled form a violent attack on the child—both the child in the book and the child who reads it. For Helen, Lewis clearly both disliked children and at the same time felt sexual pleasure in their company. She examined, among other things, Lucy's entrance into Narnia and noted the genital implications, both male and female, of the wardrobe and its contents; her incipient psychoanalytic reading was sharp enough to notice the "two mothballs" that dropped from the wardrobe when Lucy opened it. She also noted Mr. Tumnus's hairy legs, his ithyphallic associations, the reference to his bedroom, and the hints available in the books on his shelf (e.g., *The Life and Letters of Silenus* or *Nymphs and Their Ways*). She was convinced that Lewis was a threat to young readers simply because he presented himself as a guide, and his guidance could only lead to abuse. It is true that my own response to the Narnia books is cool, and it is also true that Helen and others in her class knew this. But we had not discussed Lewis formally at the time Helen handed in her essay. I can only guess that either she felt confident that I would not censure her reading or she didn't care whether I did or not. I suspect the latter is closer to the case because she was at this time in her life daring to confront aspects of her own experience that she had repressed for years.

Now Steig's point and that of many reader response critics is that we can learn valid things about literature from the subjective readings of literary works. Unlike Bleich, who, along with Holland, Louise Rosenblatt, and Wolfgang Iser, informs much of his work, Steig continues to believe in an "objective"—by which he means, in part, "shareable"—level of interpretation. He skirts the edges of solipsism without taking the plunge. Personal readings when pursued strongly lead to insights that others will share: "one of the things which has happened in teaching through reader response is that students will, in considering and objectifying their own responses, present ways of looking at a work that depend upon their individual experiences, and which yet at the same time seem to have the power to open up a whole new vein of possibility in reading for others" (137). I cannot say that Helen's way of looking at *The Lion, the Witch and the Wardrobe* opened up a whole new vein of reading for the other students in the class, because the specific issues related to adult sexual desire for children did not become part of class discussion. I can, however, say that my own sense of unease with the book was sharpened by Helen's story of reading.

And then, a year after Helen had written her essay, I came across David Holbrook's book, *The Skeleton in the Wardrobe: C. S. Lewis's Fantasies: A Phenomenological Study* (1991). I have been familiar with Holbrook's troubling and troubled reading of Lewis for years; in 1973 he published an article on the Narnia series in *Children's Literature in Education* (anthologized in *Writers, Critics, and Children*, 1976) in which he analyzed the "hate, fear and sadism" in these books (124).

But now, in 1991, we have his fuller account of Lewis's "problems." Here is Holbrook on Mr. Tumnus:

> The faun's name is Tumnus, the origins of which name now seem clear: *Tumesco*, to swell; *Tumidas*, big, protuberant; *Tumor*, a bump or bunch; also perhaps *tum* "at that time": and perhaps just the infant's "tummy." Perhaps Tumnus is the father's penis inside the mother which became a cancer? Certainly, the faun has a powerful sexual quality, which is presented as if seen by a child; and this sexuality brings at once fear of mutilation and death. (68)

Holbrook's story of reading relies on a school of psychoanalytic thought called "object-relations"; the object in question is the mother. The wardrobe, in Holbrook's scheme, is the mother's body, as is the landscape of Narnia generally; the characters are facets of Lewis's psychic makeup. By speaking to the authority of Melanie Klein, D. W. Winnicott, and of course Sigmund Freud, Holbrook gives his reading of Lewis an "objective" appearance. He also draws on details of Lewis's biography, although he tries to "restrain" himself (80) in this because he wants his analysis of the fantasies to stand on its own. We might ask ourselves whether Holbrook's very enthusiasm for his particular perspective on Lewis reflects his own psychic tendencies. My point, however, is simply that what my student found in Lewis by allowing his book to raise associations in her life does not differ radically from what Holbrook finds in the same book through his "phenomenological" method. What this proves from Steig's perspective I am not sure, but if we give any credence at all to Holbrook's reading of the Narnia books, then we must also give credence to Helen's reading. Essentially, what she felt in Lewis was a psychic disorder that threatened her, and what Holbrook wants his reader to understand is a similar psychic disorder that undetected might create psychic confusion in Lewis's reader.

The kind of interpretation Helen offered, Steig characterizes by the term "literary understanding." This refers "to an inward relationship to a text, a relationship that may be communicated to others and yet is also open to change through the communication of others' understandings." He contrasts this with "knowledge," which is "a conclusive interpretation" (xiii). Steig's understanding of the interpretive process embraces both the personal associations of all readers and the extrinsic information provided by an approach such as Holbrook's. What Steig endeavors to accomplish is a reconciliation of this apparent thesis and antithesis. No matter how personal our response to a literary text, we also carry with us extrinsic data concerning the text we read: information about the author, the history of the text or its place in history, aspects of genre. The result is that our understanding will take the form of a palimpsest.

A response-motivated reading of a literary text might take one or more of several directions: an expression of personal feelings (our likes and dislikes regarding a text), a recounting of the nonliterary association a text brings to mind (how a character reminds us of a friend or relative, or how an incident reminds us of something in our own lives), and a listing of literary associations roused by a text (how one text reminds us of another text). Whichever direction response analysis takes, it focuses on the reader as the final arbiter of a text's meaning. Everyone knows that readers differ in their response to texts, and response criticism makes this situation not an impetus for the validation of one reader's reading over another's, rather an occasion for genuine sharing of knowledge. Meaning is a function of what we know, and we all know different things; in other words, at a basic level all meaning is subjective and the reader's task is to investigate his or her own subjective responses as fully as possible and to share these with other readers in an exercise that Robert Probst terms "cooperative reading" (34). The enterprise is to create a community of readers. Why do we respond the way we respond? Why do others respond differently? Even when we are bored by a text, we have a responsibility to understand what it is about the text that bores us.

Saying that reading is an intensely subjective activity is, however, slightly disingenuous. As Stanley Fish has argued with characteristic eloquence, no one reads in a vacuum. The very creation of a community of readers creates a context within which reading occurs. Most often this context is an institutional one: a school classroom, for example. To illustrate this powerful institutional force on readers, I offer another student response to *The Lion, the Witch and the Wardrobe*. Because this student's response is shorter than Helen's, I share it in its entirety. The student's name is Nita Ross, and she titles her paper "A Surprise in Narnia."

When I saw the reading list for this course, I was really glad to see *The Lion, the Witch and the Wardrobe* on it. A few years ago we read all seven Narnia books as a family. That means we all sat around and listened as one person read out loud. It was a lot of fun, and we all enjoyed the stories immensely. My two girls played Narnia for months to come. So, I was looking forward to revisiting an old friend, one who had brought me much happiness and hours of family togetherness and enjoyment.

Over the last few months Dr. McGillis has dropped a few hints about his dislike for the Narnia books. He has also mentioned their overt Christian viewpoint. In my mind, I felt he was definitely wrong on this one. I was looking forward to showing him how much meaning this book had for me. Then I read the book, and I was surprised.

I am rather embarrassed to say that in my first reading of the book I didn't really pick up on any of the biblical motifs. By the time we got to the seventh book I was sort of certain that Aslan represented God, but that was it. After reading the book again, I wonder how I could have been so blind. It begins with the prophecies of the coming of the Messiah. Then he arrives bringing new life and warmth and love. Then he dies for the sins of others and is resurrected! To top it off we have lots of miracles thrown in: he brings stone statues to life and he gives Lucy a cordial that revives the dead. Last but not least, the male who assumes pride of place when the children become kings and queens is Peter.

I finished the book a week and a half ago and ever since I've been trying to understand my emotional response to it. What I've been feeling is outrage, anger and disappointment. I've come to the conclusion that my response is complicated. First, I think what I wanted was to hang on to my experience of the book when we read it as a family. I didn't want anything or anyone to change how I felt about the book. So I think part of my initial response was anger at McGillis for hinting at parts of the book that I hadn't understood before. I reread the book with these hints in mind and they have influenced my interpretation. It felt as if my memory shattered along with my feelings for the book. Then as I thought about it I realised that I was a different person then and *the meaning I gave the story* was different and valid for who I was then. *The meaning I give it* now is valid for who I am now.

These thoughts made me realise that part of my outrage was directed at myself. I feel sort of foolish for missing the religious overtones of the book the first time I read it. Again, I need to be aware that I am changing and accept that my interpretations change too. So, then I asked myself what is it that has changed so much in me that I bring a completely different meaning to this book. I think that part of the answer lies in the fact that I have become more aware of the patriarchal aspects of Christianity over the past year or so. These aspects of Christianity are clearly evident in this book. First we have a male God, then the evil being is a woman—the only adult woman in the book I might add (so what does this say about Christianity's view of women I ask?), and lastly the head King at the end is a male. I know all this makes me sound like a radical feminist but I don't think I am. It's just that I am in a questioning period of my life and my spirituality is something that I am questioning. I feel quite unsure about what I really do believe and about which direction I need to head in.

That brings me to the last thing that I can see that angers me about this book. Lewis gives us a glimpse of his beliefs. It appears that he feels certain in his faith. Another book of his that I have tried to read, *The Screwtape Letters*, also shows him certain in his faith. This challenges me because I am anything but certain about my spiritual life, and I feel threatened by people who are. They make me ask myself questions that I can't answer and that makes me uncomfortable.

So my revisit to Narnia was quite a surprise for me. I found things I wasn't expecting to find. They are things that challenge me to ask myself questions I don't know how to answer. However, these questions have given me an opportunity to better understand myself, and therefore I am glad I reread *The Lion, the Witch and the Wardrobe*.

I have italicized some words near the end of the fourth paragraph of Nita's essay to draw attention to her sense of empowerment. She feels that any meaning the book holds is inscribed by her. And this is to a large extent true. What she does not appear to grasp is just how formative the institutional context of her reading is. She suggests that her changing response to *The Lion, the Witch and the Wardrobe* is a result of changes in her, and this too is true. What strikes me as crucial, however, is the role of the classroom in participating in any changes taking place in Nita. In other words, she notes but does not consider the influence of the "hints" she encountered in her exposure to my classes. Her reading of the book followed these hints, and consequently it is no surprise to me that she found the Christian aspect of Lewis's book so clear. What is even more striking is her embarrassment. Why her earlier reading of the book should be invalidated or set aside remains troublesome to me. I have no doubt that Lewis's book is read and enjoyed as a fantasy adventure by countless readers. Such a reading might be prior to institutional influence, whether that institution be the Church or the school. Certainly, Helen's reading of the same book does not rest on these institutional grounds.

In any case, a response criticism often focuses directly on the reader herself or himself, and Nita provides an example of this. Her essay is less a "reading" of *The Lion, the Witch and the Wardrobe* than it is an exercise in self-understanding. The book provides the occasion for self-examination. It hardly matters that Nita does not answer the questions she asks of herself; what matters is that she has begun to ask such questions. And for others in the class who must engage with *The Lion, the Witch and the Wardrobe*, Nita's essay offers ideas to share and develop. For example, Nita's parenthetical question regarding Christianity's (and Lewis's) view of women is well worth investigating. Also well worth discussing is what Nita perceives to be Lewis's certainty of faith. How is this evident? This will necessitate an examination not only of ideas, but also of the form of Lewis's book. Who tells the story? Is the narrator, in fact, Lewis himself? How do we reconcile the book's paganism (its references to nymphs, Father Christmas, fauns, and so on) with its Christianity? If we derive nothing else from reading Nita's essay, we should derive the encouragement to think, to be active and engaged in the act of reading.

As the last of my epigraphs to this chapter indicates, response criticism has made its way into the schools. Books such as Robert Probst's *Response and Analysis* (1988) and John Willinsky's *The New Literacy* (1990) outline and argue for a response-based pedagogy. Unlike many of the other methods sketched in this book, response-based criticism should be nonthreatening to a student simply because it does not present the student with a body of knowledge she or he must learn before becoming a competent reader. The idea is that learning to read is akin to learning to speak; we acquire the grammar of literary texts simply by being immersed in them. Arthur Appleby has shown, in *The Child's Concept of Story* (1978), that children learn the conventions of story as they become more familiar with stories; they do not have to study story concepts in some neo-Aristotelian fashion. In other words, children know more than we often assume they know, and the trick is to rouse them to activity in order to give them the confidence to imagine that which they already know.

I have for several years asked my students to write response papers for class, and I too have participated in this exercise. I want to share my feelings about the exercise. First, I note that many students do not trust me when I tell them they are to investigate their own feelings, associations, and thoughts. They have been trained to suspect an agenda on the part of their instructor; they have been trained to believe, or at least to pretend to believe, that knowledge is objective and that the object of knowledge is neither the text in front of them nor their own capacity for thought, but instead the contents of their instructor's brain. Consequently, many of their reader response papers briefly examine the "meaning" of a text, its historical context, or some other acceptably academic topic. The result is perfunctory. Once in a while, however, I have seen spectacular results. If you can convince writers to write freely about what they think and feel, then you can break through the institutionalized voice that permeates so many student papers.

I ought also to make a confession: I learned quite early on in my use of the response paper that I could not write the kind of personal, intimate responses that we see and read about in the books by Bleich and Steig that I mentioned earlier. At first this bothered me. Here I was asking my students to write intimately concerning their feelings about what they read, and I was not responding in kind. But the more I thought about this, the more I realized that I was responding intimately in my own way. Frankly, I do not wish to (or have a need to) disemburden myself emotionally when I write about literature. I do find, however, that I take great delight in writing "off the top of my head" about the texts I teach. That this writing takes on something of an academic tone seems to me only natural since I am, after all, an academic. On the other hand, this writing does not sound exactly the same as the writing I have done for publication in scholarly journals.

Never having taught either *The Mysteries of Harris Burdick* or *Where the Wild Things Are*, I do not have samples of response papers on these books. But I can offer as an example of response writing a short paper I wrote on *Charlotte's Web*. I wrote this paper on April 2, 1992, and it was the sixth response paper I had written for this particular class.

The Death of a Pig

It's an hour and a quarter before class and I have yet to write my response paper on *Charlotte's Web*. As my rather laconic title suggests, I have little or nothing rattling around in my brain concerning this book. I choose the title—"Death of a Pig"—because it comes to my mind from one of White's essays, an essay in which his preoccupation with mortality is evident. This essay points out that farm pigs have one purpose in life: to adorn the dinner table, the breakfast table, or the ham sandwich for lunch. In other words, pig means *jambon*. And it is on this point that my response to this book turns.

I recall my first reading of this novel when I was about 29 years old. Sure, I found the prose exemplary: polished, clear, and lyrical. In many ways the book seemed (and seems) to me a prose poem. But that first reading left me troubled. I knew that White was trying to present death to children in an understandable and realistic fashion. And Charlotte's death is, indeed, effective in its immediacy and bluntness. For me, the scene of Charlotte's death, alone and surrounded by the left over garbage from the departed Midway tents and vehicles, is reminiscent of a scene in Charlie Chaplin's *The Circus* (1928) in which Charlie is left alone, encircled by the camera lens's iris amid a space empty and forlorn of the circus and its people. Both scenes involve a departing carnival, and both gain their effect through simplicity. The profound isolation of the individual who desires is apparent to me in both works.

This moment of isolation comes at the end of the Chaplin film, but not so in *Charlotte's Web*. This book, like other books about death for children (e.g. Katherine Paterson's *Bridge to Terabithia* (1978) or Marit Kaldhol's *Goodbye Rune* (1987)), shows continuity. To counteract the finality of death, its reminder of discontinuity, of loss and separation, White goes on to describe the birth of Charlotte's children. They carry her memory to succeeding generations, and they remind those who knew Charlotte of her grace and friendship. They are, in effect, Charlotte's last and greatest gift to Wilbur and to the life of the barn.

But what about Wilbur? Wilbur is the subject of death too. The threat of Wilbur's death is apparent in the book's first line. The main conflict in the book derives from Wilbur's anxiety over death and his desire to defeat death. Strangely, this conflict appears to be resolved successfully. As everyone knows, Charlotte fools the gullible humans in the book and saves Wilbur's bacon, so to speak. Whereas the Zuckermans of this world think of Wilbur as *jambon*, Charlotte depicts him as *cochon*. The penultimate paragraph of the book begins with this sentence: "Mr. Zuckerman took fine care of Wilbur all the rest of his days, and the pig was often visited by friends and admirers, for nobody ever forgot the year of his triumph and the miracle of the web." "All the rest of his days," might suggest that Wilbur's days are numbered, but the phrase is vague enough to leave Wilbur's death in abeyance. The rest of the sentence which points out that no one ever forgot his triumph indicates that the reason for Wilbur's stay of execution as *jambon* remains intact. In other words, the book here ends on a fantasy, the fantasy (perhaps one we would all wish were true) that pigs need not serve any other purpose than being the object of admiration. The web said Wilbur was "Some Pig" and by golly he is some pig. "Some" in the sense of "like no other," "unique," and "special." But what makes him special?

Nothing more than the words woven into Charlotte's web. Wilbur becomes some pig only after those words are woven, not before. The fact comes only after the words.

But I am running on another track here. Let me get back to Wilbur and death. I guess what irritated me on my first reading of *Charlotte's Web* was what I perceived as a fib in the book. White was trying to tell children that this funny and rather likeable pig would never die, or at least never die in the normal way for a farm pig to die: in the slaughterhouse. This spoiled the book for me. I must say, however, that my previous concern has waned. I no longer see the book as trying to pull the wool over young eyes. These are animals in this book, but this distancing from the human does not disguise the fact that Charlotte serves as a mother to Wilbur, and her death is deeply felt by him. For me, the book's most profoundly moving sentence tells us that "Wilbur never forgot Charlotte." This book is about memory and its power to hold onto the ones we love.

This is not, I regret to say, one of my better efforts at response. But it does illustrate the associative style acceptable in this type of paper. Anything goes. The reader who knows Ashraf Rushdy's "The Miracle of the Web: Community, Desire, and Narrativity in *Charlotte's Web*," an article that had recently appeared in *The Lion and the Unicorn*, and that I had read in an early draft, will hear echoes of it in my response. These echoes are, of course, simplified, but nevertheless clear. My attempt, unsuccessful as I judge it to be, was to say something useful and to be emotionally honest too. Since response can be a way of chronicling the changes in one's interests as a reader, I tried to reconstruct my first reading of *Charlotte's Web*. My comments on my feeling that the book fibbed or cheated are honest, but as the rest of this book illustrates (I hope), my interest in *Charlotte's Web* has gone far beyond the question of its fairness in presenting to children the finality and inevitability of death.

What I have learned from writing response papers for class is that we cannot escape our training. My papers nearly always swerve away from open expression and investigation of feeling toward an ostensibly disinterested academic tone. On the other hand, writing these papers does prompt the writer to find his or her own voice. I have seen this happen with some frequency in teaching: a student who cannot write a more than average term paper can and does write with verve and personality in her response papers. I want now to present a response paper written by one of my students, Bev McKay. I do this to illustrate the personal attitude to writing about literature Bev brings to her work; her writing contains a very dissimilar voice from mine.

The Likes of Me: *Alice's Adventures in Wonderland*

I'm not certain, but I think the movie *Alice in Wonderland* came to the corner show I haunted as a kid in the late '40s or early '50s. And I'm almost certain I saw the show because I rarely missed my favorite Saturday afternoon pastime, and because imprinted somewhere still are the names The Mad Hatter, The March Hare, The Queen of Hearts, The Cheshire Cat, The Mad Tea Party, and the verse that begins "The Queen of Hearts, she made some tarts." But other than a vague recollection of Alice falling down some sort of hole, I have no childhood memory whatsoever of the roles these characters played, or what the story itself was all about. What I remember very distinctly, however, was my dislike for the movie and my feelings of uneasiness toward it. And so, it was with these vague recollections and negative childhood impressions that I began my first reading of this book just two weeks ago.

By the end of the second chapter, or perhaps sooner, I found myself wallowing in those same early feelings of aversion. Admittedly, it took great effort and resolve to finish what I began, and I'm convinced that a thousand and one readings of this book would elicit the same response. It would have been so easy to revert to the child in me and simply shrug off this tale as one that failed to click. But knowing there was little to gain from a childish shrug of the shoulders, I grudgingly put my adult nose to the grindstone to search among the pages of this book for the cause or causes of my ill-feelings, and in doing so, discovered not only a greater respect for the author and his work, but a surprising connection between the Victorian Alice and myself.

Like Alice, I too need order and simplicity in my life, as well as the frequent change of events and the occasional dare to ward off boredom. And like Alice, I too feel compelled to make sense of things, to find solutions to problems, and to strive unreasonably, at times, toward perfection. But our most striking similarity is our compulsion to keep things under control. Believing these personality traits have always been a part of me, then it's easier to understand my lingering dislike for this tale. It is, after all, everything I am not.

I can't help but wonder whether the bizarreness of this story is in some way related to Lewis Carroll's Victorian upbringing, which was probably not too dissimilar from that of the 1940s. For whatever reason, parents of those eras, lovingly or not, kept unreasonably strict control over their children, and over almost every aspect of their children's lives. I clearly remember daring occasionally to break the mould of the obedient, unquestioning child by challenging my parents' authority and wisdom. And I remember those times were always met with their severe disapproval of my "cheek." Undoubtedly, the likes of me—and I'm sure there were zillions, including Lewis Carroll—longed for the day when we'd be set free from the bonds of parental oppression. And when that day finally arrived, it seemed to bring with it a lifetime of restriction, and conventional rules and regulations. It would seem Lewis Carroll was among those who took up the challenge with zealous fervour. For to me, this "off-the-wall" tale reflects not only Lewis Carroll's exuberant release from convention, authority, and emotional and intellectual restriction, but also his wish for future generations of children to be freed *as children* to seek and exercise their own identity and individuality.

Perhaps for Lewis Carroll, this work served as a kind of catharsis. And perhaps for the likes of me, it will always represent a place we entered unwillingly, and exited the richer for having been there.

Bev's response, unlike my own efforts, reflects on the relationship between Alice and herself. She is forthright in connecting her reading of the book with her own life, but at the same time she shows a predilection for what we might perceive as an "objective" reading.

She speculates on Lewis Carroll and his upbringing, and she takes an interest in Victorian conventions of child rearing. In short, Bev wrote a personal response because she thought this was what the class exercise called for. I note this because she seems to gravitate to another kind of writing. I want to illustrate this with another of her essays. This time the book was Jan Hudson's *Sweetgrass* (1984), a Canadian novel about the life of a Blackfoot Indian girl in the early nineteenth century. The book is suitable for readers of about eight to fifteen. I put it on the course list because of its historical subject matter and because it had won the prestigious Canada Council Children's Literature Prize as well as other awards. The book also receives praise for its verisimilitude in Judith Saltman's *Modern Canadian Children's Books* (75–76). Bev's response to it is especially interesting in light of the fact that I had praised the book in class.

Sweetgrass: Hard on the Heels of Julie

Had I read these two stories in reverse order, perhaps the negative impact of *Sweetgrass* would not have been as profound. For without question, my unfavourable response to Jan Hudson's work is rooted in, and coloured by, my enthusiasm and respect for Jean George's *Julie of the Wolves*. For me, *Julie* typifies the perfect literary learning tool for young readers. It offers much valuable information about the indigenous peoples of the Arctic—their barren home, the tundra, the hardy creatures that share their harsh living space, the indomitable native spirit in the face of unthinkable hardship, the ability of the human species and animals of all kinds to live in harmony with each other, the art of non-verbal communication, the natural rhythms of Arctic life, and the "gussak" influence on the traditional Inuit way of life. The inner workings of this book not only reflect a vast amount of research and an extraordinary ability to integrate fact and fiction, but also the author's personal commitment to stimulate the intellect of her reader with enriching material and ideas. This is the sort of reading that makes time fly, that roots one to a chair until the final word, that comes to an end far too soon, that lingers long after the closing page, and that becomes a tall measuring stick for similar thematic works by other authors. This brings me to *Sweetgrass*.

The outward trappings of this book are deceivingly impressive. The cover boasts a gold seal of literary acclaim; the inner leaf acknowledges an impressive-looking list of author/publisher comments; an historical footnote suggests an accurate documentation of facts for the story; and the back cover "preview" presents the author's assumed objective—to provide noteworthy historical information about the Blackfoot Confederacy, about the early nineteenth-century Western Canadian prairie, and about the lives of the Plains Indians living there during that same period. But at best, we are given minimal, superficial facts, shallow and commonplace information skimmed off the top of a deep well of rich archival material—overused information which any junior-grade student may discover after a limited amount of independent research, or may know already through incidental learning or media exposure. While "trite" seems too harsh a word for me to describe this work, no other comes to mind. In contrast to the intelligent, strong and vital Miyax, the characters Sweetgrass, Pretty Girl, and Favorite Child remind me of idle-minded Barbie Dolls. Throughout this story, I failed to find one profound, cerebral, or original thought. Originality, and depth too, are missing from the plot, a plot which seems little more than a weak series of overplayed events, undermined still further by the tiresome central theme of Sweetgrass's obsession with her unmarried status, and the inappropriate use of modern cliches and idioms. But more damaging are those references which measure human worth in terms of brawn, beauty, and materialism. Not only do these references imply misplaced values among the Blackfoot culture, but they wrongly influence young readers to judge themselves and others by similar standards. They lead to the assumption that the mid nineteenth-century Blackfoot lived by a lesser set of values than their Inuit contemporaries. For according to Jean George's *Julie*, the riches of past Inuit life are equated with intelligence, fearlessness, and love.

A work of literature, like any other art form, either clicks with its audience, or it doesn't. And while I admit Jan Hudson's first novel is not totally without merit, its tone, to me, smacks of "market appeal." For this reason, it fails to ring true. It was difficult to justify my feelings, but a little research into some doubtful historical information helped clarify my unease. For example, the suggestion that the smallpox virus was carried in blankets purchased at the Hudson's Bay Trading Post, or on the wind, or through casual contact with the Peigan messenger, stirred my curiosity. From the Communicable Disease Department in Calgary, I learned that none of these suggestions bears much weight. It's now known that this disease is transmitted primarily through contact with body fluids, and less frequently through contact with infected skin lesions, or material *recently* contaminated with the pox fluid. We are also led to believe that the medicinal calamus tea contributed to the recovery of Otter and Almost-Mother, when, in fact, there is no known cure for smallpox. And after being led to believe that a nine-day diet of fish had restored the starving members of Sweetgrass's family, I discovered that fish is not a life-sustaining food in itself because it lacks "fat," an essential dietary ingredient. The same holds true for rabbit meat, and yet the story implies otherwise.

I wondered, too, about Hudson's depiction of the Indian women as subordinate to men—for example, the lowering of the eyes, the lack of choice for women, the term "slavewife," and the suggestion that women's accomplishments were unworthy of acknowledgement or praise. Information from a staff member at the Glenbow Museum (in Calgary) revealed the opposite to be true; women in Blackfoot society were not only equal in status to their male counterparts, but they were highly revered by their mates as the entrusted holders of the family's most sacred possession—the medicine bundle. Having discovered this much regarding the Blackfoot women, I question Hudson's uncomplimentary reference to women as commodities. She states on page 14 that a husband's gifts of marriage were used to "purchase" a wife. And once again I was surprised to learn that this idea is a common misconception, that, in fact, these gifts were given to the woman's father to *honour* her. I also questioned the frequent use of the word "luck." From my source at the Glenbow, I learned that the concept of chance was totally foreign to early Indian cultures. The Blackfoot, like all the tribes mentioned in this story, believed the events in their lives happened by design, that all happenings were caused by explainable things, things that were often associated with their spirits.

My greatest disappointment was the chapter devoted to the Sun Dance. Here was a perfect opportunity to teach children a wealth of information about the most complex of all Blackfoot rituals.

Instead, the richness and importance of this sacred and social event were buried under a mountain of trivia. One of the most unforgivable examples of this is the incidental, inaccurate and incomplete reference to the Sun Dance Woman (see page 63). She was *not*, as the story defines her, simply a "sponsor"; she was a chosen holy woman. She was *not* on view by other members of the tribe during her four-day period of fasting and praying, but she remained in seclusion, only to come out from her tipi once during the morning and evening. She did *not* fast and pray alone, but rather with her mate. And they did not *just* fast and pray; they chanted and sang ancient songs to their creator. And they cut and dried buffalo tongues which, at the end of the four-day ritual, were passed from the hands of the Sun Dance Woman during a sacred ceremony into the hands of each member of the tribe as a holy blessing.

Having said all this, I'm not sure what it all means, or if it means anything at all. I do know, however, that I feel deceived and shortchanged by this book, and that my ill-feelings toward it have led to the opinion that this work not only does a disservice to its young readers, but also to our Canadian history, and to the people of the Blackfoot Confederacy.

This response paper differs from the first of Bev's reproduced here in that she feels more at ease examining the book the way she wants to examine it. For Bev, this means engaging in research relevant to the book. This essay's strength derives from Bev's willingness to pursue her feelings of unease despite the apparent institutional approval of this book. She offers material to share and debate with other readers of *Sweetgrass*. This essay, like the others I have included here, differs notably from ones you will find included in the books by Bleich or Steig. But they nonetheless reveal useful and shareable things about both the works the writers discuss and the writers themselves. This type of writing is perhaps the most pedagogically useful since it removes the anxiety of "getting it right." The writer writes without the burden of formality that comes with the traditional form of academic writing; the only responsibility we have is to write honestly that which we feel and think in response to the stimulus of a text without the disguise of objectivity.

My examples of response writing are to some extent misleading since they imply that a response must follow the usual pattern of discursive writing. This is not, however, mandatory. As my discussion of Anno's *Twice Told Tales* in the preceding chapter should indicate, response may employ other forms of discourse: either the writing of another story or even the illustration of a story. Children do this all the time when they write or draw pictures in response to what they read, see, or hear. As my discussion of parody in chapter 5 might also have indicated, parody is a form of critical comment. One text invariably interprets another text, as the elaborate theory of influence associated with the work of Harold Bloom teaches us. Everything we create, whether this be a formal critical article, a story or drawing, or a spontaneous response, is a critical reading of some other text. We never, even when we are practicing the hermetically closed reading of a formalist or a New Critic, write without a context, and that context is intensely textual. By this I mean that all response—objective or subjective—is a response not only to a work, but also to a text, that is, to the connections that what we used to think of only as a "work of art" must have to the larger world. Text is everything. In this sense, then, the separation of intrinsic and extrinsic is artificial. This might be seen in Wellek and Warren's call for a comparative literature, or Cleanth Brooks's references to Freud or Sir James Frazer in that most New Critical of books, *The Well Wrought Urn*. I might also cite a sentence from this book; in his chapter on Wordsworth's "Immortality Ode," Brooks writes: "But I must confess that I feel the solution is asserted rather than dramatized" (148). Here we do, in fact, come full circle.

9

A Beginning Again

We heard Wally wail through the whole neighborhood,
as his mother whaled Wally as hard as she could,
she made Wally holler, she made Wally whoop,
for what he had spelled in the alphabet soup.

(Jack Prelutsky, New Kid on the Block)

Here is a simple poem by one of the best-known writers of children's verse. I offer it as a final example for critical examination. What follows is a response to the poem that contains (implicitly as well as explicitly) nearly all the methodological approaches I have outlined earlier in the book: formal, thematic, structural, deconstructive, political, and reader response. I have not attempted either an archetypal or a psychoanalytical reading of the poem. The point is not simply to reprise these several approaches, but to show that they connect. The previous chapters should also contain enough cross-fertilization to indicate that few theoretical approaches are pure. Theory is like other aspects of a living world; it thrives on miscegenation.

Prelutsky tells us that poetry is "communication, right up there with sculpture and photography and painting and music" ("In Search of," 103). Okay, let us see what "We Heard Wally Wail" has to communicate. What immediately strikes me are the whacking sounds, the onomatopoeic effect of the alliteration. "W," "h," and "wh" compete for attention here. Sounds work through assonance, too, as the first line brilliantly indicates; the modulated ah-ay sound in "Wally wail" is balanced by the oo-oh sound in "through the whole," and both of these sounds are tucked between the erd-ood of "heard . . . neighborhood," which begins and ends the line. This line contains the most spectacular of the poem's aural effects, but the reader cannot remain untuned to sound throughout the poem: "whaled Wally . . . hard," "Wally holler . . . Wally whoop," "spelled . . . soup." Aiding and abetting this alliterative effect is the insistent metrical beat that I hear as "We *heard Wally wail* through the *whole neigh*borhood." We could, I think, stress just about every word in the poem. The heavy stresses are, of course, standard fare in poetry for younger children, the idea being, I guess, that children need to rumba. We might also note that aiding and abetting the poem's strong rhythm are the masculine rhymes. In fact, nearly every word in the poem, with the exception of "Wally," has a masculine ending. This helps the poem to thud a little. After all, Wally's mother is whacking him as hard as she can. True, children are unlikely to spend their time finding out what gives the poem its effect, but this is no reason for us not to.

Why, you might ask? Well, for one reason because it is there. For another, because we might want to know whether form and content are in harmony; in other words, we might want to know whether this is a good poem or not. Here things get tricky. I like to think form *is* content and therefore as long as the poet shows good form everything will be hunky-dory. I often tell students that children's poetry has one function: to draw the child's attention to language in its metaphoric and musical power. Really, the important thing about poetry for children is that it keeps alive the instinct for linguistic play, for a language that is free from the pretend clarity of the marketplace. But, of course, nothing is this simple. Language communicates because words have lexical and contextual meanings. But perhaps this is the crucial point: in literature, the fun is precisely that language drawing attention to itself has no design on its reader, whereas the language we encounter in most other aspects of our life does have designs upon us. We might even go further and speculate that any literature that has nothing but a design upon us is weak as literature. Strong poetry—"On the Ning Nang Nong," for example—is strong because it keeps the mind open; it does not attempt to close the mind.

What about "We Heard Wally Wail"? Some might decry the corporal punishment inflicted on Wally by his irate mother. On the other hand, some might applaud this paragon of discipline for giving it to her son for his disrespectful behavior. Whichever position we take, we might agree that the poem actively works to negate the seriousness both of Wally's actions and of his mother's reaction, through its bounce and its verbal pyrotechnics. If we like the poem, then we will focus on these verbal pyrotechnics; if we do not like the poem, then we will criticize its presentation of an abusive parent or the vulgarity of Wally.

But we still have not got to what Prelutsky might be communicating to his young readers. What is in this poem for them? Obviously, I can only speculate here since I am no longer a young reader, but I can and do recall something from my own childhood that seems to me relevant to this poem. When I was a kid growing up on Russell Street, I regularly spent Saturday mornings staring out our bathroom window. To put you at ease, let me say that this was the only room in the house that had a window onto our backyard and the Perkins's house behind ours. I usually went to the bathroom on Saturday morning to stare out the window. I stared in some awe at the back door of the Perkins's house because I knew that at precisely nine o'clock Dick Perkins would come bursting out of that door, still in his pajamas, closely followed by Mrs. Perkins. Dick would run down the few steps and then turn to face his mother. She would stand on the stoop with a broom in her hand; she always yelled at Dick and flailed the broom in his direction. Often he would grab it from her and flail it back in her face. This would send her back into the house, slamming and locking the door behind her. In his pajamas, Dick would come over to our house and ask my mother for a cigarette; he had, he would say, to wait until his mother cooled off.

Now I do not know why Dick Perkins's mother chased him from the house every Saturday morning, but I like to think he did something as transgressive (probably more so) as Wally's indelicacy with the alphabet soup. One of the nice things about Prelutsky's poem is its silence on just what it was that Wally spelled with his wet pasta letters; one of the nice things about seeing Dick flee from his house was the mystery of his transgression. And just as Dick fled from his frazzled mother, I can envisage Wally fleeing from his harridan of a mother. Note the ambiguity through the placement of the phrase "through the whole neighborhood." Following "wail" as it does, this phrase might indicate that Wally's cries emanate from his house, or it might indicate that Wally is wailing his way (a variation on wending his way) through the neighborhood, followed closely by his incensed mother. However we read this, one thing is clear to me. Prelutsky is having fun with the idea of transgression. He knows his reader will get a giggle from the notion of naughty language. Maybe he thinks his reader will share the mildly sadistic delight in Wally's punishment that we might sense in the speaker. Or perhaps he suspects the reader will react the way I reacted to Dick Perkins: with envy at this guy's sand. Imagine strolling the neighborhood in your pajamas with the broom you had snatched from your angry mother's hands! Imagine sitting at the lunch or dinner table with your parents, eating alphabet soup, and spelling right there on your spoon for everyone at the table to see some taboo word, some word forbidden to the vocabulary of polite people! Sure kids will like this.

I have not spoken about what is, perhaps, the most obvious aspect of the poem: its voice. The speaker uses the first person "We." He or she is obviously someone in the neighborhood—child or adult. How do we know whether this is a child or an adult speaking? I do not think we do for certain, but the delight the person takes in Wally's discomfort (I think of "holler" and "whoop") makes me think the speaker is supposed to be a child. Is this convincing? Is the poem any good? Frankly, I do not have pat answers to these questions. The truth is, the poem does not do a lot for me. What's more, children's poetry generally does not do a lot for me. I think much of it is ephemeral; I think "We Heard Wally Wail" is ephemeral. I would like to think our children had more to challenge them than this kind of thing. Now that I have written what I have, I think of an obvious analogue for this poem. Here is the analogue:

A Beginning Again

> There was an old woman
> Who lived in a shoe.
> She had so many children
> She didn't know what to do.
> She gave them some broth
> Without any bread,
> Then whipped them all soundly
> And sent them to bed.

I can still hear the relish in my voice as I read the word "whipped" to my kids years ago. Perhaps Prelutsky's little poem partakes of the spirit of this nursery rhyme. The exasperation of overworked and overstressed parents might lie behind both poems, although this is more obvious in the nursery rhyme. Here poverty, cramped quarters, and the cacophony of a house full of children go some way to explaining the woman's desperate measure to ensure some quiet at bedtime. For me, the mother's reaction in the Prelutsky poem has much less justification. The exaggeration is forced and, for me at least, not very effective. The middle-class delicacy that would object to four wobbly letters on a soup spoon pales alongside the weary round the poor welfare-fated mother in the nursery rhyme must take.

Having raised this analogy with "The Old Woman Who Lived in a Shoe," I have also raised the idea of economic hardship. This seems of little relevance to Prelutsky's poem, especially in light of the fact that most of his poetry for children takes for its context a decidedly middle-class milieu. But his use of alphabet soup is loaded. Alphabet soup is the creation of our capitalist consumerism; soup companies turn their pasta into letters in order to sell soup. In this poem, Wally finds himself trapped between imagination and commercialism. His imaginative use of the letters in his soup is only possible because his society creates products that invite such play. We might extrapolate from this to notice that many of the products designed especially for children encourage a dubious form of play: dolls that demand consumer goods related to fashion and wealth (I think of Barbie and her flashy clothes and fast cars), dolls that eat and that evacuate what they eat, costume jewelry, automobiles made to crash, and so on.

But I return to my initial point: what matters at the early stages of a child's literary education is sound more than sense. Capture them with dance. I despair how language holds little or no power for older students; I despair because what everyone should realize is that language is power, as much (maybe even more so) as money or muscle or machine guns. We live in a world in which the debasement of language proceeds at an alarming rate. Just the other day, I read a student essay in which the student said that she preferred to read prose because it was more natural than poetry. She went on to say that prose is more familiar to us because we come to it earlier in life than we do poetry. Do we really encounter prose before we encounter the old woman who lives in a shoe? Do children not babble and coo before they speak in sentences? Do children not chant and sing in the schoolyard and on the street at least as early as their first encounters with prose? Too soon they give up their singing. Too soon they accommodate a prosaic world.

So what good is literary theory? Will it keep our children singing? Well perhaps not. But understanding something of literary theory will give us some understanding of how the literature we give to our children works. It might also keep us engaged with the texts that surround us, keep us singing even if it is a more mature song than we sang as youthful readers of texts. And as long as we keep singing, we have a chance of passing along our singing spirit to those we teach. What we teach when we teach literature to children is not, then, themes and structures, but rather the desire to examine, analyze, re-create, perform, and understand the forces that shape our own lives. In this sense, the reading of literature and the study of text is both a form of play and a deeply political activity.

Had I used an epigraph for this last chapter, I would have chosen the following from Wayne Booth's "A Hippocratic Oath for the Pluralist": "I will not write any history of criticism, or analysis of *the* types of criticism, unless driven to it by thirteen demons and unless I decide to spend the lifetime required to do the job decently" (*Critical Understanding*, 352). We need to marshall these thirteen demons in the service of teaching children to spend a lifetime reading.

Children's Books Cited

Ahlberg, Janet and Allan. *The Jolly Postman or Other People's Letters*. Boston: Little, Brown, 1986.

Aiken, Joan. The Dido Twite series. Harmondsworth, England: Puffin.

Alexander, Lloyd. The Prydain series. New York: Dell.

Anno, Mitsumasa. *Anno's Twice Told Tales by the Brothers Grimm and Mr. Fox*. New York: Philomel, 1993.

Bang, Molly. *The Grey Lady and the Strawberry Snatcher*. New York: Four Winds, 1980.

Bawden, Nina. *The Peppermint Pig*. Harmondsworth, England: Puffin, 1988 (1977).

Briggs, Raymond. *Fungus the Bogeyman*. London: Hamish Hamilton, 1977.

———. *Gentleman Jim*. London: Hamish Hamilton, 1980.

———. *Jim and the Beanstock*. London: Puffin, 1988 (1970).

———. *The Man*. Toronto: Douglas and McIntyre, 1992.

———. *The Snowman*. London: Hamish Hamilton, 1978.

———. *The Tin-Pot Foreign General and the Old Iron Woman*. London: Hamish Hamilton, 1984.

Brooks, Walter R. The Freddy series. New York: Knopf.

Browne, Anthony. *Willy and Hugh*. London: Julia MacRae, 1991.

Browne, Frances. *Granny's Wonderful Chair*. Harmondsworth, England: Puffin Classics, 1985 (1856).

Bunyan, John. *The Pilgrim's Progress*. Oxford: Oxford World's Classics, 1984 (1678).

Burnett, Frances Hodgson. *The Secret Garden*. New York: Dell, 1973 (1911).

Burningham, John. *Grandpa*. London: Puffin, 1988 (1984).

Carroll, Lewis. *Alice's Adventures in Wonderland* and *Through the Looking Glass*. Oxford: Oxford World's Classics, 1982 (1865, 1872).

Chambers, Aidan. *Breaktime*. London: The Bodley Head, 1978.

Childe-Pemberton, Harriet. "All My Doing; or Red Riding-Hood Over Again" (1882). In *Victorian Fairy Tales*, ed. Jack Zipes. New York: Methuen, 1987: 211–48.

Cleary, Beverly. The Ramona series. New York: Dell.

Coolidge, Susan. *What Katy Did*. Harmondsworth, England: Puffin Classics, 1982 (1872).

Cooper, Susan. The "Dark is Rising" series. New York: Atheneum.

Cormier, Robert. *I Am the Cheese*. New York: Dell, 1977.

Day, Thomas. *The History of Sandford and Merton* (1783–1789) (abridged). In *Masterworks of Children's Literature*, vol. 3, ed. Robert Bator. New York: Stonehill, 1983: 131–80.

Fielding, Sarah. *The Governess, or Little Female Academy*. London and New York: Pandora, 1987 (1749).

Fleischman, Paul. *Shadow Play*. Pictures by Eric Beddows. New York: Harper and Row, 1990.

Fox, Paula. *Lily and the Lost Boy*. New York: Dell, 1987.

French, Fiona. *City of Gold*. London: Oxford University Press, 1974.

———. *The Princess and the Musician*. London: Evans Brothers, 1981.

———. *Snow White in New York*. Oxford: Oxford University Press, 1986.

Gág, Wanda. *Millions of Cats*. New York: Coward, McCann and Geoghegan, 1928.

Garner, Alan. *Red Shift*. New York: Macmillan, 1973.

George, Jean Craighead. *Julie of the Wolves*. New York: Harper and Row, 1972.

Gibbons, Alan. *Pig*. London: Dent, 1990.

Grahame, Kenneth. *The Wind in the Willows*. New York: Scribner's, 1983 (1908).

Grimm Brothers. *The Complete Grimm's Fairy Tales*. New York: Pantheon, 1972 (1944).

———. *Household Stories by the Brothers Grimm*. Tr. Lucy Crane. New York: Dover, 1963 (1866).

Hamilton, Virginia. *M. C. Higgins the Great*. New York: Laurel-Leaf, 1981 (1974).

History of Little Goody Two-Shoes, The (1765). In *Masterworks of Children's Literature*, vol. 3, ed. Robert Bator. New York: Stonehill, 1983: 73–111.

Horwitz, Elinor Lander. *When the Sky Is Like Lace*. Pictures by Barbara Cooney. New York: Lippincott, 1975.

Hudson, Jan. *Sweetgrass*. Edmonton: Tree Frog, 1984.

Hunt, Peter. *Backtrack*. London: Julia MacRae, 1986.

Hunter, Mollie. *A Sound of Chariots*. New York: Harper Trophy, 1988 (1972).

Ingelow, Jean. *Mopsa the Fairy* (1869). In *A Christmas Carol by Charles Dickens and Other Victorian Fairy Tales*, selected by U. C. Knoepflmacher. Toronto: Bantam, 1983: 235–346.

Ionesco, Eugene. *Story Number 1*. Pictures by Etienne Delessert. Harlin Quist, 1968.

Kaldhol, Marit, and Wenche Oyen. *Goodbye Rune*. Tr. by Michael Crosby-Jones. St. John's, Newfoundland: Breakwater, 1987.

King-Smith, Dick. *The Sheep-Pig*. Harmondsworth, England: Puffin, 1985 (1983).

Kozikowski, Renate. *Titus Bear Goes to School*. New York: Harper and Row, 1984.

Lear, Edward. *The Complete Nonsense of Edward Lear*. Collected by Holbrook Jackson. New York: Dover, 1951 (1947).

LeGuin, Ursula. The "Earthsea" series. Harmondsworth, England: Puffin.

Lewis, C. S. The Narnia series. Harmondsworth, England: Puffin.

Lobel, Arnold. *The Book of Pigericks*. New York: Harper and Row, 1983.

Macaulay, David. *Black and White*. Boston: Houghton Mifflin, 1990.

McCloskey, Robert. *Time of Wonder*. New York: Viking, 1957.

MacDonald, George. *The Light Princess and Other Tales*. London: Victor Gollancz, 1967.

———. *Phantastes*. London: Smith, Elder, 1858.

———. *The Princess and the Goblin/The Princess and Curdie*. Oxford: Oxford World's Classics, 1990 (1872 and 1881).

Milne, A. A. *The House at Pooh Corner*. London: Methuen, 1973 (1928).

———. *Winnie-The-Pooh*. Toronto: McClelland and Stewart, 1972 (1926).

Montgomery, L. M. *Anne of Green Gables*. Toronto: McClelland and Stewart, 1983 (1908).

Munsch, Robert. *Giant or Waiting for the Thursday Boat*. Willowdale, Ontario: Annick Press, 1989.

———. *Good Families Don't*. Toronto: Doubleday, 1990.

Nesbit, E. *Five Children and It*. Harmondsworth, England: Puffin, 1971 (1902).

Opie, Iona and Peter. *The Oxford Dictionary of Nursery Rhymes*. Oxford: Oxford University Press, 1984 (1951).

Paterson, Katherine. *Bridge to Terabithia*. New York: Avon, 1977.

————. *The Great Gilly Hopkins*. New York: Avon, 1978.

Pearce, Philippa. *Tom's Midnight Garden*. London: Oxford University Press, 1969 (1958).

Perrault, Charles. *Little Red Riding Hood*. Illustrated by Sarah Moon. Mankato, Minn.: Creative Education, 1983.

Potter, Beatrix. *The Tale of Peter Rabbit*. New York: Dover, 1973 (1903).

————. *The Tale of Pigling Bland*. London: Frederick Warne, 1913.

Prelutsky, Jack. *The New Kid on the Block*. New York: Greenwillow, 1984.

Raskin, Ellen. *Figgs and Phantoms*. New York: Dutton, 1977 (1974).

————. *The Westing Game*. New York: Avon, 1978.

Richler, Mordecai. *Jacob Two-Two Meets the Hooded Fang*. New York: Bantam, 1975.

Saint-Exupéry, Antoine de. *The Little Prince*. New York: Harbrace-Harcourt, 1971 (1943).

Scieszka, Jon, and Lane Smith. *The Stinky Cheese Man and Other Fairly Stupid Tales*. New York: Viking, 1992.

Sendak, Maurice. *In the Night Kitchen*. New York: Harper and Row, 1970.

————. *Kenny's Window*. New York: Harper and Row, 1956.

————. *Outside Over There*. New York: Harper and Row, 1981.

————. *Where the Wild Things Are*. New York: Harper and Row, 1963.

Seuss, Dr. *The Lorax* (1971). In *Six By Seuss*. New York: Random House, 1991: 282–345.

Sinclair, Catherine. *Holiday House*. London: Hamish Hamilton, 1972 (1839).

Spier, Peter. *Fast-Slow/High-Low*. New York: Doubleday, 1972.

Steig, William. *The Amazing Bone*. Harmondsworth, England: Puffin, 1977 (1976).

————. *Amos and Boris*. Harmondsworth, England: Puffin, 1978 (1971).

————. *Caleb and Kate*. New York: Scholastic, 1977.

————. *Roland the Minstrel Pig*. London: Hamish Hamilton, 1968.

————. *Shrek!* New York: Farrar, 1990.

————. *Sylvester and the Magic Pebble*. New York: Windmill, 1969.

————. *Yellow and Pink*. New York: Farrar, 1984.

————. *The Zabajaba Jungle*. New York: Farrar, 1977.

Stevenson, Robert Louis. *Treasure Island*. Harmondsworth, England: Puffin, 1972 (1883).

Switzer, Margaret. *Existential Folktales*. Berkeley, Calif.: Cayuse, 1985.

Tennyson, Alfred, Lord. *The Lady of Shalott*. Illus. by Charles Keeping. Oxford: Oxford University Press, 1986.

Tolkien, J. R. R. *The Hobbit*. London: Unwin, 1972 (1937).

Van Allsburg, Chris. *Ben's Dream*. Boston: Houghton Mifflin, 1982.

———. *The Mysteries of Harris Burdick*. Boston: Houghton Mifflin, 1984.

White, E. B. *Charlotte's Web*. New York: Dell, 1973 (1952).

Wiesner, David. *Free Fall*. New York: Mulberry Books, 1988.

Wollstonecraft, Mary. *Original Stories from Real Life* (1788). In *Masterworks of Children's Literature*, vol. 3, ed. Robert Bator. New York: Stonehill, 1983: 353–406.

Wordsworth, William. *Wordsworth's Poems for the Young*. London: Alexander Strahan, 1866.

Zindel, Paul. *The Pigman*. New York: Dell, 1968.

Anthologies of Children's Literature Cited

Fadiman, Clifton. *The World Treasury of Children's Literature*. 2 vols. Boston: Little, Brown, 1984.

Griffith, John W., and Charles H. Frey. *Classics of Children's Literature*. 2nd edition. New York: Macmillan, 1987 (1981).

Lee, Alvin A., and Hope Arnott. *Circle of Stories*. 2 vols. New York: Harcourt, 1972.

Moss, Anita, and Jon C. Stott. *The Family of Stories: An Anthology of Children's Literature*. New York: Holt, Rinehart and Winston, 1986.

Opie, Iona and Peter. *The Classic Fairy Tales*. London: Oxford University Press, 1974.

———. *The Oxford Book of Children's Verse*. London: Oxford University Press, 1973.

Saltman, Judith. *The Riverside Anthology of Children's Literature*. 6th edition. Boston: Houghton Mifflin, 1988.

Works of Literary Theory and Criticism Cited

Abrams, M. H. *Natural Supernaturalism*. Oxford: Oxford University Press, 1971.

Alberghene, Janice M. "Writing in *Charlotte's Web*," *Children's Literature in Education* 16 (1985): 32–44.

Althusser, Louis. *Lenin and Philosophy*. New York: The Monthly Review Press, 1971.

Appleby, Arthur N. *The Child's Concept of Story: Ages Two to Seventeen*. Chicago: University of Chicago Press, 1978.

Bachelard, Gaston. *The Poetics of Space*. Tr. Maria Jolas. Boston: Beacon, 1969 (1958).

Bakhtin, M. M., and P. N. Medvedev. *The Formal Method in Literary Scholarship*. Tr. Albert J. Wehrle. Baltimore: The Johns Hopkins University Press, 1978.

Bal, Mieke. *Narratology: Introduction to the Theory of Narrative*. Toronto: University of Toronto Press, 1985.

Barber, Benjamin R. *An Aristocracy of Everyone: The Politics of Education and the Future of America*. New York: Ballantine, 1992.

Barthes, Roland. *S/Z*. Tr. Richard Miller. New York: Will and Wang, 1974.

Bataille, Georges. *Visions of Excess: Selected Writings, 1927–1939*. Tr. Allan Stoekl. Minneapolis: University of Minnesota Press, 1985.

Baudrillard, Jean. *Simulations*. Tr. Paul Foss, Paul Patton, and Philip Bietchman. New York: Semiotext(e), 1983.

Belsey, Catherine. *Critical Practice*. London: Methuen, 1980.

Bettelheim, Bruno. *The Uses of Enchantment: The Meaning and Importance of Fairy Tales*. New York: Knopf, 1976.

Bleich, David. *Subjective Criticism*. Baltimore: The Johns Hopkins University Press, 1978.

Bloom, Harold. *Agon: Toward a Theory of Revisionism*. Oxford: Oxford University Press, 1982.

Booth, Wayne C. *Critical Understanding: The Powers and Limits of Pluralism*. Chicago: University of Chicago Press, 1979.

Borges, Jorge Luis. "Pierre Menard, Author of the 'Quixote,'" *Labyrinths: Selected Stories and Other Writings*, ed. Donald A. Yates and James E. Irby. New York: New Directions, 1962: 36–44.

Bottigheimer, Ruth. *Grimms' Bad Girls and Bold Boys: The Moral and Social Vision of the Tales*. New Haven, Conn.: Yale University Press, 1987.

Bowie, Malcolm. *Lacan*. London: Fontana, 1991.

Brooks, Cleanth. *The Well Wrought Urn*. New York: Harcourt, Brace, 1947.

—— and Robert Penn Warren. *Understanding Poetry*. 4th edition. New York: Holt, 1976 (1st edition, 1938).

Caudwell, Christopher. *Romance and Realism: A Study in English Bourgeois Literature*. Princeton, N.J.: Princeton University Press, 1970.

Chatman, Seymour. *Story and Discourse: Narrative Structure in Fiction and Film*. Ithaca, N.Y.: Cornell University Press, 1978.

Cixous, Helene. "The Laugh of the Medusa," *New French Feminisms*, ed. Elaine Marks and Isabelle de Courtivron. New York: Schocken, 1980: 245–64.

Coleridge, S. T. *Biogaphia Literaria*. Ed. George Watson. London: Everyman-Dent, 1965 (1817).

Coles, Robert. *The Political Life of Children*. Boston: Houghton Mifflin, 1986.

Culler, Jonathan. *On Deconstruction: Theory and Criticism After Structuralism*. Ithaca, N.Y.: Cornell University Press, 1982.

——. *The Pursuit of Signs: Semiotics, Literature, Deconstruction*. London: Routledge, 1981.

——. *Structuralist Poetics: Structuralism, Linguistics and the Study of Literature*. London: Routledge, 1975.

Cullinan, Bernice. *Literature and the Child*. 2nd edition. San Diego: Harcourt, 1989 (1981).

Daly, Mary. *Gyn/Ecology: The Metaethics of Radical Feminism*. Boston: Beacon, 1978.

Deleuze, Gilles, and Felix Guattari. *Anti-Oedipus: Capitalism and Schizophrenia*. Tr. Robert Hurley, Mark Seem, and Helen R. Lane. Minneapolis: University of Minnesota Press, 1983.

DelFattore, Joan. *What Johnny Shouldn't Read*. New Haven, Conn.: Yale University Press, 1992.

Dixon, Bob. *Catching Them Young 2: Political Ideas in Children's Fiction*. London: Pluto Press, 1977.

Works of Literary Theory and Criticism Cited

Dylan, Bob. *Lyrics, 1962–1985*. New York: Knopf, 1985.

Eagleton, Terry. *Literary Theory: An Introduction*. Oxford: Basil Blackwell, 1983.

Edinger, Edward F. *Ego and Archetype*. Baltimore: Penguin, 1974 (1972).

Egan, Kieran. *Primary Understanding: Education in Early Childhood*. New York: Routledge, 1991 (1988).

Empson, William. *Some Versions of Pastoral*. London: Chatto and Windus, 1935.

Fish, Stanley. *Is There a Text in This Class? The Authority of Interpretive Communities*. Cambridge, Mass.: Harvard University Press, 1980.

Foulkes, A. P. *Literature and Propaganda*. London: Methuen, 1983.

Freud, Sigmund. "The Case of the Wolf-Man," *The Wolf-Man by the Wolf-Man: The Double Story of Freud's Most Famous Case*. Ed. Muriel Gardiner. New York: Basic Books, 1971: 153–262.

———. *A General Introduction to Psychoanalysis*. Tr. Joan Riviere. New York: Pocket Books, 1972 (1920).

———. *The Interpretation of Dreams*. Tr. James Strachey. Harmondsworth, England: Penguin, 1977 (1905).

———. "The 'Uncanny,'" *Art and Literature*. Tr. Alex Strachey. Harmondsworth, England: Penguin, 1985 (1919): 335–76.

Frye, Northrop. *Anatomy of Criticism*. New York: Atheneum, 1966 (1957).

———. *The Critical Path*. Bloomington: Indiana University Press, 1971.

———. *The Educated Imagination*. Toronto: Canadian Broadcasting Corporation, 1963.

———. *Fearful Symmetry: A Study of William Blake*. Boston: Beacon, 1967 (1947).

———. *The Great Code: The Bible and Literature*. Toronto: Academic Press, 1981.

———. *Myth and Metaphor: Selected Essays 1974–1988*. Ed. Robert Denham. Charlottesville: University Press of Virginia, 1990.

———. *Northrop Frye on Culture and Literature*. Ed. Robert Denham. Chicago: University of Chicago Press, 1978.

———. *The Stubborn Structure: Essays on Criticism and Society*. Ithaca, N.Y.: Cornell University Press, 1970.

Gauthier, Xaviere. "Is There Such a Thing as Women's Writing," *New French Feminisms*, ed. Elaine Marks and Isabelle de Courtivron. New York: Schocken, 1980: 161–64.

Genette, Gerard. *Narrative Discourse: An Essay in Method*. Tr. Jane E. Lewin. Ithaca, N.Y.: Cornell University Press, 1983 (1980).

Georgiou, Constantine. *Children and Their Literature*. Englewood Cliffs, N.J.: Prentice-Hall, 1969.

Gilbert, Sandra M., and Susan Gubar. *The Madwoman in the Attic: The Woman Writer and the Nineteenth-Century Literary Imagination*. New Haven, Conn.: Yale University Press, 1984 (1979).

Golden, Joanne M. *The Narrative Symbol in Childhood Literature: Explorations in the Construction of Text*. New York: Mouton de Gruyter, 1990.

Gose, Elliott. *Mere Creatures: A Study of Modern Fantasy Tales for Children*. Toronto: University of Toronto Press, 1988.

Graff, Gerald. *Beyond the Culture Wars: How Teaching the Conflicts Can Revitalize American Education*. New York: W. W. Norton, 1992.

———. *Literature Against Itself: Literary Ideas in Modern Society*. Chicago: University of Chicago Press, 1979.

———. *Professing Literature: An Institutional History*. Chicago: University of Chicago Press, 1987.

Hagstrum, Jean. *William Blake: Poet and Painter*. Chicago: University of Chicago Press, 1978 (1964).

Hartman, Geoffrey H. *Beyond Formalism: Literary Essays 1958–1970*. New Haven, Conn.: Yale University Press, 1970.

Helms, Randall. *Tolkien's World*. Boston: Houghton Mifflin, 1974.

Helsinger, Elizabeth K., Robin Lauterbach Sheets, and William Veeder. *The Woman Question: Society and Literature in Britain and America 1837–1883*. Vol. 1, *Defining Voices*. Chicago: University of Chicago Press, 1983.

Hentoff, Nat. "Among the Wild Things," *Only Connect: Readings on Children's Literature*, ed. Sheila Egoff, G. T. Stubbs, and L. F. Ashley. Toronto: Oxford University Press, 1969: 323–46.

Hirsch, E. D. *A First Dictionary of Cultural Literacy: What Our Children Need to Know*. Boston: Houghton Mifflin, 1989.

———. *Validity in Interpretation*. New Haven, Conn.: Yale University Press, 1967.

Holbrook, David. "The Problem of C. S. Lewis," *Writers, Critics, and Children*, ed. by Geoff Fox et al. New York: Agathon Press, 1976: 116–24.

———. *The Skeleton in the Wardrobe: C. S. Lewis's Fantasies: A Phenomenological Study*. London: Bucknell University Press, 1991.

Holland, Norman N. *Dynamics of Literary Response*. New York: Norton, 1975 (1968).

Hollindale, Peter. "Ideology and the Children's Book," *Signal* 55 (1988): 3–22. Reprinted in Peter Hunt, ed. *Literature for Children: Contemporary Criticism*, London: Routledge, 1992: 19–40.

Homans, Margaret. *Bearing the Word: Language and Female Experience in Nineteenth-Century Women's Writing*. Chicago: University of Chicago Press, 1989 (1986).

Huck, Charlotte S. *Children's Literature in the Elementary School.* 3rd edition. New York: Holt, Rinehart and Winston, 1976 (1961).

Hunt, Peter. *Criticism, Theory, and Children's Literature.* Oxford: Basil Blackwell, 1991.

————, ed. *Children's Literature: The Development of Criticism.* London: Routledge, 1990.

Hutcheon, Linda. *The Politics of Postmodernism.* London: Routledge, 1989.

Inglis, Fred. *The Promise of Happiness: Value and Meaning in Children's Fiction.* Cambridge, England: Cambridge University Press, 1981.

Iser, Wolfgang. *The Act of Reading: A Theory of Aesthetic Response.* Baltimore: The Johns Hopkins University Press, 1978.

Jameson, Fredric. *The Political Unconscious: Narrative as a Socially Symbolic Act.* Ithaca, N.Y.: Cornell University Press, 1981.

————. *Postmodernism or, The Cultural Logic of Late Capitalism.* Durham, N.C.: Duke University Press, 1991.

Jauss, Hans Robert. *Toward an Aesthetic of Reception.* Tr. Timothy Bahti. Minneapolis: University of Minnesota Press, 1982.

Johnson, Barbara. "Writing," *Critical Terms for Literary Study*, ed. Frank Lentricchia and Thomas McLaughlin. Chicago: University of Chicago Press, 1990: 39–49.

Juvenile Review; or, Moral and Critical Observations on Children's Books; Intended as a Guide to Parents and Teachers, in Their Choice of Books of Instruction and Amusement, The. London: N. Hailes, Juvenile Library, 1817.

Kent, David, and D. R. Ewen, eds. *Romantic Parodies, 1797–1831.* London: Associated University Presses, 1992.

Kermode, Frank. *The Genesis of Secrecy: On the Interpretation of Narrative.* Cambridge, Mass.: Harvard University Press, 1979.

Kernan, Alvin. *The Death of Literature.* New Haven, Conn.: Yale University Press, 1990.

Kinghorn, Norton D. "The Real Miracle of *Charlotte's Web*," *Children's Literature Association Quarterly* 11 (1986): 4–9.

Klein, Melanie. *Love, Guilt and Reparation: And Other Works 1921–1945.* London: Virago, 1975.

Knapp, Mary and Herbert. *One Potato, Two Potato: The Folklore of American Children.* New York: Norton, 1976.

Lacan, Jacques. *Ecrits: A Selection.* New York: Norton, 1977.

Laing, R. D. *The Politics of Experience and The Bird of Paradise.* Harmondsworth, England: Penguin, 1970 (1967).

Landes, Sonia. "E. B. White's *Charlotte's Web*: Caught in the Web,"

Touchstones: Reflections on the Best in Children's Literature, vol. 1, ed. Perry Nodelman. West Lafayette, Ind.: Children's Literature Association, 1985: 270–80.

———. "Picture Books as Literature," *Children's Literature Association Quarterly* 10 (1985): 51–54.

Landsberg, Michele. *Michele Landsberg's Guide to Children's Books.* Markham, Ontario: Penguin, 1985.

Lanes, Selma. *The Art of Maurice Sendak.* New York: Abrams, 1980.

Leach, Edmund. *Claude Lévi-Strauss.* New York: Viking, 1970.

———. *Culture and Communication: The Logic by Which Symbols Are Connected.* Cambridge, England: Cambridge University Press, 1976.

Leeson, Robert. *Reading and Righting: The Past, Present and Future of Fiction for the Young.* London: Collins, 1985.

Lemon, Lee T., and Marion J. Reis. *Russian Formalist Criticism: Four Essays.* Lincoln: University of Nebraska Press, 1965.

Lévi-Strauss, Claude. *The Savage Mind.* Chicago: University of Chicago Press, 1966.

Lieberman, Marcia K. "'Some Day My Prince Will Come': Female Acculturation Through the Fairy Tale," *Don't Bet on the Prince*, ed. Jack Zipes. New York: Methuen, 1986: 185–200.

Lukens, Rebecca J. *A Critical Handbook of Children's Literature.* Glenview, Ill.: Scott, Foresman, 1976.

Lyotard, Jean-Francois. *The Postmodern Condition: A Report on Knowledge.* Tr. Geoff Bennington and Brian Massumi. Minneapolis: University of Minnesota Press, 1984.

MacCann, Donnarae and Gloria Woodard, eds. *The Black American in Books for Children: Readings in Racism.* Metuchen, N.J.: Scarecrow Press, 1972.

MacDonald, Greville. *George MacDonald and His Wife.* London: Unwin, 1924.

McGavran, James Holt, Jr. "'The Children Sport upon the Shore': Romantic Vision in Two Twentieth-Century Picture Books," *Children's Literature Association Quarterly* 11 (1986–87): 170–75.

McGillis, Roderick, ed. *For the Childlike: George MacDonald's Fantasies for Children.* Metuchen, N.J.: Scarecrow, 1992.

———. "Novelty and Romancement: Fantasy in Children's Literature," *The English Quarterly* 9 (1976–77): 27–43.

———. "Repetitions: Oral and Written Story," *Sitting at the Feet of the Past: Retelling the North American Folktale*, ed. Gary D. Schmidt and Donald R. Hettinga. Westport, Conn.: Greenwood Press, 1992: 137–53.

————. "Tenniel's Turned Rabbit: A Reading of *Alice* with Tenniel's Help," *English Studies in Canada* 3 (1977): 326–35.

————. "'What *Is* the Fun' Said Alice," *Children's Literature in Education* 17 (1986): 25–36.

Marcuse, Herbert. *One-Dimensional Man.* Boston: Beacon, 1964.

Minard, Rosemary, ed. *Womenfolk and Fairy Tales.* Boston: Houghton Mifflin, 1975.

"MLA Survey Casts Light on Canon Debate," *MLA Newsletter* (winter 1991): 12–14.

Morris, John S. "Fantasy in a Mythless Age," *Children's Literature* 2 (1973): 77–86.

Myers, Mitzi. "Impeccable Governesses, Rational Dames, and Moral Mothers: Mary Wollstonecraft and the Female Tradition in Georgian Children's Books," *Children's Literature* 14 (1986): 31–59.

————. "'A Taste for Truth and Realities': Early Advice to Mothers on Books for Girls," *Children's Literature Association Quarterly* 12 (1987): 118–24.

Nelson, Claudia. *Boys Will Be Girls: The Feminine Ethic and British Children's Fiction, 1857–1917.* New Brunswick, N.J.: Rutgers University Press, 1991.

Nodelman, Perry. "Children's Literature as Women's Writing," *Children's Literature Association Quarterly* 13 (1988): 31–34.

————. *The Pleasures of Children's Literature.* New York: Longman, 1990.

————. "Text as Teacher: The Beginning of *Charlotte's Web*," *Children's Literature* 13 (1985): 109–27.

————. *Words About Pictures: The Narrative Art of Children's Picture Books.* Athens: University of Georgia Press, 1988.

————, ed. *Touchstones: Reflections on the Best in Children's Literature.* 3 vols. West Lafayette, Ind.: Children's Literature Association, 1985–1989.

Perrot, Jean. "Maurice Sendak's Ritual Cooking of the Child in Three Tableaux: The Moon, Mother, and Music," *Children's Literature* 18 (1990): 68–86.

Piaget, Jean. *Structuralism.* Tr. Chaninah Maschler. New York: Harper Torchbooks, 1968.

Prelutsky, Jack. "In Search of the Addle-pated Paddlepuss," *The Art and Craft of Writing for Children,* ed. William Zinsser. Boston: Houghton Mifflin, 1990: 99–120.

Prince, Gerald. *A Dictionary of Narratology.* Lincoln: University of Nebraska Press, 1987.

Probst, Robert E. *Response and Analysis: Teaching Literature in Junior and Senior High School*. Portsmouth, N.H.: Boynton/Cook, 1988.

Propp, V. *Morphology of the Folktale*. Tr. Laurence Scott. Austin: University of Texas Press, 1979 (1975).

Rabkin, Eric. *The Fantastic in Literature*. Princeton, N.J.: Princeton University Press, 1976.

Reed, Michael D. "The Female Oedipal Complex in Maurice Sendak's *Outside Over There*," *Children's Literature Association Quarterly* 11 (1986–87): 176–80.

Richardson, Alan. "Wordsworth, Fairy Tales, and the Politics of Children's Reading," *Romanticism and Children's Literature in Nineteenth-Century England*, ed. James Holt McGavran, Jr. Athens: University of Georgia Press, 1991: 34–53.

Rose, Jacqueline. *The Case of Peter Pan, or the Impossibility of Children's Fiction*. London: Macmillan, 1984.

Rosenblatt, Louise M. *The Reader, the Text, the Poem: The Transactional Theory of the Literary Work*. Carbondale: Southern Illinois University Press, 1978.

Rowe, John Carlos. "Structure," *Critical Terms for Literary Study*, ed. Frank Lentricchia and Thomas McLaughlin. Chicago: University of Chicago Press, 1990: 22–38.

Rowe, Karen E. "Feminism and Fairy Tales," *Don't Bet on the Prince*, ed. Jack Zipes. New York: Methuen, 1986: 209–26.

Rushdy, Ashraf H. A. "'The Miracle of the Web': Community, Desire, and Narrativity in *Charlotte's Web*," *The Lion and the Unicorn* 15 (1991): 35–60.

Ruskin, John. *Sesame and Lilies*. London: Cassell, 1907 (1865).

Rustin, Margaret and Michael. *Narratives of Love and Loss: Studies in Modern Children's Fiction*. London: Verso, 1987.

Sale, Roger. *Fairy Tales and After: From Snow White to E. B. White*. Cambridge, Mass.: Harvard University Press, 1978.

Saltman, Judith. *Modern Canadian Children's Books*. Toronto: Oxford University Press, 1987.

Sassure, Ferdinand de. *Course in General Linguistics*. Tr. Wade Baskin. New York: The Philosophical Library, 1959.

Sayre, Henry. "Performance," *Critical Terms for Literary Study*, ed. Frank Lentricchia and Thomas McLaughlin. Chicago: University of Chicago Press, 1990: 91–104.

Shaloo, Sharon. "'Get With the Program!': The Mass- and Direct-Marketing of Children's Literature," *The Lion and the Unicorn* 17 (1993): 1–14.

Shavit, Zohar. *Poetics of Children's Literature*. Athens: University of Georgia Press, 1986.

Shelley, Percy Bysshe. *A Defence of Poetry*. Indianapolis, Ind.: Bobbs-Merrill, 1965 (1840).

Skura, Meredith Anne. *The Literary Use of the Psychoanalytic Process*. New Haven, Conn.: Yale University Press, 1981.

Sloan, Glenna Davis. *The Child as Critic: Teaching Literature in Elementary and Middle Schools*. 3rd edition. New York: Teachers College Press, 1991 (1984).

Steig, Michael. *Stories of Reading: Subjectivity and Literary Understanding*. Baltimore: The Johns Hopkins University Press, 1989.

Stephens, John. *Language and Ideology in Children's Fiction*. London: Longman, 1992.

Stewig, John Warren. *Children and Literature*. 2nd edition. Boston: Houghton Mifflin, 1988.

Stone, Kay. "The Misuses of Enchantment: Controversies on the Significance of Fairy Tales," *Women's Folklore, Women's Culture*, eds. Rosan A. Jordan and Susan J. Kalcik. Philadelphia: University of Pennsylvania Press, 1985: 125–45.

Sutton-Smith, Brian. *The Folkstories of Children*. Philadelphia: University of Pennsylvania Press, 1981.

Swinfen, Ann. *In Defense of Fantasy: A Study of the Genre in English and American Literature Since 1945*. London: Routledge, 1984.

Thompson, Stith. *The Folktale*. Berkeley: University of California Press, 1977 (1946).

Todorov, Tzvetan. *The Fantastic: A Structural Approach to a Literary Genre*. Ithaca, N.Y.: Cornell University Press, 1975.

Tolkien, J. R. R. *Tree and Leaf*. London: Unwin, 1970.

Townsend, John Rowe. "Standards of Criticism for Children's Literature," *The Signal Approach to Children's Books,* ed. by Nancy Chambers. Harmondsworth, Middlesex: Kestrel Books, 1980: 193–207.

Vickery, John B., ed. *Myth and Literature: Contemporary Theory and Practice*. Lincoln: University of Nebraska Press, 1973 (1966).

von Franz, M.-L. "The Process of Individuation," *Man and His Symbols*, ed. Carl G. Jung. New York: Dell, 1973 (1964): 157–254.

Waelti-Walters, Jennifer. *Fairy Tales and the Female Imagination*. Montreal: Eden, 1982.

Warner, Marina. *From the Beast to the Blonde*. London: Chatto & Windus, 1994.

Wellek, Rene, and Austin Warren. *Theory of Literature*. New York: Harcourt, Brace, 1956 (1942).

Willinsky, John. *The New Literacy: Redefining Reading and Writing in the Schools*. New York: Routledge, 1990.

Wimsatt, W. K. *The Verbal Icon: Studies in the Meaning of Poetry*. London: Methuen, 1970 (1954).

Wollstonecraft, Mary. *Vindications of the Rights of Woman* (1792). Harmondsworth, England: Penguin Classic, 1985.

Wordsworth, William. *Poetical Works*. Ed. Ernest de Selincourt. London: Oxford University Press, 1965 (1904).

———. *The Prelude: A Parallel Text*. Ed. J. C. Maxwell. London: Penguin, 1986 (1971).

Wright, Elizabeth. *Psychoanalytic Criticism: Theory in Practice*. London: Methuen, 1984.

Zipes, Jack. *Breaking the Magic Spell: Radical Theories of Folk and Fairy Tales*. London: Heinemann, 1979.

———. *Don't Bet on the Prince: Contemporary Feminist Fairy Tales in North America and England*. New York: Methuen, 1986.

———. *Fairy Tales and the Art of Subversion: The Classical Genre for Children and the Process of Civilization*. New York: Wildman, 1983.

———. *The Trials and Tribulations of Little Red Riding Hood*. South Hadley, Mass.: Bergin and Garvey, 1983.

Index

Index

Index

Index

The Author

Roderick McGillis is Professor of English at the University of Calgary.
His research interests range from popular culture to children's literature
to nineteenth-century British literature, and he has published in all these
areas. His articles deal with the work of Lewis Carroll, George
MacDonald, Charles Dickens, William Wordsworth, and William Blake.
He has also published on film, literary theory, and fairy tales. Journals in
which his work appears include *English Studies in Canada, Children's
Literature in Education, Studies in the Literary Imagination, The Journal
of Popular Culture, The Durham University Journal, Scottish Literary
Journal, Canadian Children's Literature,* and *The Inklings.* He is the
author of a forthcoming volume in Twayne's Masterworks series on
Frances Hodgson Burnett's *A Little Princess.* Currently President of the
Children's Literature Association, in his spare time McGillis performs as
a storyteller for both adults and children.